DATE DUE

SEP 1 0 2012	

BRODART, CO.   Cat. No. 23-221

GAME DEVELOPMENT ESSENTIALS

ONLINE GAME DEVELOPMENT

Rick Hall

Jeannie Novak

DELMAR
CENGAGE Learning

Australia • Brazil • Japan • Korea • Mexico • Singapore • Spain • United Kingdom • United States

Game Development Essentials:
Online Game Development
Rick Hall & Jeannie Novak

Vice President, Technology and Trades ABU:
  David Garza

Director of Learning Solutions: Sandy Clark

Managing Editor: Larry Main

Senior Acquisitions Editor: James Gish

Product Manager: Sharon Chambliss

Editorial Assistant: Sarah Timm

Marketing Director: Deborah Yarnell

Marketing Manager: Bryant Chrzan

Marketing Specialist: Victoria Ortiz

Director of Production: Wendy Troeger

Production Manager: Mark Bernard

Content Project Manager: Michael Tubbert

Technology Project Director: Joe Pliss

Technology Project Manager:
  Christopher Catalina

Cover Image: *City of Heroes* courtesy of NCsoft.

For product information and technology assistance, contact us at
Cengage Learning Customer & Sales Support, 1-800-354-9706

For permission to use material from this text or product, submit all requests online at **www.cengage.com/permissions**
Further permissions questions can be emailed to
permissionrequest@cengage.com

Library of Congress Control Number: 2007942514

In-Publication Data has been applied for.

ISBN-13: 978-1-4180-5267-6

ISBN-10: 1-4180-5267-1

Delmar
5 Maxwell Drive
PO Box 8007
Clifton Park, NY 12065-8007
USA

Cengage Learning is a leading provider of customized learning solutions with office locations around the globe, including Singapore, the United Kingdom, Australia, Mexico, Brazil, and Japan. Locate your local office at:

international.cengage.com/region

Cengage Learning products are represented in Canada by Nelson - Education, Ltd.

For your lifelong learning solutions, visit **delmar.cengage.com**

Visit our corporate website at **cengage.com**

Notice to the Reader

Publisher does not warrant or guarantee any of the products described herein or perform any independent analysis in connection with any of the product information contained herein. Publisher does not assume, and expressly disclaims, any obligation to obtain and include information other than that provided to it by the manufacturer. The reader is expressly warned to consider and adopt all safety precautions that might be indicated by the activities described herein and to avoid all potential hazards. By following the instructions contained herein, the reader willingly assumes all risks in connection with such instructions. The publisher makes no representations or warranties of any kind, including but not limited to, the warranties of fitness for particular purpose or merchantability, nor are any such representations implied with respect to the material set forth herein, and the publisher takes no responsibility with respect to such material. The publisher shall not be liable for any special, consequential, or exemplary damages resulting, in whole or part, from the readers' use of, or reliance upon, this material.

Printed in Canada
1 2 3 4 5 6 7 11 10 09 08 07

CONTENTS

Part I: Origins & Planning 1

Chapter 1 History: where did online games come from? 3

Part II: Design & Marketing 89

Chapter 4 Content:
a structural approach 91

Chapter 5 Gameplay:
multiplayer expectations 117

Chapter 6 Spin: keep community & marketing in mind 155

Part III: Launch & Beyond 179

Chapter 7 Live!: life after launch 181

Chapter 8 The Business: understanding the bottom line 211

Introduction

Online Game Development:
risk & reward

Massively multiplayer online games (MMOGs) are not quite as new as people have been led to believe. Tracing back to their roots, we can see a pattern of slow evolution over the course of nearly 30 years. What is new, however, is the way these games are being utilized in a business sense. Unlike games of just 10 years ago, MMOGs have shown an ability to become the juggernauts of the digital entertainment industry. They have the potential to dominate revenues in a way that no previous games could ever compete with.

With great rewards, however, come great risks. Although MMOGs have the potential to generate many times the revenues of their standalone counterparts, they also cost a proportional amount more to build. As the reward increases, so too does the risk. MMOGs can represent spectacular successes or incredible failures. In today's competitive world, where so much money is riding on development, we can't afford to fail. The goal of this book is to help navigate the reader through the incredibly complex process of creating one of these amazing projects.

Readers will learn how to organize the development of a MMOG from multiple vital perspectives—including technological, management, financial, marketing, organizational, and creative. By being exposed to MMOGs from a high level—where all of the essential building blocks can be understood—the risks associated with their construction can be mitigated down to a manageable level. Readers will come to understand that, although they are very different from standalone games, MMOGs can nonetheless be approached in a manner that makes them every bit as achievable.

Rick Hall   Jeannie Novak
Longwood, FL   Santa Monica, CA

About the *Game Development Essentials* Series

The *Game Development Essentials* series was created to fulfill a need: to provide students and creative professionals alike with a complete education in all aspects of the game industry. As more creative professionals migrate to the game industry, and as more game degree and certificate programs are launched, the books in this series will become even more essential to game education and career development.

Not limited to the education market, this series is also appropriate for the trade market and for those who have a general interest in the game industry. Books in the series contain several unique features. All are in full-color and contain hundreds of images—including original illustrations, diagrams, game screenshots, and photos of industry professionals. They also contain a great deal of profiles, tips and case studies from professionals in the industry who are actively developing games. Starting with an overview of all aspects of the industry—*Game Development Essentials: An Introduction*—this series focuses on topics as varied as story & character development, interface design, artificial intelligence, gameplay mechanics, level design, online game development, simulation development, and audio.

Jeannie Novak
Lead Author & Series Editor

About *Game Development Essentials: Online Game Development*

This book provides an overview of online game development—complete with historical background, dimensions, strategies, and future predictions.

This book contains the following unique features:

- Key chapter questions that are clearly stated at the beginning of each chapter
- Coverage that surveys the topics of online game development concepts, process, and techniques
- Thought-provoking review and study exercises at the end of each chapter suitable for students and professionals alike that help promote critical thinking and problem-solving skills
- Case studies, quotations from leading professionals, and profiles of game developers that feature concise tips and techniques to help readers focus in on issues specific to online game development
- An abundance of full-color images throughout that help illustrate the concepts and practical applications discussed in the book

There are several general themes that are emphasized throughout this book, including:

- Distinguishing between online multiplayer game development and single-player games
- Exploring design, technology, and business considerations associated with massively multiplayer online games
- Illustrating a structural approach to game design and gameplay mechanics associated with online game development
- Investigating marketing and community management issues specific to online game development
- Evaluating existing online games with emphasis on the risks and rewards associated with their development

Who Should Read This Book?

This book is not limited to the education market. If you found this book on a shelf at the bookstore and picked it up out of curiosity, this book is for you, too! The audience for this book includes students, industry professionals, and the general interest consumer market. The style is informal and accessible with a concentration on theory and practice—geared toward both students and professionals.

Students that might benefit from this book include:

- College students in game development, interactive design, entertainment studies, communication, and emerging technologies programs
- Art, design, programming, and production students who are taking game development courses
- Professional students in college-level programs who are taking game development courses
- Game development students at universities

The audience of industry professionals for this book include:

- Graphic designers, animators, and interactive media developers who are interested in becoming game artists
- Programmers and interactive media developers who are interested in becoming game programmers
- Professionals such as writers, producers, artists, and designers in other arts and entertainment media—including film, television, and music—who are interested in transferring their skills to the game development industry

How Is This Book Organized?

This book consists of three parts—focusing on origins/planning, design/marketing, and launch/beyond.

Part I   Origins & Planning—Focuses on providing a historical and structural context to online game development. Chapters in this section include:

- ■ **Chapter 1   History: where did online games come from?**—discusses the history of online games, the development of the MMOG business model, and the evolution of a new player lifestyle
- ■ **Chapter 2   Constraints: understand the issues before designing**— explores business, technology, and gameplay constraints specific to MMOG development
- ■ **Chapter 3   Organization: make a plan before you start**—reviews pre-production issues such as the development team, phases, and documentation

Part II   Design & Marketing—Focuses on how game design and marketing concepts can address the needs of online players. Chapters in this section include:

- ■ **Chapter 4   Content: a structural approach**—discusses game design concepts such as second-order ideas, tone words, core mechanics, production values, and the uncanny valley
- ■ **Chapter 5   Gameplay: multiplayer expectations**—discusses gameplay features such as player types, balance, level grinding, feedback, and player groups
- ■ **Chapter 6   Spin: keep community & marketing in mind**—focuses on marketing, community management techniques, and player demographics

Part III   Launch & Beyond—Focuses on post-launch and business issues, along with thoughts on the future of online game development. Chapters in this section include:

- **Chapter 7   Live!: life after launch**—explores post-launch features such as the live team, expansion packs, security issues, and developer-to-player communication
- **Chapter 8   The Business: understanding the bottom line**—explores business issues such as costs, monetization models, and overseas considerations
- **Chapter 9   Endgame: bringing everything together**—highlights future predictions, career paths, and education related to online game development

The book also contains a **Resources** section—which includes a list of game development news sources, guides, directories, conferences, articles, and books related to topics discussed in this text.

How to Use This Text

The sections that follow describe text elements found throughout the book and how they are intended to be used.

key chapter questions

Key chapter questions are learning objectives in the form of overview questions that start off each chapter. Readers should be able to answer the questions upon understanding the chapter material.

sidebars

Sidebars offer in-depth information from the authors on specific topics—accompanied by associated images.

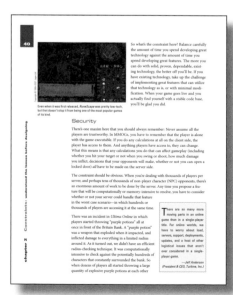

quotes

Quotes contain short, insightful thoughts from industry professionals, observers, players, and students.

notes

Notes contain thought-provoking ideas provided by the authors that are intended to help the readers think critically about the book's topics.

tips

Tips provide advice and inspiration from industry professionals and educators, as well as practical techniques and tips of the trade.

case studies

Case studies contain anecdotes from industry professionals (accompanied by game screenshots) on their experiences developing specific game titles.

profiles

Profiles provide bios, photos and in-depth commentary from industry professionals and educators.

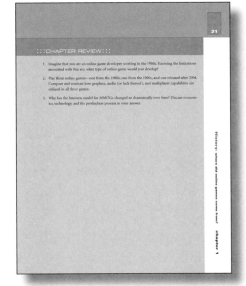

chapter review

Chapter review exercises at the end of each chapter allow readers to apply what they've learned. Annotations and guidelines are included in the instructor's guide, available separately (see next page).

About the Companion DVD

The companion DVD contains the following media:

- Game engines: Torque (Windows and Mac versions 1.5.1) and Game Maker (version 7)
- 3D modeling and animation software: Autodesk 3ds Max (version 9) and Autodesk Maya (version 8.5 PLE)
- Game design documentation: Gas Powered Games (Chris Taylor GDD template), Torn Space (Michael Black *Sub Hunter* GDD), Wizards of the Coast (*Uncivilized: The Goblin Game* [code name: *Salmon*] call for game design/ submission), NCsoft (*City of Heroes / City of Villains / Dungeon Runners / Tabula Rasa: Caves of Donn* developer diaries, *Guild Wars: Eye of the North* dungeons & quests), CCP Games (*EVE Online*), and Dragon's Eye Productions (*Furcadia*)
- Game design articles: Harvey Smith/Witchboy's Cauldron and Barrie Ellis/ One-Switch Games

- Concept Art: NCsoft (*Tabula Rasa, City of Heroes, City of Villains, Dungeon Runners, Aion, Guild Wars, Lineage II*), Capcom (*Viewtiful Joe 2, Devil May Cry 3: Dante's Awakening, Resident Evil 4*), Valve (*Half-Life 2*), Sony Online Entertainment (*EverQuest, EverQuest II*), CCP Games (*EVE Online*), and Dragon's Eye Productions (*Furcadia*)

- Game demos/trial versions: Take Two Interactive Software (*Prey*), Blizzard (*Diablo II*), Firaxis (*Civilization IV, Sid Meier's Railroads!*), Stardock (*Galactic Civilizations II: Gold Edition*), THQ (*Company of Heroes*), Enemy Technology (*I of the Enemy: Ril'Cerat*), Star Mountain Studios (*Bergman, Weird Helmet, Frozen, Findolla*), GarageGames (*Marble Blast: Gold, Think Tanks, Zap!*), Max Gaming Technologies (*Dark Horizons: Lore Invasion*), Chronic Logic (*Gish*), Large Animal Games (*Rocket Bowl Plus*), 21-6 Productions (*Tube Twist, Orbz*), CDV (*City Life, Glory of the Roman Empire, War Front: Turning Point*), Last Day of Work (*Virtual Villagers, Fish Tycoon*), Hanako Games (*Cute Knight*), Microsoft (*Zoo Tycoon 2: Marine Mania*), U.S. Army (*America's Army*), Cyan Worlds, Inc. (*Myst Online*), CCP Games (*EVE Online*), Wizards of the Coast (*Magic: The Gathering Online, Acquire, RoboRally*), NCsoft (*Dungeon Runners*), and Sony Online Entertainment (*EverQuest, EverQuest II*)

About the Instructor's Guide

The instructor's guide (e-resource, available separately on DVD) was developed to assist instructors in planning and implementing their instructional programs. It includes sample syllabi, test questions, assignments, projects, PowerPoint files, and other valuable instructional resources.

Order Number: 1-4180-5268-X

About the Authors

Rick Hall is a 15-year veteran of the gaming industry with experience as a producer, studio head, programmer, and game designer. During his time in the game industry, he has worked on MMOGs, RPGs, adventure games, RTSs, flight sims, fighting games, sports sims, and even a fishing simulation. Rick has developed games for the PC, PlayStation, N64, PS2, Sony PSP, and Nintendo DS. He started his career at Paragon Software, a studio that eventually became the core development group for Take 2's initial 1994 startup. After leaving Take 2, Rick joined EA's Origin studio in Austin, Texas where for five years he served as a live producer on *Ultima Online*—and later as executive producer on *Ultima X Odyssey*. In 2004, Rick joined EA's Tiburon studio in Orlando, Florida, where he has been a Senior Producer on the *Madden Football* handheld products. Rick currently teaches Production at The University of Central Florida's FIEA program—and he is a founding member of 360 Ed, a company that makes educational software.

Photo credit: Luis Levy

Jeannie Novak is the founder of Indiespace—one of the first companies to promote and distribute interactive entertainment online—where she consults with creative professionals in the music, film, and television industries to help them migrate to the game industry. In addition to being lead author and series editor of the *Game Development Essentials* series, Jeannie is the co-author of *Play the Game: The Parent's Guide to Video Games* and three pioneering books on the interactive entertainment industry—including *Creating Internet Entertainment.* Jeannie is the Online Program Director for the Game Art & Design and Media Arts & Animation programs at the Art Institute of Pittsburgh – Online Division, where she is also Producer & Lead Designer on a educational business simulation game that is being built within the *Second Life* environment. She has also been a game instructor and curriculum development expert at UCLA Extension, Art Center College of Design, Academy of Entertainment and Technology at Santa Monica College, DeVry University, Westwood College, and ITT Technical Institute—and she has consulted for the UC Berkeley Center for New Media. Jeannie has developed or participated in game workshops and panels in association with the British Academy of Television Arts & Sciences (BAFTA), Macworld, Digital Hollywood, and iHollywood Forum. She is a member of the International Game Developers Association (IGDA) and has served on selection committees for the Academy of Interactive Arts & Sciences (AIAS) DICE Awards. Jeannie was chosen as one of the 100 most influential people in high-technology by *MicroTimes* magazine—and she has been profiled by CNN, *Billboard Magazine,* Sundance Channel, *Daily Variety,* and the *Los Angeles Times.* She received an M.A. in Communication Management from the University of Southern California (USC), where she focused on using massively multiplayer online games (MMOGs) as online distance learning applications. She received a B.A. in Mass Communication from the University of California, Los Angeles (UCLA)—graduating summa cum laude and Phi Beta Kappa. When she isn't writing and teaching, Jeannie spends most of her time recording, performing, and composing music. More information on the author can be found at *http://jeannie.com* and *http://indiespace.com.*

Acknowledgements

The authors would like to thank the following people for their hard work and dedication to this project:

Jim Gish (Acquisitions Editor, Delmar/ Cengage Learning), for making this series happen.

Sharon Chambliss (Product Manager, Delmar/Cengage Learning), for moving this project along and always maintaining a professional demeanor.

Michael Tubbert (Content Project Manager, Delmar/Cengage Learning), for his helpful pair of eyes and consistent responsiveness during production crunch time.

Sarah Timm (Editorial Assistant, Delmar/ Cengage Learning), for her ongoing assistance throughout the series.

Christine Clark & Nina Hnatov, for their thorough and thoughtful copyediting.

David Ladyman (Image Research & Permissions Specialist), for his superhuman efforts in clearing the many images in this book.

Patricia Shogren (Project Manager, GEX Publishing Services), for her diligent work and prompt response during the layout and compositing phase.

Per Olin, for his organized and aesthetically pleasing diagrams.

Ben Bourbon, for his clever and inspired illustrations.

David Koontz (Publisher, Chilton), for starting it all by introducing Jeannie Novak to Jim Gish.

A big thanks also goes out to the people who contributed their thoughts, ideas, and original images to this book:

Aaron Marks (On Your Mark Music Productions)

Barrie Ellis (One-Switch)

Ben Noel (Electronic Arts)

Bill Louden (Austin Community College)

Bryan Walker (Retro Studios)

Chris Kirmse (Xfire)

Chris Taylor (Gas Powered Games)

Christian Lange

Damion Schubert (BioWare)

David Javelosa (Academy of Entertainment & Technology/Santa Monica College)

Deborah Baxtrom (The Art Institute of Pittsburgh – Online Division)

Denis Papp (TimeGate Studios)

Frank T. Gilson (Wizards of the Coast)

Gordon Walton (BioWare)

Graeme Bayless (Kush Games/2K Sports)

Harvey Smith (Midway Games)

Jason Spangler (Electronic Arts)

JB Shoda (Electronic Arts)

Jeff Anderson (Turbine)

Jessica Mulligan (Sunflowers GmbH)

John Comes (Gas Powered Games)

Kenneth C. Finney (Art Institute of Toronto)

Mario "Thunderbear" Orsini (Team Orbit/ Academy of Game Entertainment Technology)

Mark Seremet

Michael Black (Torn Space)

Milan Petrovich (The Art Institute of San Francisco)

Phil Trumbo (Digipen Institute of Technology)

Raph Koster (Areae)

Rich Vogel (BioWare)

Richard Allen Bartle (Essex University)

Rob Martyn (Electronic Arts)

Ryan Brant

Starr Long (NCsoft)

Thanks to the following people and companies for their tremendous help with referrals and in securing permissions, images, and demos:

Adrian Wright (Max Gaming Technologies)

Ai Hasegawa & Hideki Yoshimoto (Namco Bandai)

Al Corey (Playnet)

Alex Kierkegaard (insomnia.ac)

Alexandra Miseta (Stardock)

Andrea Silva

Andrew Tepper (eGenesis)

Annie Belanger (Autodesk)

Brad Lineberger (DrakkarZone Inc.)

Brian Green (Near Death Studios)

Brian Hupp (Electronic Arts)

Brianna Messina (Blizzard Entertainment)

Briar Lee Mitchell (Star Mountain Studios)

Carla Humphrey (Last Day of Work)

Charles Moncrief (TorilMUD)

Chris Brooks

Chris Glover (Eidos Interactive)

Chris Keswani (OnNet USA)

Christian Lange (Conundrum Studios)

Christian Schweitz (Game Secrets)

Daniel James (Three Rings)

Darren Robertson (Starpeace)

David Greenspan (THQ)

David Rosén & Marcus Andrews (Lockpick)

David Swofford (NCsoft)

Dennis Shirk (Firaxis)

Don McGowan & Genevieve Waldman (Microsoft Corporation)

Dr. Cat & Emerald Flame (Dragon's Eye Productions)

Eric Fritz (GarageGames)

Estela Lemus (Capcom)

Gena Feist (Take-Two Games)

Georgina Okerson (Hanako Games)

Gina Bovara (Intel)

Heidi Schulz, Bill Money & Denis Loubet (Pixel Mine)

Jagex Limited

Jana Rubenstein, Makiko Nakamura & Eijirou Yoshida (Sega of America)

Jason Holtman (Valve)

Josiah Pisciotta (Chronic Logic)

Kate Ross (Wizards of the Coast)

Kelly Conway & Olivia Malstrom (Sony Online Entertainment)

Kristin Kwasek & John Golden (Turbine)

Linda Carlson

Lori Mezoff (U.S. Army)

Maggie the Jackcat

Mario Kroll (CDV Software)

Mark Overmars, Sandy Duncan & Sophie Russell (YoYo Games)

Mark Rein & Kelly Farrow (Epic Games)

Mark Temple (Enemy Technology)

Michael Fahey

Navy Field

Nexon

Nintendo

Nstorm

Dr. Richard Bartle

Rusty Williams (Flying Lab Software)

Ryan Mette & Justin Mette (21-6 Productions)

Shane Davis (Pixel Mine)

Sophie Jakubowicz (Ubisoft)

Ted Brockwood (Calico Media)

Terri Perkins (Funcom)

Tony Fryman (Cyan)

Valerie Massey (CCP Games)

Vikki Vega (Sony Computer Entertainment America)

Wade Tinney (Large Animal Games)

Questions & Feedback

We welcome your questions and feedback. If you have suggestions that you think others would benefit from, please let us know and we will try to include them in the next edition.

To send us your questions and/or feedback, you can contact the publisher at:

Delmar Learning
Executive Woods
5 Maxwell Drive
Clifton Park, NY 12065
Attn: Graphic Arts Team
(800) 998-7498

Or the series editor at:

Jeannie Novak
Founder & CEO
INDIESPACE
P.O. Box 5458
Santa Monica, CA 90409
jeannie@indiespace.com

DEDICATION

To everyone who wants to see with new eyes.

—Rick

To Luis, who takes the risks and shares the rewards with me.

—Jeannie

Part I: Origins & Planning

CHAPTER

History

where did online games come from?

Key Chapter Questions

- How are *massively multiplayer online games (MMOGs)* different from other electronic games?

- How long did it take to go from a few dozen *simultaneous players* to millions?

- What are some significant *technology considerations* that impact MMOGs?

- How has a new *player lifestyle* evolved out of online multiplayer games?

- How has the MMOG *business model* changed over time?

This chapter discusses the evolution of online games from design, technology, and monetization perspectives. It will show how early massively multiplayer online games (MMOGs) evolved from niche experiments to global businesses and address the need for a fundamentally sound development approach.

What Is an MMOG Anyway?

Ask most game developers this question, and don't be surprised if you get a wide variety of slightly different answers. The acronym MMOG implies subtly different things to different people. However, the core concepts are generally similar. A massively multiplayer online game (MMOG) is one in which a large number of people can participate simultaneously over a network, interact with each other (and usually interact with the game world), join in or leave at any time, and expect everything they've achieved to "persist" while they are offline.

This last part, *persistence*, is extremely important. A key component for any MMOG is the feeling that it is a continuous world. Players should be able to jump in at any time, play for a while, and leave—secure in the knowledge that when they log back on, they'll find things just as they left them, more or less.

Conundrum Studios Inc.

Any change a player makes in an MMOG such as *Project Visitor* will "persist" after that player logs off.

It doesn't matter whether you're talking about an MMORPG (massively multiplayer online role-playing game), MMORTS (massively multiplayer online real-time strategy game), MMOFPS (massively multiplayer online first-person shooter), or any other MMOG variant. Whether it is the player character, souped-up hot rod, intergalactic smuggler ship, or membership in a gang of bounty-hunting Smurfs, an MMOG assures players that anything they achieved in the game world will still be there no matter how long it has been since they last logged in.

Most people can agree on the preceding definition, but opinions start to diverge from there. Speaking a bit more philosophically, many believe that an MMOG is something more. They believe that an MMOG should be a *virtual world*—a place that at least *feels* like it is real, and is somehow larger and more complete than a simple game map. They want their environment to feel as limitless and diverse as the Earth on which they live (or at least the one where they *wish* they lived). They want everything in their environment to feel like it is *alive*—behaving in its own unique-but-predictable manner and living in its proper place.

These players also believe that MMOGs should focus significantly on the concepts of socialization and community; it's not enough for there to always be a human opponent. An MMOG must be a *place of being*. It must be a community, perhaps a little cozier than a "world" per se, and it may be better described as a virtual *neighborhood* or *village* than a virtual *world*. For them, the game must contain all of the tools necessary to form friendships and communities, work together, social-ize, and thrive as a group—while still allowing them to stand out as individuals.

Still others will insist that an MMOG is further defined by the open-endedness of its gameplay. They think there must be a nearly unlimited list of possible activities, and a sense that there is always something new to try just over the horizon. Even if the game itself must necessarily be finite, players want the feeling that they can do anything they can think of and not be *limited* in the same sense that they might be in a traditional game.

In *Guild Wars,* the game world is rich, detailed, and seemingly limitless.

It doesn't take much thought to realize that if not carefully controlled, an MMOG with the preceding broad definition can quickly become a development project of infinite and overwhelming scope. Clearly, we don't possess the technology, resources, or time to make a genuine virtual world where players can do anything and go anywhere. And in truth, that sort of game would probably be directionless, tedious, and much less interesting than it sounds. The trick is to create a game that provides a *feeling* of vastness and open-endedness—but that is in actuality strictly limited in its scope.

Evolution, Not Revolution

Quite a few MMOGs have come close to achieving an idealistic model of appar-ent vastness and open-endedness. But before you go thinking that this was some titanic leap of ingenuity by a brilliant game developer, it wasn't. The evolutionary path of MMOGs has taken almost 30 years to tread—and the changes along the way have been numerous, small, and subtle. We still have trouble identifying the "exact moment of change."

For years, game industry professionals, journalists, and rabid MMOG aficionados have continued to debate the utterly pointless question, "When was the first massively multiplayer online game launched?" The debate seems to center on the word "massively." There have been single-player "online" games since the 1980s, and "multiplayer" games have been around for even longer than that—but when did they first become "massively" multiplayer online games? To answer this question, we have to decide how many players a game must support simultaneously before it's considered *massive*. Is it 32? 64? 128? 256? More? It's funny how heated the debate gets. Presumably, the reason for the bickering is a matter of deciding who gets to plant their flag on the credit.

The simple fact is the number of players that a game supports is just an arbitrary number. That's all. Once there are more than two players, multiplayer games start to have more similarities than differences. Taking a look at the history of MMOGs will show us that there was no *revolutionary* game that magically supported a massive number of players. Rather, it was a process of *evolution* whereby the number of players kept methodically increasing until one day we realized that there were an awful lot of people playing all at once—and the term "massively multiplayer online game" suddenly seemed appropriate.

Illustration by Ben Bourbon

Dude, every single member of my D&D group was online playing last night. That's MASSIVE!

Determining the exact moment multiplayer games became *massive* isn't nearly as interesting as the story of how we reached that point. Along the way, it is important to understand the numerous changes in graphics, technology, game design, production techniques, and business models that have occurred. The timeline in the following section shows early games that were mostly developed by hobbyists and college students. These games were free to anyone who wanted to play them, unsophisticated, and often considered "illegal" (i.e., the owners of the servers on which the games were played didn't like the "waste of resources" and often deleted games as soon as they found them).

The early business models began by charging players by the hour but quickly graduated to monthly subscriptions. Games in the mid-to-late 1980s were able to attract a limited niche of subscribers measured in the hundreds, while games now garner literally millions of subscribers worldwide. In the space of 25 years, games have gone from being a niche, slightly illegal hobby, to becoming a worldwide industry, generating literally billions of dollars per year—and the explosive growth shows no signs of slowing.

::::: The New Lifestyle

"My guildies were helping me twink my alt, and we totally pwned all the pats in the zone by repeatedly kiting them into the standard mez/AOE DOT trap, all the way to the boss. We didn't wipe once. We're so L337!"—Typical MMOG player comment

Although completely incomprehensible to most people, the preceding comment is nothing new to anyone who regularly plays MMOGs. Roughly translated, it means: "Some members of my club were helping me to rapidly advance my secondary character, and we accomplished this by repeatedly getting wandering monster patrol groups to chase us, whereupon we cast spells to paralyze each group in its entirety, and then killed them en masse with spells that inflict damage over time across a wide area. We did this all the way to the boss monster, without ever getting everyone in the party killed off simultaneously. We're incredible!"

Courtesy of Blizzard Entertainment, Inc.

An example of a typical incomprehensible-looking "l33t-speak" from *World of Warcraft*

The fascinating thing about MMOGs is that longtime players have evolved their own *language* over time. In many ways, this is reminiscent of people's real-life occupations. Have you ever tried listening to a sailor speaking aboard a ship? How about a computer programmer describing his code? Have you ever listened to a police scanner or a ham radio operator? What you undoubtedly would hear is a confusing series of acronyms, shorthand words, and slang that make almost no sense the first time around. These *languages* came into being because people in these professions needed effective ways to communicate, often as quickly as possible, with concise and exact instructions, descriptions, and orders.

Similarly, MMOG players have also found it necessary to develop their own language—and it's just as efficient, precise, and descriptive as the language of any other occupation. But think about the word "occupation" for a moment. Almost any MMOG player will tell you, "It's not just a game; it's a lifestyle." And that's highly significant. MMOGs are more than just hobbies. They're a commitment. They're a way of life. Many players spend more time in their favorite MMOG world than they spend at the office. They make new friends there, form relationships, and sometimes even marry other players. They spend tremendous amounts of time and money establishing and improving their characters. Their game is often a rabid obsession for them. The fact that they've developed their own language, one that is fairly independent of the specific MMOG that is being played, is rather telling. MMOGs are fundamentally different from other types of computer games—and, if you want to learn how to build one, you need to understand that.

A Historical Timeline

Let's take a look at how this incredible industry came into existence. The table on the following page lists some games from 1969 through 2004 that have contributed a significant evolutionary step on the path of MMOGs. This list is not intended to represent every game between 1969 and the present. It simply points out a series of evolutionary changes that have gotten us to where we are today.

Ultima Online

EverQuest

PlanetSide

Phantasy Star Online

1969	**Spacewar** First 2-player computer game.	1974	**Pedit5** First game allowing persistence, but allowing almost no interaction between players.
1975	**Dungeon** Text-based multiplayer RPG dungeon crawl.	1977	**Mines of Moria** Multiplayer RPG using wireframe graphics and persistence.
1977	**Oubliette** Predecessor to *Wizardry*, this was a multiplayer RPG dungeon crawl.	1978	**Empire** Military economic game, supported up to 32 simultaneous players.
1978	**MUD1** Text-based RPG, initially supported 36 users per server, began charging subscribers $4/hr in 1980, often considered the grandfather of MMORPGs.	1979	**Avatar** RPG with advanced graphics, supporting up to 15 players per server.
1981	**Islands of Kesmai** Text-based multiplayer RPG, one of the first to charge an hourly rate ($12 per hour) to play, it supported 100 players per server.	1982	**Megawars** Multiplayer, team-based space exploration game, ran as a commercial product for eighteen years until the year 2000.
1983	**Scepter of Goth** Text-based, commercial MUD supporting up to 15 simultaneous players.	1984	**Aradath** Text-based multiplayer RPG, this was the first game to charge a monthly subscription fee, $40 per month.
1987	**Habitat** The first graphical character-based interactive environment, supported up to 64 simultaneous players.	1987	**Air Warrior** First multiplayer air combat simulator. With wireframe graphics, it initially supported 50 players per server. The game reached 25,000 paying subscribers in 1996.
1987	**Gemstone** Text-based MUD that was able to support 650-1000 players, each paying $14.95 per month.	1988	**Kingdom of Drakkar** Graphical RPG that supported 122 players per server, each paying $4 per hour. The game achieved 10,000 subscribers at its height.
1988	**Federation** Text-based intergalactic economy game, replaced by *Federation II* in 2003.	1990	**Dragon's Gate** Text-based RPG MUD, this is one of the longest running pay-per-play games still active.
1991	**Neverwinter Nights** Graphical RPG based on *AD&D*, charging $6 per hour to play, the game could initially support 50 players per server, increased to 500 by 1995.	1992	**Shadow of Yserbius** Graphical RPG, featuring Player-vs.-Player combat, initially supported up to 30 players per server.
1996	**Meridian 59** The first game to actually use the term "MMOG" in describing itself. This graphical RPG initially supported 250 players per server, reaching a max subscriber level of about 12,000, each paying $9.95 per month.	1997	**Ultima Online** The first truly global MMORPG, *UO* could initially support 1000 players per server each paying $9.95 per month, and reached a maximum worldwide subscriber level of 250K with 80K in Japan.
1998	**Lineage** Graphical RPG made for South Korean Internet game rooms, players paid hourly rates, reportedly reached a maximum of 3,500,000 subscribers.	1999	**EverQuest** The first fully 3D MMORPG, achieved 550,000 subscribers mostly in the U.S. For a time this was the biggest U.S. MMOG.
2000	**Phantasy Star Online** The first MMOG made specifically for a console system (Sega Dreamcast), featuring both solo and multiplayer modes, reached 600K subscribers.	2001	**Dark Age of Camelot** One of the first 3D games in the U.S. to depend strongly on Player vs. Player combat, this MMORPG reached a peak of 250K subscribers worldwide.
2001	**Majestic** Although it never exceeded 17K subscribers, this conspiracy-based Alternative Reality Game featured game play across cell phones, IM, email, and FAXes.	2001	**RuneScape** Developed entirely in Java, offering both free and pay-to-play accounts, currently has 800K subscribers.
2001	**The Legend of Mir II** 2D graphical MMORPG, almost unknown in the west, reached 1,000,000 peak simultaneous users mostly in China.	2001	**Motor City Online** The first 3D MMOG car racing game, reached a peak of 35,000 subscribers.
2002	**Ragnarok Online** Another extremely popular MMORPG in South Korea, reached 800,000 subscribers.	2002	**Earth & Beyond** An MMOG featuring exploration, spaceflight, and serialized fiction, reached a maximum of 39K subscribers.
2003	**Fantasy Westward Journey** Perhaps the biggest MMORPG to date, this 2D Chinese game has reached 56 million subscribers.	2003	**PlanetSide** A 3D First-Person-Shooter MMOG, reached a peak of 60,000 subscribers.
2003	**Toontown** The first MMOG designed specifically for children and family audiences, it reached 110K subscribers in 2006.	2004	**World of Warcraft** The undisputed financial heavy-weight champion of MMOGs, this 3D RPG has over 10 million worldwide subscribers, generating perhaps $700 million in annual revenues.

History: where did online games come from?   chapter 1

Design

Until one puts together even a small list like this, many people seem to hold the erroneous belief that the only game genre that is possible for an MMOG platform is a role-playing game (i.e., an MMORPG). But even a quick glance at this small list will show you that this notion is not true now—and it hasn't been for many years.

There have been MMOGs that were economic simulations, military simulations, combat flight sims, racing games, alternative reality games, and first-person shooters—just to name a few. We'll look at what has made this possible in upcoming sections. But let's first examine the evolution in design thinking.

MMOGs are not always MMORPGs. Consider the historic first-person shooter (MMOFPS), *World War II Online.*

The earliest multiplayer games weren't all that different from single-player games. There was very little interaction between players; in fact, most of it took place between the players and the environment or creatures. Players could chat and sometimes gang up on a bad guy, but that was about all the interaction they could have. It didn't take long before new forms of interaction were introduced. Games quickly allowed players to trade items, customize their appearance, and even fight against each other. And as with any innovation, each of these exposed problems.

Allowing players to trade items introduced the rudiments of "virtual economy" into MMOGs. This is a broader subject for another chapter, but it should suffice to say that virtual economies have had a profound impact on long-term gameplay. A poorly balanced virtual economy can have disastrous effects on an MMOG within just a few months of being launched. This was something that early developers had very little chance of understanding without being specialists in economics. As a result, new virtual economies experienced some interesting issues of inflation, hoarding, supply and demand, and stratification (in which a veteran player's bankroll might be so far beyond that of a new player that it was almost impossible to ever catch up).

Perhaps the best example of customization comes from Cryptic/NCsoft's *City of Heroes.* With the game's hero-generation feature, players can create a superhero character that looks and acts like nearly anything you've ever seen in a comic book. The result is stunning—but this kind of innovation isn't without its share of technical hurdles.

As any developer will tell you, customization can involve complex non-linear bone scaling, procedural textures, blended animations, geometry stitching, and a host of other techniques—each of which takes up processing power on the computer. And while that isn't necessarily an insurmountable problem, remember that we can't predict how many characters will be standing together in a scene in an MMOG. Sure, if one or two characters are standing next to each other, we can happily provide all the processor-hogging customizations we want. But what if there are 10? 50? 100? Suddenly we find all of that processor-intensive customization is creating nightmarish performance issues.

Courtesy of NCsoft

Character creation (such as the superhero-generation feature in *City of Heroes*) is a common element of MMOGs.

And then there was the innovation of "player vs. player" (PvP) combat. It was easy to predict that it would be a *lot* more fun to fight against other players instead of computer-controlled enemies. And, in fact, it doesn't sound like that would create any difficulties that hadn't been seen before. After all, coin-operated arcade machines had been offering PvP for many years already.

But there's where the word "massively" really starts to assert its significance in the label "MMOG." Think about it for a minute. When you make a game that pits one player against another, all you have to do is provide the same tools for each side and the game is fair. But what happens when there are three players? Invariably, two of them will gang up on the third—and one of them will be at a serious disadvantage. This problem simply magnifies itself exponentially as you add more and more players to the mix.

People are inherently eager to win. In an environment that allows players the opportunity to form gangs and pick on individuals, they will do so. Players will view it as an easy way to guarantee victory. Your virtual world can quickly devolve into a society such as that in *The Lord of the Flies*—which won't be very much fun for those individuals who are systematically victimized. PvP is a tremendously fun concept—but in an MMOG environment, the "mob mentality" must be dealt with or players who aren't in a strong gang simply won't want to play.

We can see that as MMOGs became more sophisticated and feature-rich, a set of problems evolved that had never been considered in single-player (or two-player) games. The issues we've described represent merely the tip of the iceberg. MMOGs

Courtesy of Blizzard Entertainment, Inc.

Player-vs.-player battle in *World of Warcraft*

have also encountered design challenges as a result of being played via the Internet. Within days after any MMOG is launched, players are posting web sites that expose bugs and design flaws that give them advantages, cheat sites that provide all of the best solutions to any mission or quest, and third-party software that extends the features of the game in such a way that any player who doesn't have this modification will be at a disadvantage. That's the blessing and curse of MMOGs. Large numbers of people playing simultaneously create a richer and more interesting environment—but they also create situations that are difficult to predict due to the number of people involved. In a way, it's like pitting the foresight of a 20-person development team against the ingenuity of a few hundred thousand sneaky players who spend every waking moment trying to find flaws in the design. The developers can't fight this with brute force; it requires a fundamentally different way of thinking.

Technology

Let's take a look at how MMOG technology has evolved. The three main components that significantly distinguish MMOGs from other kinds of games include latency, throughput, and databases. Each component has its own way of impacting MMOGs, and each has both reflected and driven the available technology in the marketplace.

Latency

Latency is perhaps the single most important technical hurdle that needs to be overcome in MMOG development. It has always impacted MMOGs, and in one way or another it *will* impact your game as well. Sometimes referred to as *ping time*, latency is the amount of time it takes a signal to travel from your computer across the Internet to the server and back. Unfortunately, this is not a constant value. On slow modems, such as dial-ups, this can be anywhere from 110 to 150 milliseconds (ms), and sometimes far greater. On a cable modem, it might be from 10 to 50 ms—but again, it's not consistent from one Internet connection to the next or even from one *moment* to the next on the same connection. In any case, except when dealing with the fastest ping times, an impact on the game will be felt.

Consider trying to play a fighting game on an MMOG platform. Typical fighting games involve very fast-performing software. At 30 frames per second, it only takes 33 ms for every frame to play. That means that on a dial-up modem, it would take 3–5 animation frames before the server could provide the appropriate response to your computer for whatever button is pressed. That's simply unacceptable to anyone used to playing high-performance fighting games, where it is expected that the response will be "instant" (i.e., the next frame). The same logic is used when considering first-person shooters (FPSs) and racing games; both are fast game genres requiring quick responses from the server.

Courtesy of Lorax (Wikipedia Commons)

We've come a long way from the days of the 110-baud modem!

In the early days of MMOGs, action games would have been nearly unplayable with the existing latency—so RPGs and slow-moving simulations were all that was realistically feasible. If the server takes a little time to provide a response in their case, it doesn't impact gameplay negatively. In fact, some of the earliest multiplayer games were playable on teletype speeds (110 baud).

Used with permission of Sony Online Entertainment

Massively multiplayer online first-person shooters such as *PlanetSide* are possible now that latency has improved.

But as technology has advanced, the options available to MMOG developers have increased significantly. With ping times falling, new genres of games have opened up to the MMOG platform. Since the year 2000, we've seen more than one MMOFPS (such as *PlanetSide* and *World War II Online*)—and there are a number of others under development. As latency has improved, new possibilities have become available.

Throughput

Throughput is defined as the amount of data that is transferred across a channel in a specified period of time. Some of us are old enough to remember that modems used to be classified as 2400 baud, 9600 baud, 14.4 Kbps, 28.8 Kbps, etc. However, even the average technically minded person was only vaguely aware of what baud or Kbps meant, and these days we don't even bother with these labels. Modems are simply DSL modems, cable modems, T1 lines—and a host of other devices that have their own unique, mystifying throughput speeds. Happily, the specific details don't really matter much for purposes of our discussion. What does matter is the way in which throughput impacts the game. Let's consider an example to better illustrate the point.

Say we're making an early MMORPG where the only thing players can do is move around in a text-based world. What data must be sent back and forth across the Internet to support this feature? Well, if players want to move anywhere, they have to inform the server. Perhaps the player presses the F key for Forward. This key press requires only a few bytes of information to be sent to the server: the key press itself, and some header information that makes it more intelligible to the server. That's it, right?

Wrong. Once the player moves, the server must indicate that the move has been accepted. After all, what if there's a wall in front of the player? There may not be an option to move forward. So the server has to send back verification that the move was accepted. Great. Just a few more bytes. Now we're done, right?

Courtesy of TORIL MUD

```
outside the city walls.  The reception area has large brick fireplaces
on the north and south side and a wide stair that leads up to the
private rooms.  A reception desk sits on each side of these stairs
with the inn's offices tucked underneath.
Exits: - East
A broken arrow lies here, discarded.
The beautiful innkeeper stands here beaming at you from ear to ear.

Emissary Lane 8v/121V P: std > e
  Small granite stones have been laid side by side forming a
roadway through this city. The stones are off-white and have
been mortared together with a dark gray mixture.  Large torch
holders have been bolted into the walls of several buildings
about the area.  A group of merchants pass by, too intent on
their conversation to pay any heed to your passing.  The
mention of exotic goods and caravan heading west are all of
the conversation that you could catch.  A strong scent of
honey and nectar lingers here.  The lane continues north
into the center of town, south towards the caster guilds;
west is a small building of some type.
Exits: - North - South - West

< 185h/185H 120v/121V P: std >
```

Description of a new location for a player in *TORIL MUD*—one of many multi-user dungeons (MUDs) that are considered the text-based precursors to the graphics-rich massively multiplayer online games.

Nope. Don't forget the other players. Anytime players move, their computers have to be informed, and the new location has to be provided to *all* of them. It's always relevant for everyone to know where everyone else is at any given point in time. So let's say there are a dozen players. Each time the player character moves, a small packet of data (such as 10 bytes) must be sent to 11 other people. And every time any of them moves, the movement data must be sent to the players. If we assume the player can move, at most, once per second, then we're talking about 120 bytes of data that must be used every second to support 12 players (with 10 bytes going out for the player, and 110 bytes coming in for the other 11 players).

Now throw in combat, chat, and customization. (After all, players want every other player to see the cool outfits they've designed.) What about changes to the environment itself (such as non-player characters [NPCs] that can move around, talk, react to the player character, react to each other, etc.)? At this point, it's not hard to envision that our throughput needs to be up in the hundreds of bytes per second to keep up with everything.

But only being able to update the player character's position once per second simply isn't adequate. Fighting games, racing games, and FPSs need the player character's position to be updated 30 times a second or more. So multiply your estimates by 30. It's nowhere near this simple in reality, but you get the idea. The throughput that is required gets very large very quickly, especially when you try to imagine being in a crowded virtual urban center, with 100 people standing around you—talking, fighting, jumping up and down, and all wearing their own unique costumes. The critical concept here is that when you do anything at all, that action must be transmitted to everyone within visual range of you. And likewise, anything someone near you does must be transmitted to you. So when large numbers of people stand near each other, the problem of throughput expands exponentially.

```
Narrow road between lands.
You are stood on a narrow road between The Land and whence you came.
To the north and south are the small foothills of a pair of majestic
mountains, with a large wall running round. To the west the road
continues, where in the distance you can see a thatched cottage
opposite an ancient cemetery. The way out is to the east, where a
shroud of mist covers the secret pass by which you entered The
Land. It is raining.
*w
Narrow road.
You are on a narrow east-west road with a forest to the north and
Gorse scrub to the south. It is raining. A splendid necklace lies
on the ground.
?
```

The start screen of *MUD1,* considered to be the oldest virtual world in existence—was created by Richard Bartle and Roy Trubshaw in 1978.

In early MMOGs, it wasn't necessary to update position very often (once per second was fine), and transactions such as chat and barter use relatively low bandwidth. With clever optimizations, 20 or 30 players could be supported on a 110-baud modem (as accomplished by the game *MUD1* in 1978).

As time marched on, more features contributed to throughput needs—as did faster and more accurate positional data. As MMOGs became more complex, the amount of throughput per player increased. To demonstrate this clearly, refer to the accompanying diagram—which has been compiled from information provided by a number of early MMOG developers. The diagram doesn't include every MMOG ever made, but it shows how trends have been increasing over time. It is interesting to note how although the numbers bounce around a bit, the trend shows a gradual evolution over time—rather than major revolutionary leaps. As stated earlier, the advancement of MMOGs has been an evolutionary process.

Diagram by Per Olin

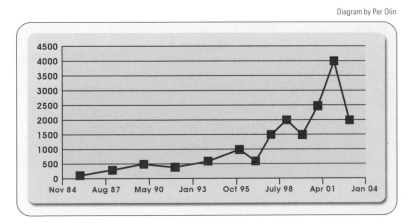

The increase in required bandwidth per player over the last 20 years

Databases

Recall that in the definition of an MMOG, the concept of "persistence" was introduced. This was described as the need for the players' achievements, physical positions in the world, and possessions to be maintained when they log on and off over the course of time. In early MMOGs, developers simply stored these things directly in the server's RAM and transferred all of the data to a text file at the end of the day. It wasn't very elegant, but it wasn't considered a complicated problem either.

As the number of players began to increase, so did the number of things they could do, objects they could acquire, and achievements they could make. The problem started to magnify. With a few thousand players all wandering around in a server killing bad guys, trading objects, finding treasure, completing missions, firing bullets or arrows, drinking potions, using gasoline, or burning up antimatter crystals, the need for a transactional *database* became apparent.

Courtesy NCsoft

NCsoft (Austin) technical customer support representative Lance Schibi

In fact, not only was player data on the rise, but a new MMOG requirement really crystallized the need for databases: customer support. As MMOGs became big business, it became necessary to keep better records. Developers had to know all kinds of information about, for example, the player's accounts, billing records, and complaint records. (Unfortunately, any time there is a large crowd of people, some of them will enjoy harassing those around them, and customer support needs to keep a record of how often complaints are lodged, and against whom.) Customer support representatives need to be able to access, sort, and query this information as rapidly as possible to service the vast numbers of people subscribing to their games.

Since 2000, MMOGs have evolved the need for extremely powerful transactional databases, capable of logging tens of thousands of changes per second. In some cases, MMOG databases have become as advanced as the most powerful databases of national financial institutions. We've come a long way from posting text files at the end of each business day.

Business Model

Most developers tend to consider the MMOG only from the two perspectives presented earlier: design and technology. A more subtle and perhaps more powerful way to consider the MMOG is from the business model perspective. After all, we need more money to create sophisticated designs with powerful technology. However, no one is going to *spend* more money on development unless they're sure to see greater revenues when the game ships. If they can't realize a profit, then it's not a business venture worth taking. It is fair to say that an MMOG is not just a different kind of game; it's a different kind of business entirely. Unlike typical games, you don't just pay for the game in the box, play it, and move on. In the MMOG model, the revenues generated by the box sales only account for roughly 20% of the total. The vast majority of revenues are brought in by the monthly subscription fees.

It's fascinating to see how the monetization model has evolved over time. In the earliest online games, players were charged an hourly fee to play. In some cases, this was as much as $12–14 per *hour*. If we break out our abacus for a moment, we see that it will cost between $480 and $560 a month to play this sort of game for 10 hours per week! That's a staggering sum for a game, and yet some players paid that and more.

But really, who were these crazy people? What kind of fanatic would pay $500 a month to play a game? Most of them weren't wealthy, bored aristocrats with a lot of spare time on their hands. No, the fanatics were known as "early adopters"—those few pioneering souls who are so enthusiastic about new technology that they're willing to pay anything they can afford (sometimes more than they can afford) to be on board before the rest of the world.

While this sounds attractive to some people, it represents a small fraction of the player universe. The overwhelming majority of players simply won't pay that much, no matter how *cool* it is to be on the leading edge of technology. The result? Hourly fees started coming down and the number of players increased.

The trick was to understand the model. Is it better to have 1,000 players paying $500 a month or 50,000 players paying $10 a month? Since the revenues generated by both are identical, we might intuitively say, "Well, 1,000 players a month will only require five customer support representatives, while 50,000 players will take 25 customer support representatives, so I'll make more profit on the 1,000 players each paying $500 a month."

That's true, but there's a problem. People come and go from MMOGs. A new one starts up, and they abandon the old game to try the new one. And when your customer base is small, every player that leaves the game is a huge revenue hit. It's much easier to deal with attrition in the second option: 50,000 players paying $10 a month. So prices started falling, and the number of subscribers started rising. However, as games became deeper and more time consuming, players realized that with an hourly fee they had the choice of either playing less or going broke. But when they played less, the addiction wasn't as strong, and they tended to eventually stop playing altogether.

Thus, the monthly subscription fee was born. Instead of paying by the hour, players were charged by the month—regardless of how many hours they played the game. This opened up the marketplace considerably. One of the first games to charge a monthly subscription fee was *Aradath*, in 1984, which charged players $40 a month.

Over the ensuing decade, even monthly subscription fees dropped, until they eventually bottomed out in the mid-1990s at an average of around $10 a month. Since then, they've slowly crept back up. The accompanying diagram shows the evolution of how much money certain players paid to play their respective MMOGs. To make it easy, the chart assumes each player spends 10 hours per week playing their game.

Diagram by Per Olin

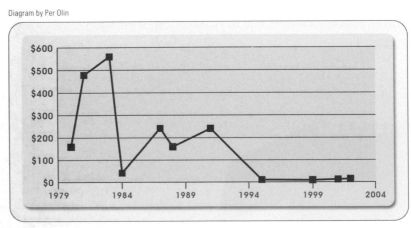

Average cost to play an MMOG per month

The information in the previous diagram isn't that different from the cost decreases we would expect to see for any innovation entering the marketplace. It doesn't look much different from, say, the evolution for the cost of a calculator over a 20-year span. In the early 1970s, a calculator used to cost about $500. These days, they give away more powerful calculators for free when you open a new checking account with a bank. And, as expected, when the cost of the product decreases, the number of people who are willing to pay increases proportionately. Of course, better features, better technology, and better marketing all contribute to the equation as well.

Diagram by Per Olin

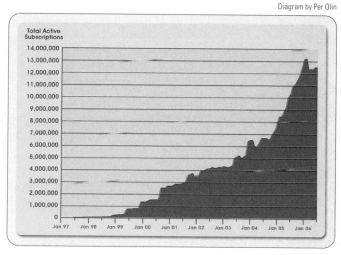

The explosion of MMOG players from 1997 to 2006

And finally, as noted earlier, the cost of developing MMOGs has increased over time as well. As MMOGs have become larger, more sophisticated, and more content rich, it has required systematically larger development teams and longer schedules to build them. For example, in 1980, Richard Bartle finished *MUD1* with a total of roughly 24 months of effort. By 2004, a typical MMOG consumed roughly 1,400 months of labor. Made possible by quite a number of industry friends and acquaintances, the accompanying diagram shows how development costs have been rising.

Diagram by Per Olin

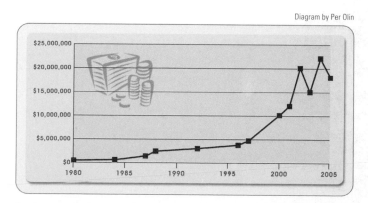

As the complexity of the development effort increases, so do the costs.

So now that you have a feel for the incredible potential of the MMOG market, it's time to start learning exactly how these games are made. The days when a couple of college students can slap together a niche hobby project in a few months are over. Given the revenues they generate, MMOGs have become big business, and are being treated accordingly. They are breathtakingly risky, expensive gambles for game developers. They often require teams of 50–100 developers typically consuming 3–6 years of development time, at a cost in the tens of millions of dollars. They are the ultimate game development gamble, with the proverbial pot of gold at the end of the rainbow.

Throughout the remainder of this book, we'll discuss what goes into building one of these behemoths. You'll learn what separates them from single-player games, how the design must be approached, planning, managing communities, and handling the business and service once the game launches. From start to finish, you'll see that far from being the nightmarishly complex, overwhelming monster that they might appear at first, MMOGs are actually just a fascinating new frontier to explore. To be sure, they require fundamentally different thinking and much more careful planning, but MMOGs are the wave of the future of computer gaming, and well worth the effort.

:::CHAPTER REVIEW:::

1. Imagine that you are an online game developer working in the 1980s. Knowing the limitations associated with this era, what type of online game would you develop?

2. Play three online games—one from the 1980s, one from the 1990s, and one released after 2004. Compare and contrast how graphics, audio (or lack thereof), and multiplayer capabilities are utilized in all three games.

3. Why has the business model for MMOGs changed so dramatically over time? Discuss economics, technology, and the production process in your answer.

2

CHAPTER

Constraints

understand the issues before designing

Key Chapter Questions

- What are *constraints* and why do you need to understand them?

- How does a *business model* impact design?

- How does *technology* impact design?

- In what ways must *gameplay* be distinct in games involving thousands of players?

- Is more work involved in building the game itself, or the *infrastructure* that supports it?

Before charging off to start designing the next great massively multiplayer online game (MMOG), it's best to *create the box* within which you'll be working. You need to understand the nature of the differences between a single-player game and one that will be played by thousands of players simultaneously. There are many such differences—which we'll call *constraints*—and each one will impact the way you think about your design. You need to look at the game from a very high level—and understand how each component of the game, infrastructure, and online service interacts with the players. Failure to recognize and understand the constraints that are involved may result in your MMOG collapsing like an expensive house of cards.

Constraint is Not a Four-Letter Word

Constraint is one of those words that seem to have generated a bad reputation for itself. When most designers hear this word, it conjures up a dictionary definition that makes them cringe. *A constraint is a limitation of possibilities,* or (our favorite) *it is the threat or use of force to control the thoughts or behavior of others* (actually found in a dictionary)! Designers see the long list of ugly synonyms—restraint, restriction, limitation, limit, control, or a lack of freedom—and they start to get angry.

When designers hear about having to design around the constraints of a problem, many immediately assume there's an intent to assert dictatorial control over their creativity. They see constraints as an artificial imposition of limits that will curb their creativity and squelch their much prized, right-brained freedom. A puff of smoke drifts off the tops of some designers' heads, and they grumble off into the next room—hoping this is just being said to satisfy the "suits" and they'll be rejoined in the land of imagination tomorrow.

But the reality is that constraints aren't limitations at all. In fact, they're a series of guideposts that will help you explore a design idea more fully. Constraints do that. They focus your thinking in ways that help you to take a concept deeper and explore it more fully. Ah, but that statement sounds ambiguous at best—so let's consider an example.

Illustration by Ben Bourbon

Think of a brilliant game design. Right now. Make it something new, something that even *you* haven't considered before (i.e., not something that's been sitting percolating in the back of your head for the past five years). Take five minutes and consider it now. Physically put this book down and think for a few minutes.

We're going to assume that five minutes wasn't enough time to come up with an innovative, brilliant idea. But that's not important. What *is* important is the thought process you went through to start that effort. If you're a designer who's worth your salt, you had to ask yourself a few questions (or provide answers to questions) right from the start. Your questions probably involved the following: What is the game's hardware platform? What is the primary genre? What's the target audience demographic? Am I working with an existing intellectual property or trying to develop something new?

You may or may not have mentally asked these specific questions—but somewhere in your head, you had similar questions and knew the answers. For instance, maybe you decided you were going to design a vampire-themed online role-playing game (RPG). Well, guess what? That's a *constraint*. The answers to all of the preceding questions are constraints. Each one shapes limitations on your project, whether you like it or not. It makes a difference whether your game will be built for hand-held, computer, or online via Xbox Live. Limits exist—whether you're making an RPG, racing game, simulation, or sports game. Making a game for 5–10 year olds or 18–35 year olds impacts the kinds of choices allowed.

Courtesy of Starpeace

Navy Field

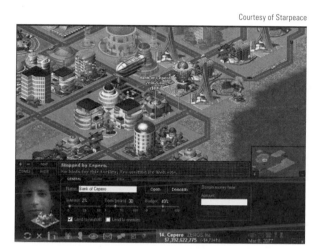 

Focusing on a specific genre, such as massively multiplayer online real-time strategy games *Starpeace* (business) and *Navy Field* (Navy combat), is a type of constraint.

But somehow, the *obvious* constraints don't seem to bother us. We turn them into an advantage. They give us direction and free us from having to waste time thinking about nonsensical possibilities. Knowing that we're designing an adventure game for, say, 8-year-old kids, we start to ask ourselves questions about what 8-year-olds like. We watch a bunch of *Power Rangers* and *Rugrats* cartoons just to get us into the right mental groove. A good designer will try to explore the world of the 8-year-old and understand what makes it fun to design a game for that audience.

So think about that for a minute. The demographic constraint just did something for us. It acted like a guidepost. It gave us a specific path to explore. It gave us focus and direction. It told us where to look. Yes, technically, it acted like a limitation in that it *disallowed* a large range of possible content—but we didn't really view that as a bad thing because we know there's still a huge realm of options open to us.

In point of fact, this is how you should think of all constraints. Don't treat them as limitations. Instead, think of them as sign posts that will point you in the direction of unexplored territory that will have its own unique set of issues and challenges. The more creatively you deal with those challenges, the more interesting your game will be.

Illustration by Ben Bourbon

Yes! An RTS about Intergalactic Amish Space Marines!

If you spend enough time working on these solutions, turning them into solid features, the effort often drives intriguing and innovative ideas. It actually makes sense. Most ideas are only problems because they haven't been properly explored. Creating features in underexplored areas leads to innovation almost by definition.

With all this in mind, let's go out and *look for* constraints. The more we can find, the more focused our thinking will be—and the deeper we can take our subject matter. Let's see what kinds of constraints are built-in for MMOGs and how they will impact designs. The accompanying diagram lists some basic considerations, which have been divided into three categories. Each item constitutes a constraint to consider (or a new territory to explore) in the development process. If we're smart about it, we can turn these constraints into creative *features* rather than simply have them serve as limitations.

Diagram by Per Olin

Business	Technology	Gameplay
The Revenue Model	Current State-of-the-Art	Community
Usability	Security	Troublesome Players
Monetization Model	Latency	Sacred Cows
Customer Support	Bandwidth	A Virtual Economy
Development Time	Infrastructural Needs	Cultural Considerations
	AI Performance	Quantifying Ourselves

This isn't intended to be a comprehensive list. It's just the most basic list of common constraints. Every project will have its own unique collection of constraints; it's up to you to identify what they are and develop your game with them in mind. The first step to doing that is to identify those constraints. We'll learn how to deal with them later.

Business Constraints

The first type of constraint that can affect any design is the *business constraint*. Although we idealistically tend to think of a game design as a purely creative endeavor, it actually isn't. Like it or not, much like a Hollywood film, the point of making a game is to make money. That means we have to understand exactly how much the game will cost to build and operate and consider this against how much money we can make from it. Understanding these issues will provide us with important considerations for the game's design, as we will see.

Revenue Model

MMOGs have captured the attention of all segments of the game industry. Looking at MMOGs superficially, we see a dream come true. Typical single-player games involve paying for two years of development costs, followed by a few months of sales—and then the cycle repeats. It's a very spiky revenue model that looks something like the accompanying diagram, which assumes a 25-person development team for two years, contractors, marketing costs, and manufacturing costs —all fairly typical of a development effort where one is attempting to make a AAA single-player game. The bars indicate how much money the developer currently has in the bank. Right off the bat, we can see that for two years, the developer is in the red. Then there's a massive spike as the game hits the shelves, the debt is erased, and we're swimming in money. It looks great, although it's scary for the first two years. Why? Because this chart assumes that the game in question will sell one million units. But there's no guarantee of that. Two more graphs follow that show what the situation looks like with half a million units sold and a quarter of a million units sold, respectively. It's not quite so rosy.

Diagram by Per Olin

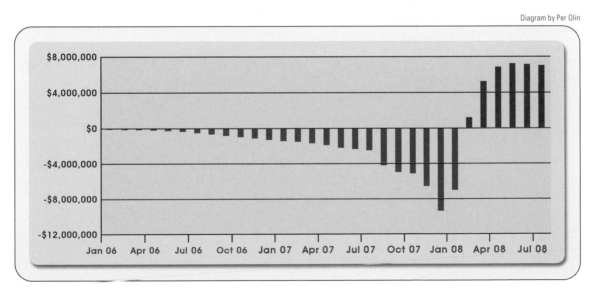

Cash flow model for a single-player game selling one million units

Diagram by Per Olin

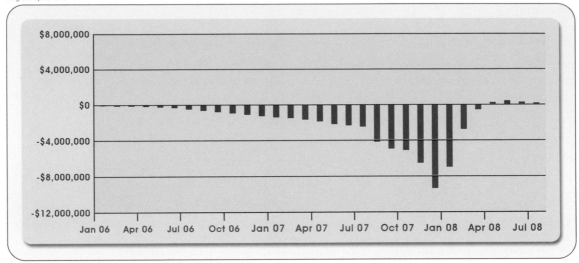

Same game at 500,000 units sold

Diagram by Per Olin

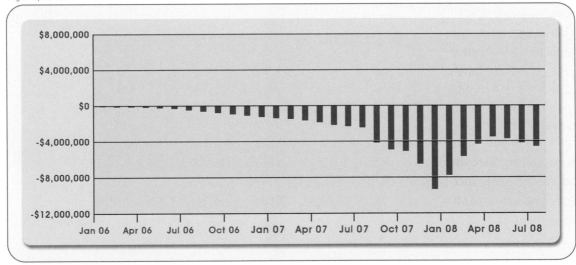

Same game at 250,000 units sold

At 500,000 units, the developer barely breaks even—and at 250,000 units, it never gets any better than $3 million in debt. Of course, these models assume that we're going all-out—spending the money and time to make a AAA title. There are ways to decrease development costs and time, but the charts still demonstrate the point of how risky and volatile the cash flow model is for a single-player game. So now let's look at how an MMOG cash flow model works.

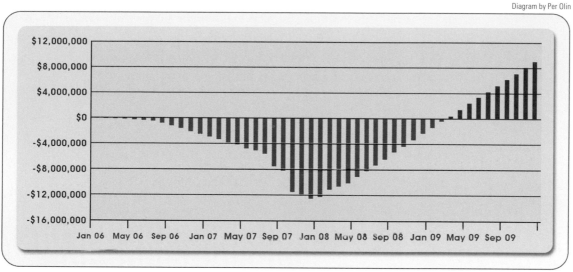

MMOG selling a total of 250,000 units over the course of two years

In the accompanying diagram, we've increased the development team to a size of 50, spent several million dollars on servers, and factored in elements such as "newbie churn" and "veteran churn" (the rates at which players opt not to pay for subscriptions or cancel their subscriptions). We've stretched out the unit sales over a two-year period and have approximated the cost of running the service. Still, with a total of 250,000 units sold, this game covers all development and service costs and winds up showing a $9 million bank balance within two years after launch—and the curve is still rising (sometimes continuing for many more years).

It's not hard to see why the business model for MMOGs is so attractive. You don't have to be wildly successful to make money. Oh, and in case you were wondering: In the event our MMOG sells one million units over the same time period, our bank account two years after launch would be just over $100 million. Compare this with the $16 million you'd have in the bank after making a pair of million-unit single-player games in the same time period, and you can see what has the game industry so worked up. It's big business.

But before we get too excited, let's look at the other side of the coin. The accompanying diagram shows our MMOG with the same 250,000 units sold over two years, but with one major change: a dramatically decreased retention of players (i.e., an MMOG that doesn't give players a reason to stay very long).

As you can see, there is a cost associated with running the service—and, if players don't have a reason to stick around, the game actually *loses* money over time. The only difference between this chart and the other two-year cash flow chart is the desire for players to stick around and pay a subscription fee. Everything else remains exactly the same. This chart looks similar to the single-player game that sells 250,000 units, except it loses roughly four times as much money. You get the picture. It's enormously important to provide an experience that gives players incentive to play for a much longer time than in a typical single-player game.

Diagram by Per Olin

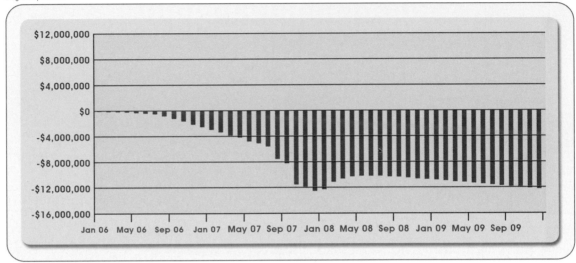

MMOG selling a total of 250,000 units over two years, but where players don't stay very long

But now the question on your mind might be: How is all this a *constraint*? It looks more like a business model. It's a constraint for one huge reason. The success or failure of the entire model depends on subscription revenues. As you saw in the difference between the two-year cash flow examples, the desire for players to stick around and play longer than 40 hours makes a difference of over $20 million dollars in the bank account. That's the key. The *cash flow* model for MMOGs forces us to fundamentally change our goals in game design. The design is no longer about a compact, powerful, 40-hour experience. It's about crafting a *lifestyle* for people. *That* is a constraint.

In the MMOG world, you can't design a game that entertains a player for a mere 20–40 hours. An MMOG has to entertain the player for *thousands* of hours. The player has to want to keep playing month after month, and keep shelling out a subscription fee. This is a fundamentally different kind of experience from what we'd design in a single-player game, but it's one we *have* to deal with. If we don't get MMOG players to pay a subscription fee every month, the revenue model breaks down disastrously.

Given this information, how do we deal with this constraint? Well, first and foremost we try to understand how it limits the kind of game we can build. Think about some of the great story-based games you've played. Games such as *The Legend of Zelda, Metal Gear Solid, Fable, Prince of Persia*, or anything in that vein, wouldn't work as designed in a massively multiplayer setting. Why? Because they involve a story with a beginning, middle, and end. You *can't* end the story in a massively multiplayer game. If you end the story, people will have no reason to stick around and play. So even though all of these games were quite successful, their heavy dependence on stories with a climactic ending makes them inappropriate for an MMOG.

Will adventure games such as *Monkey Island, Full Throttle, Day of the Tentacle, Myst,* or *The Longest Journey* work? Nope. Once the player has solved all of the puzzles, no matter how imaginative and cool they were, the game isn't interesting to play anymore; there's no *replayability* value. To make them work for a long-term MMOG experience, you'd have to design thousands of puzzles, and that simply isn't practical.

Plot-driven stories, found in games such as *Prince of Persia: The Sands of Time*, can present problems in MMOGs

Funcom

Adventure games such as *Dreamfall: The Longest Journey* don't translate well into massively multiplayer online games—primarily because of their linear gameplay and lack of replayability.

In fact, any game that has a distinct objective as the core gameplay element—whether that's beating a boss, solving puzzles, finding hidden treasure, or living an epic story—won't work "as is" in an MMOG environment. You can't ever get to an end point of any kind in an MMOG. Give players a feeling of finality, and they're sure to wander off and play something else. And, as we've already seen, that breaks our attractive revenue model and will make the executives very, very angry with us. Climactic endings or ultimate objectives don't work in MMOGs. This conclusion might seem rather obvious. You might think, "Yeah, yeah. I get it. MMOGs have to go on forever. No biggie." But this is not as easy as it sounds. Consider a level-based RPG. Your character kills monsters, collects experience, and raises level by level. But there's always a maximum level. Whether that maximum is level 20, 50, 100, or 1,000, the players will reach it eventually. Then what? If you don't have compelling things for them to do when they max out their character level…off they go, along with subscription revenues.

And while you're thinking about that, recall that an MMOG has to entertain the player for thousands of hours. The word "entertain" is critical here. It's also highly relative. Something that works in a 40-hour experience probably won't work in a 1,000-hour experience. The concept of leveling a character shouldn't be monotonous in an MMOG. It might be fun to kill orcs for a while and switch to monsters that are more and more difficult to kill after a few dozen hours—but that in itself can't possibly entertain a player for *thousands* of hours. Players need a greater diversity of things to do. Players need breaks in the game, where they're not constantly out in the field killing things. Your design must compensate for a natural rhythm and pacing that will last a very long time—mixing tension with humor, fear, rest, socialization, environment, and a plethora of other activities.

Aaron Marks on MMOG Constraints :::::

Aaron Marks
(Composer; Founder,
On Your Mark Music)

Practically falling into the game industry almost 10 years ago, Aaron Marks has amassed music and sound design credits on touch-screen arcade games, class II video bingo/slot machines, computer games, console games—and over 70 online casino games. Aaron has also written for *Game Developer Magazine,* Gamasutra.com, and Music4Games.net. He is the author of *The Complete Guide to Game Audio,* an expansive book on all aspects of audio for video games—and of the forthcoming *Game Audio Development,* part of the *Game Development Essentials* series. He is also a member of the advisory board for the Game Audio Network Guild (GANG)—and he continues his pursuit of the ultimate soundscape, creating music and sound for various projects.

Unlike the developer who creates a "standard" video game, the developer of an MMOG must also be willing and able to provide continuous support and resources to keep the community active. Not only is the technical aspect of running servers with sufficient bandwidth to prevent lag, security, and bug fixes necessary—but an entire creative team must be in continuous motion to create new content in order to keep players happy and engaged. It's a tremendous commitment and not for the weak at heart!

Usability

In this book, we'll define *usability* as a set of techniques for making the game easier to learn and understand. This can be accomplished by making more intuitive user interfaces (UIs), simpler game mechanics, and rich content that appeals to the broadest possible audience. You might think that usability is a gameplay constraint, but this is not necessarily the case. Many games are a lot of fun for hardcore audiences, but they're just too obscure and complex for the casual player. This doesn't make them bad games. It just means that they cater to a niche audience. Usability is a constraint born from the desire to sell to a larger customer base. A usable game is clear, focused, usually fairly simple, and invites players into a place that feels comfortable and familiar. It's a business-driven decision that is designed to maximize retention, and thus maximize profits.

The "game design purists" who scoff at the idea of a simple, clear game design are often amusing. Many designers feel like complexity is a *must* in MMOGs, and they look down upon the "casual gamer." They might tell you that "an MMOG player is, by definition, someone who is willing to devote large portions of their life to playing this game. They want depth, complexity, and a limitless number of things to do. They want realism and difficult challenges. They wear their suffering through the steep learning curve like a medal of honor around their necks." There are so many things wrong with this sentiment that it's hard to know where to begin. While it's true that the goal of an MMOG is to provide an incentive for people to play as much as possible, this has utterly nothing to do with complexity—but *immersion*. Making a game that's friendly and inviting, easy to learn, and a *place* where players want to be is the goal. Most players don't want to have to research to play a game. They don't want to feel like it would be less work to pass the bar exam. They just want to have fun.

As for *realism*, again, this is bewildering. Simulation games aside, who wants reality? Games are fun because in them you can *escape* from reality, not live through more of it. You don't want a world of tedious details and number crunching. Honestly, if you were learning to cast magic, all the fantasy novels tell you there are *years* of study involved. Clearly none of us wants *that* reality. So where do we draw the line? When it stops being fun, it's too much reality.

The details of making a game more usable will be covered in the design sections. For now it will suffice to say that there are three main areas on which to focus attention: user interface, atmosphere, and gameplay mechanics. The goal will be to make these three areas intuitive, aesthetically appealing, simple, logical, consistent, and clear.

Illustration by 3en Bourbon.

Creating games for small, hardcore audiences may be more personally interesting to the game designer, but it's not very good business.

> When I create an activity in a game that I know people are going to try to make a macro to overcome, that's a feature I remove from the design. If it was a fun feature, people would want to play it, not start a macro running and go grab a sandwich.
>
> —Rick Hall

Monetization Model

Monetization is a concept that game developers often don't need to consider unless they are developing MMOGs. For a typical single-player game, you get money by selling the box. That's all there is to it. But MMOGs turn out to be very different. There are several ways to get money from the customer. The basic subscription model is more involved than you might think at first glance. Sure, you ask the players for $15 a month—and if they like your game, they pay the fee. But how do they pay it?

Remember, *monthly subscription fees* don't require a trip to the game store. Players can just submit their credit card numbers into your billing system and have the fee deducted every month. But some folks don't like to have recurring bills on their credit cards. Some players aren't old enough to have them. In some countries, such as Japan, credit cards are fairly unusual—and many people simply don't have them. So how do all of those people pay?

- *Game Time Cards*: With game time cards, players can go to the store every month and spend $15 to buy a card—much like a phone card. It has a registration code in it that players punch into the system when it's time to pay the bill. Some players don't want to have to go to the trouble of buying a game time card every month, so they buy a three-month card or a six-month card. Some games now allow billing to be done through cell phones.
- *Pay-to-Play*: This model works just fine in the United States and Japan. But in South Korea (one of the most wired nations on earth), players don't buy the games at all. The overwhelming majority of players just go to Internet game rooms, where the computers are all set up—with games installed and connections ready to go. These people don't buy the game, but they pay $1 an hour to play any game they want.
- *Micro-Transactions*: Some companies are leaning toward what's known as a micro-transaction billing system. The game has no monthly subscription fee. Instead, players can buy from a selection of digital actions, paying for them in small chunks. Players might buy a laser blaster for $0.50 or a rocket booster for $1.50. There are thousands of items from which to choose, and players can just "go shopping" anytime they like.

Each of the billing models involves slight differences to how you design your game. We've already seen how the standard billing model affects the way we have to approach the design. But how do the other monetization methods change this? The two models that impact design most significantly are the game room and the micro-transaction models. Let's consider each separately.

Game Room Model

Why does it matter if you're playing from a *game room* instead of your system at home? Well, first and foremost, game rooms are big open spaces—with players actually close enough to talk to each other. Team communication becomes far more efficient when players can shout instructions and call for help verbally, rather than having to type tedious text chat messages. And when you can count on your players all having more effective teamwork, it opens up more possibilities for tactics and strategies. You can actually use tougher creatures and harder challenges when you know for sure that a tightly communicating group will be dealing with them.

Courtesy of Hachimaki (Wikipedia Commons)

Courtesy NCsoft

Just by looking at an Internet game room, you can tell it's a different environment. MMOGs in an Internet game room play more like a LAN party game than the typical MMOG.

Lineage subscriber numbers are incredibly high, in part because it's free to open an account in a game room (*Lineage: The Blood Pledge,* shown).

Since players pay per hour to play in game rooms, they don't pay a subscription fee. The game room pays a set fee per month to carry the game, and players can open accounts and create characters anytime they want. And because you don't know if they'll quit for six months and then come back, the account can never close. (That's why *Lineage* subscriber numbers are so insanely high, by the way; since it's free to open an account in a game room, some people have *dozens* of accounts. And since the accounts can never be closed, then everyone who has ever been opened is counted as an "active subscriber.") This tends to put a lot more stress on the database than a typical MMOG, and it requires more careful architecture. It also opens loopholes for various kinds of *griefers* (people who derive their entertainment from ruining other players' experiences). Game room designs and development require some extra care and thought before being undertaken.

Micro-Transaction Model

Now let's switch gears and think about *micro-transaction* billing. This type of billing scheme has quite a bit of impact on game design. Think about it. If players can *buy* any item in the game instead of working or fighting for it, then not only will

Illustration by Ben Bourbon

We started deleting their characters and then charging to get them restored!

many players have everything of value on the day the game launches, but it reduces the ways in which you can reward your players for hard-fought victories. Why fight for something when you can just spend $1 and buy it?

The game industry is often pretty clever when it comes to dreaming up new ways to get more money out of players. Sooner or later, someone will come up with yet another monetization scheme. Your job as a developer will be to find out up front what type of scheme will be used, figure out how it will affect your game, and design accordingly.

Some companies will do *anything* to make money.

Customer Support

One of the biggest costs associated with running an MMOG once it goes live is *customer support (CS)*. Players have come to expect that when they encounter difficulties in the game, they can call upon a service representative who has the tools to assist them. CS representatives are traditionally available at least during "prime time" playing hours—but often support is offered 24/7 (because the game is being played 24/7). To support several hundred thousand players, perhaps 20–30 (or more) CS representatives will be employed in shifts. It's easy to see how the expense can mount. CS representatives are called upon to resolve issues such as helping players who have gotten stuck somewhere on the map, addressing software bugs that have "eaten" items, mediating disputes, dealing with troublesome players, providing technical support, and even sometimes explaining the workings of the game to novice players.

The constraint here is to try to anticipate all of the various reasons (or as many as you can) players might need customer support—and provide in-game tools that allow players to resolve their own problems without having to call on the reps. These tools can appear in many forms—such as automated help systems, teleport features, and automatic hardware profiling tools. Each type of problem will require thought and careful solutions. Remember that every tool you give to a player can affect game balance. For instance, it's almost impossible to create a 3D world map that has no *stuck points* (unintentional glitches in the world where your character can get stuck, unable to move or escape). No matter how carefully you build the world, players will ingeniously hunt with ferret-like determination, until they manage to get stuck somewhere that they can't escape.

A common solution to this problem is to give players buttons they can push that will teleport them to known safe spots. Sounds straightforward, right? What could go wrong? Well, if you give players unrestricted use of this particular feature, they'll use it as a means of transportation—possibly undermining the reasons for "travel time." They'll also probably start using this tool as a means of escaping a fight when needed. So to solve these problems, you have to limit how often the tool can be used, and under what circumstances it's not available. (For instance, it can't be used if you're currently engaged in combat.)

Of course, many games already have various means of teleportation (such as hearthstones, runes, and teleport spells), and this feature is included partly to resolve the "stuck point" problem so players don't have to resort to calling CS reps. Even though it's a common feature, it still demonstrates how even the simplest tools that are intended as a means of assisting CS can be turned into game unbalancing problems if care isn't taken to design them properly.

> Someone just used the automated help system to teleport the entire crafter's guild to the bottom of the ocean.

Illustration by Ben Bourbon

Some players get more fun out of misusing the game system than actually playing the game.

Nonetheless, the more tools that you provide players to help resolve traditional "CS problems," the more you'll reduce the strain on your CS reps. Clearly, if you can get by with fewer representatives, it will have a positive impact on the profitability of the game. Use care, and devise tools that reduce the CS strain in as many ways as you can—but don't let the tools be turned against you.

Development Time

Despite the wishes of most developers, it is not a good thing to have an unlimited amount of development time. Aside from the obvious reason that more development time equals more development costs, unlimited development time has other negative effects.

- *Projects with excessive development schedules tend to lose focus.* The longer you take to develop a game, the more likely you are to "wander off into the weeds" creating features that have nothing to do with the core concept; this eventually detracts from the game.
- *Longer development can result in constant modifications and "tweaking."* This tends to make the code base start to turn into a Frankenstein mess.
- *The longer you look at something, the more you become convinced that its imperfections are glaring and horrible, increasing the temptation to make more and more changes.* Remember, you'll probably work on the game longer than most players will spend playing it. In essence, you'll get tired of it, and have a tendency to make unjustified adjustments.

When you settle on a development schedule, you should make every effort to stick to it. That means you should exercise great care in scoping your project appropriately. Go with the rule of quality over quantity. Give yourself plenty of time to polish the features you build. Make them deep, clear, intuitive, and clean. This will give you much better results than building an enormous number of features, only to see them all implemented half-heartedly. Despite popular belief, a smaller set of well-executed features is better than a larger number of average ones. Avoid the temptation of trying to make your game encompass "everything." Just do what you do well, and you'll be fine.

Technology Constraints

Let's start by defining "technology constraints" as any issue of technology that impacts the design of the game. In some cases, you'll begin development with an existing game engine like *Unreal* or *Quake*, and the software architecture of the engine will impose certain limitations on what you can and can't do. In other cases, you'll develop your own engine, and you will encounter things you don't have the technical expertise or time to develop. And in yet other cases, the platform itself (whether PC, handheld, or console) will produce limitations. Understanding right from the beginning how your software engine and hardware platform can affect your game design will save you a lot of rework time later on.

Current State of the Art

Some single-player games have made their mark by being technological marvels. Some of the latest 3D and physics engines are so stunning that people play the games just for the thrill of staring slack-jawed at the incredible technology on the screen. Some of these games don't even have particularly interesting or innovative gameplay, but they are still successful for their sheer "shock and awe" value.

Be very careful about pursuing this "state-of-the-art" approach for MMOGs. While it works just fine for single-player games, it is a rather dubious approach for MMOGs. As you learned in the Business Constraints section, an MMOG has to keep people entertained for thousands of hours if the revenue model is to work. There are two huge reasons why leading edge technology doesn't help us achieve that goal.

1. *No matter how amazing the graphics or physics systems might be, they won't keep an average player entertained for very long.* They're fine for a compact, 20–40 hour experience. However, eventually we become accustomed to the "shiny object" and our fascination wears off. After that, if there isn't gameplay value, the player will move on. In the big scheme of things, 30–40 hours is less than 2% of the amount of time you should hope for a player to subscribe to your MMOG. But more often than not, developing that killer new technology requires *far more* than 2% of the development schedule and budget. Pursuing state-of-the-art technology in an MMOG is likely to be a poor allocation of resources.

2. *No matter how cutting-edge your technology might be, it won't take long for the rest of the industry to duplicate it.* Even if your big claim to fame is some incredible marvel of engineering, someone else will have something better a year later. The hope for MMOGs is that they'll last for many years. If your only redeeming value is great technology, you're sunk as soon as someone comes along with something better.

This isn't to say you should ignore state-of-the-art technology. It's just that, unlike single-player games, great technology can't be your main selling point. It simply doesn't have the "legs" to carry you through the long haul.

During the *Day of the Tentacle* and *Full Throttle* days, it was amazing how companies such as LucasArts could make such great games with yesterday's technology. Blizzard has had similar success. Rather than fuss with twitchy, poorly performing, CPU-crushing software, they've taken code that's solid and proven and have applied tremendous personality and production value to it. This same philosophy has also reaped significant rewards at Lionhead and Maxis. It can definitely be done. Some of the best game developers in the world understand that great production value is easier to achieve and just as effective (if not more so) than great technology. If anything, this is even truer for MMOGs.

Illustration by Ben Bourbon

Consider the benefit to your game before committing to expensive, time-consuming features.

Even when it was first released, *RuneScape* was pretty low-tech, but that doesn't stop it from being one of the most popular games of its kind.

So what's the constraint here? Balance carefully the amount of time you spend developing great technology against the amount of time you spend developing great features. The more you can do with solid, proven, dependable, existing technology, the better off you'll be. If you have existing technology, take up the challenge of implementing great features that can utilize that technology as is, or with minimal modification. When your game goes live and you actually find yourself with a stable code base, you'll be glad you did.

Security

There's one maxim here that you should always remember: Never assume all the players are trustworthy. In MMOGs, you have to remember that the player is alone with the game executable. If you do any calculations at all on the client side, the player has access to them. And anything players have access to, they can change. What this means is that any calculations you do that can affect gameplay (including whether you hit your target or not when you swing or shoot, how much damage you inflict, decisions that your opponents will make, whether or not you can open a locked door) *all* have to be made on the server side.

The constraint should be obvious. When you're dealing with thousands of players per server, and perhaps tens of thousands of non-player character (NPC) opponents, there's an enormous amount of work to be done by the server. Any time you propose a feature that will be computationally or memory-intensive to resolve, you have to consider whether or not your server could handle that feature in the worst case scenario—in which hundreds or thousands of players are accessing it at the same time.

There was an incident in *Ultima Online* in which players started throwing "purple potions" all at once in front of the Britain Bank. A "purple potion" was a weapon that exploded when it impacted, and inflicted damage to everything in a limited radius around it. As it turned out, we didn't have an efficient radius-checking technique. It was computationally intensive to check against the potentially hundreds of characters that constantly surrounded the bank. So when dozens of players all started throwing a large quantity of explosive purple potions at each other

> There are so many more moving parts in an online game than in a single-player title. For online worlds, we have to worry about load, servers, support, deployments, updates, and a host of other logistical issues that aren't ever considered in a single-player game.
>
> —*Jeff Anderson*
> (President & CEO, Turbine, Inc.)

all at the same time, the server became buried in tens of thousands of simultaneous radius checks. The Live Team eventually fixed the problem, but when players first discovered it, they were able to bring the server to its knees any time they wanted.

Here's how all of this relates to network security: There are several things you have to secure when developing an MMOG:

Courtesy NCsoft

- Client side code
- Network traffic (as in encryption)
- Server access
- Account access
- Customer support tool
- Patch server

A look inside an MMOG server collocation facility at NCsoft

As you can see, there are several things to consider. Such considerations become a different kind of constraint on the development process. You have to spend a lot of time and effort handling this area properly. You have to compensate for this (and other infrastructural needs) when you start determining the scope of your design. If you don't think about these things—and you fill up all of your development schedules with nifty features—you'll either wind up having to cut them later, or you'll have a game that gets destroyed by hackers. Don't let anyone fool you. If you're not well secured, hackers will find *any* hole in your defenses almost immediately.

Latency

Another obvious and well-known constraint for MMOGs is the issue of *latency*. In short, latency is the time it takes a signal to travel from your computer to the server and back again. This is significant, because we don't want calculations to take place on the client side. So if you want to shoot your neutron blaster at the alien cyborg, you click your mouse, the blaster fires, and you won't know whether you hit it or how much damage you inflicted until after the results come back from the server. Let's see how that impacts us.

On broadband connections, latency is around 60 ms (milliseconds), and on dial-up modems it averages around 200 ms. A fifth of a second might not seem like a very long time, but when compared to something like, say, frame rate, we can see pretty clearly how it affects the game. Imagine if your game played at five frames per second! A fighting game such as *Tekken* would be virtually unplayable.

Courtesy of NAMCO BANDAI Games America Inc.

Fighting games in particular (*Tekken 4,* shown) require response times that create nearly insurmountable difficulties given current Internet latencies.

Almost any game genre that is "twitch" in nature (relying on fast reflexes and rapid action as the main gameplay mechanic) becomes problematic when we have to factor in latency. The problem is less pronounced on broadband connections— but even there, we find problems. There are no guarantees about response times on the Internet. Often, the latency drifts around—sometimes responding quickly, sometimes experiencing long delays. Players who lose a tough fight because there was an Internet issue don't like it. The potential market size for a given game drops dramatically when the game gets the reputation that players with the fastest connection speeds have a distinct advantage. Until technology solves the problem by guaranteeing low latency, this issue will continue to be a constraint. It will limit the types of games we can apply to the MMOG model.

Bandwidth

Bandwidth is a constraint that is subtler, but nonetheless affects our long-term decisions for developing MMOGs. Bandwidth is the rate at which data can be transmitted over an Internet connection. On a broadband connection, we typically see a bandwidth of around 3 Mbit/s (megabits per second)—while on dial-up connections, we see 56kbit/s (kilobits per second). Keep in mind, those are pretty optimal numbers. Lots of things can slow them down.

Regardless, it's still clear that bandwidth is much more of a problem for dial-up users than for broadband users. To demonstrate this in practical terms, let's consider an example. Let's say that after your game goes *live*, you have additions you want to

Illustration by Ben Bourbon

make. Maybe these additions are new maps for exploration, more sound and music, new animations, new creatures, or changes to data files. It's not uncommon for these changes to get fairly large in size. We've seen patches for MMOGs before that have weighed in at 150 Mb. Even on a broadband connection, that patch can take 10–20 minutes or more to download to the player. But what happens with a player who's using a dial-up connection? A download like this can take the better part of a day. You definitely don't want to be answering CS telephone calls the day you tell all your dial-up users they can't play because it's going to take all day to download the patch! Patches like this will invariably cost you subscribers.

Huge downloads on a dial-up connection can be a deadly drag.

In addition to affecting patch sizes, bandwidth can also affect your decisions to include features such as voiceover Internet protocol (voiceover IP or VOIP), dynamic background content, user-generated content, streaming audio and video, and a host of other ideas.

There's one final issue to consider that's much more far-reaching than user-side problems. You have to think about the *service side* in all of these instances. On the service side, you have to pay an ISP for all of that data you're sending to the user. It's not free. When you create huge patches and have hundreds of thousands of players downloading them at the same time, you have to have a *massive* pipe to support it. The same holds true for any "bandwidth-heavy" in-game feature. The bigger the pipe, the more it costs you as a game service provider.

Always keep in mind that an MMOG is a business. Controlling costs through your design decisions will have a significant impact on your bottom line. When you start developing an MMOG, you need to create a bandwidth limit per player that works with your financial model. You need to understand how much money you're going to be spending every month to keep each player in the game. If you wanted to have 250,000 simultaneous players all drawing maximum bandwidth from their broadband connections, then your outgoing pipe has to have 250,000 times the capacity of a single broadband connection! The cost of this would make your MMOG service not financially viable unless you had a very high monthly subscription rate.

Courtesy of Shane Davis (Pixel Mine)

Games with VoIP *(Firearm: Reloaded*, shown) can be a lot of fun, but they can add substantial bandwidth costs to the game.

Illustration by Ben Bourbon

Costs are too high. I need you to build a game where people will pay their monthly fee, but never actually log in and play.

One businessman's idea of the perfect MMOG design

Infrastructure Needs

Infrastructure is a huge constraint that could be the subject of an entire book all by itself. Unlike some of the other constraints, this one doesn't usually affect the *design* of the game—but it does profoundly affect the development effort. The first time most developers undertake an MMOG project, they invariably underestimate the infrastructure requirements in epic proportions. If you haven't done this before, you really need to spend a lot of time understanding the *big picture* before commencing with your design and development. It turns out the implementation of the game itself is probably less than 50% of the total work that is required to build an MMOG. The bulk of the work and cost comes from building the infrastructure that is required to support one of these massive undertakings.

Diagram by Per Olin

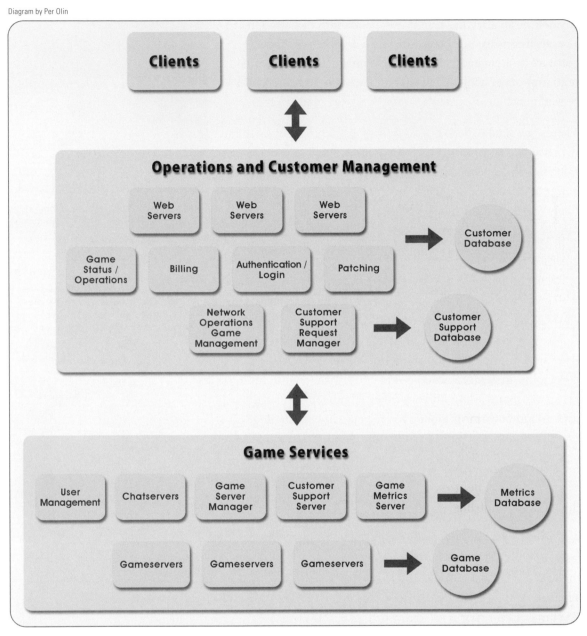

The infrastructure for a typical MMOG

As you can see, there are a *lot* of supporting systems that go into an MMOG. Login servers, authentication, billing, customer support tools, databases metrics collection, patch servers, server monitoring tools, and web services must all be implemented.

As you plan the project, you should leave plenty of time and development resources available to build out your service infrastructure. Remember, your game will perform differently on a full server than on Windows or Linux boxes that you use to develop code in-house. Once your full-sized server is operational, expect to spend considerable time adjusting your game code to work well on the bigger architecture.

If you decide to try to improve development time by building your game to fit pre-existing server architecture, realize that this will affect your game designs and software implementation. You'll either have to customize the server hardware to accommodate your game code, or modify the game code to accommodate your server architecture. Either way, it will impact your decisions, timing, and budget —so plan accordingly.

The Importance (& Expense) of Infrastructure

The backbone infrastructure required to maintain player statistics is specific to MMOG development. Some clever programmers have attempted to force gamer stats to remain on the gamer's local machine, but this leaves the product wide open for hackers and cheaters. Backbone infrastructures of this type are historically expensive, and complex to maintain. New technologies and optional development paths are now starting to dispel the perceived stigma.

—Mario "Thunderbear" Orsini
(Executive Producer, Team Orbit / Academy of Game Entertainment Technology (AGET))

AI Performance

Artificial intelligence (AI) is a much underappreciated constraint of most MMOGs. AI is an area that could stand vast improvement in almost all computer games, but it's one that must be considered very carefully for MMOGs. First, we should consider the tactics and intelligence of computer-controlled opponents.

As we've noted more than once, an MMOG is intended to be an experience that lasts a great deal longer than a single-player game. Despite this, we constantly hear many MMOGs described as "a level grind." In other words, the act of permanent advancement isn't very interesting. It's a "grind" to just methodically move from one target to the next, pressing the same buttons over and over, depending on your statistical superiority to defeat the opponent. There isn't much strategy or even thought required on the player's part. Avoid designs that require relentlessly repetitive action. Remember: you want players to subscribe to your game for months or even years. Try to constantly give them lots of decisions to make, and things to do that require actual thought and interaction. Don't build one of those games that allows the player to win simply by pressing the F2 key 27 times in a row.

A roar of approval emanates from the crowd as you score your 811th straight victory in the arena

Better AI would alleviate some of this. If the computer opponents were capable of recognizing and adapting to player tactics, much as human opponents can do, then the act of fighting them might be much more interesting—and the length of time players subscribe to the MMOG would increase. There are two reasons this hasn't been explored in much depth yet:

First, there aren't enough talented AI programmers in the industry. Our notion of "good AI" has been, at best, a complex set of conditional statements that cover the NPC opponents' basic options in typical situations. It's always easy to find the flaws, and opponents quickly follow easily recognizable patterns that players exploit. The result? After encountering a given type of opponent a couple of times, the player picks up the "pattern" and combat becomes boring. Yet because we want MMOG experiences to last many months, this boring pattern must be repeated endlessly.

The second reason good combat AI hasn't been explored much is again due to the fact that all computations must take place on the server. AI is often costly to calculate. There are lots of variables that must be constantly evaluated. But for every player on a map, there are many more computer opponents. A typical server that accommodates 2,500 players might have 10,000 or more opponents at any given time. Controlling the behavior of all of them—everything from pathfinding to combat AI—is very costly in terms of CPU overhead. AI programming must be efficient, so it tends to be rather sparse in depth and flexibility.

There is another issue regarding AI that has received virtually no consideration in MMOGs. The NPCs in non-combat situations generally receive no AI at all. They are mindless automatons that are either completely stationary or roam around the map in random patterns. If there's a dog in the street, it should *act* like a dog. It should scratch at fleas, chase cats, maybe bark at passersby, or perhaps be frightened of characters wearing bulky metal armor. But when such "ambiance creatures" appear in MMOGs, they are invariably robot-like and break the immersion.

Consider a village like you might find in the game *Fable*. The NPCs in the village know who you are. They are aware of your exploits, victories, and defeats, and whether you're good or evil—and they react accordingly. The world is alive with sycophants and antagonists. Your character develops admirers, enemies, and love interests. The world is far richer and more interesting than the zombie-like NPCs you'll find in any MMOG.

Ironically, this sort of AI should be much less "expensive" in terms of CPU overhead than combat AI. The requirements don't have to be timed with nearly the split-second precision, and it should be expected that NPC opinions will change slowly over time—unlike the ever-changing nuances of a combat situation. Unfortunately, it is an area that has received little to no attention.

Whether you decide to work on NPC and "ambiance creatures" or combat AI, a CPU overhead budget must be determined—and careful planning must be done. This is an area where some MMOG developer is going to shine one day, and that game will enjoy considerable success. That world will be much richer and deeper, and players will be more willing to spend time there. And some executives will be happily counting their subscription dollars.

Reprinted with permission from Microsoft Corporation

Used with permission of Sony Online Entertainment

In *Fable,* it's the behavior of the NPCs more than anything else that brings the game to life.

Interesting characters in *EverQuest II*

Gameplay Constraints

A "gameplay constraint" is any issue where the nature of an MMOG itself will affect game play. It's important to remember that an MMOG is *played* much differently from a single-player game. The presence of thousands of other players in your world creates a social dynamic that profoundly alters the way the game is perceived. To properly design an MMOG, you must first identify what differentiates it from a single-player game, and then design ways to accentuate the resultant strengths and avoid the weaknesses.

Community

Community is one of the most well-known constraints of MMOGs. Everybody knows that the heart and soul of MMOGs lies in the ability of players to socialize with each other. The most recognizable positive effects of good community include:

- "Living world" feeling to the virtual world—in part due to crowds of people chatting
- *"Peer pressure"* to return to the game world regularly
- *Assistance* provided by the group when a member encounters difficulty in combat (such as fighting as a team, trading objects, and casting beneficial spells on one another)
- *Dissemination of information* between anyone in the game world—which relieves some of the customer support stress

These are all solid reasons to provide tools for community. To that effect, the most common community tools provided in MMOGs are:

- various forms of chat (including general, party, guild, trade)
- ability to form temporary parties
- ability to form permanent groups or guilds
- tools to manage and communicate both with parties and with guilds
- buddy lists and ignore lists
- customized costumes or guild/group insignias
- in-game email
- auction systems
- want ads and bounty boards
- player-run governments
- voiceover IP "TeamSpeak"

All of these systems combine to achieve the positive effects mentioned earlier—and, if you have the ability to do so, it is strongly recommended that you include as many of these tools as possible in your game. However, no matter how many tools developers provide for players to communicate and socialize, players inevitably want more. Most games see player-developed software soon after launch that enhances existing game systems, and the vast majority of these tools are either for communicating or gathering information.

Currently, one particular area that still has room for improvement is the inclusion of tools that enhance teamwork. Since most combat systems are frenetically paced by design, there is often little time to type complex instructions, pleas for assistance, or strategies during a fight. Players must rely on previously devised strategies, and hope that unforeseen circumstances don't result in their plans going awry.

Many player-created tools now include software that can track designated team responsibilities and communicate them automatically to all members of the group. Certain players can have designated responsibilities—such as tanks, healers, or sappers. Teammates are assigned roles for support, protection, offense, and defense—and their targeting systems can be made to automatically select the desired target. This can be very handy when there are so many opponents onscreen that it's hard to click on the proper target. It's easy to visualize many other tools in similar veins that facilitate team play.

Some player-created tools, such as RaidAssist (highlighted) in *World of Warcraft*, can significantly improve the ability of players to act in large groups.

A good constraint for any MMOG would be to consider the dynamics of your particular core game mechanic, especially as it relates to coordinated team play, and prepare a comprehensive set of tools to facilitate actions and communication for groups of various sizes. (Small groups of 2–8, medium groups of 20–60, and larger groups are all common.) The simple fact is that it's virtually impossible to provide too many tools for community.

Troublesome Players

Every MMOG suffers from a variety of difficult people, or *troublesome players*. There are several different flavors of these players. The common thread between most of them, however, is that they seem to derive their main form of entertainment from ruining the experiences of other players. They are at their absolute happiest when they can frustrate other players to the point that they'll quit the game and never come back. This is done in a variety of ways. Some troublesome players like to make their characters powerful and then roam around the world attacking any player that is significantly lower level than them—following them around and killing them over and over. Others are con artists, finding ways to trick gullible people out of their hard-earned money or items. Still others are *spoilers*. They lie in wait for another player to get to a critical point in a battle or quest, and then rush in to kill the boss out from under the quester, or spoil the fight in some other way, causing the quester to have to start his mission over. Then there are loot stealers, spawn campers, kill stealers, kiters, and just generally verbally abusive people.

Phil Trumbo on Effective MMOGs :::::

Phil Trumbo
(Director, Trumbo
Studio; Instructor,
Digipen Institute of
Technology)

Phil Trumbo has provided creative and artistic input to nearly 100 high-profile games, with retail sales of over a billion dollars. Many of his notable successes come from adapting prestigious film and television properties into highly successful games, including *Pirates of the Caribbean, Chronicles of Narnia, Lord of the Rings, Harry Potter, Shrek, Spiderman, The Sims, Star Wars, Lego, Finding Nemo, X-Men,* and *Ice Age.* Trumbo won an Emmy Award for directing the animated opening title sequence for CBS's *Pee Wee's Playhouse.* He has also served as a director, designer, and animator for clients, including Electronic Arts, Activision, Buena Vista Games, Hidden City Games, Vivendi Universal Games, NBC, ABC, CBS, Procter & Gamble, General Foods, Ralston Purina, General Mills, Nickelodeon, and MTV.

■ *World of Warcraft*: Blizzard has done everything right by creating an exciting social gaming network with cool realms, unique races, classes, and professions—all tied together with excellent performance and elegant player control.

■ *Guild Wars*: Wonderfully rich worlds and totally killer character design.

■ *City of Heroes:* A great concept that is well-executed. It's so much fun to create your player character, design your fortress, and team up with other players.

This is an obvious constraint. It's something you absolutely must deal with, but the solution to the problem isn't necessarily obvious. The first instinct might be to either a) just ignore it, or b) instruct CS to locate and ban the offensive players. However, neither of these solutions is effective. Ignoring the offending players doesn't make them go away and eventually costs you subscribers. Trying to have CS act as police won't work either. Not only is this very time-intensive, but the offensive players will simply open new accounts under different names and come back—and they'll probably be even more offensive. They'll actually get entertainment out of making CS chase them in circles. Harassing CS is more fun than harassing players for some people.

There is also a third alternative: Arm the players with the necessary tools to implement their own police functions. In theory, this sounds like a good idea—but in practice, it invariably fails quickly. Whoever is chosen to lead the policing group quickly devolves in some virtual parody of *Lord of the Flies* to become a power-crazed thug. Hence, new bullies replace our old ones, and the new bullies have the legitimacy of having been *elected* for the job.

But rather than ponder the failed solutions, think about what these troublesome players might *provide*. Yes, they do provide something. Most of the people who play MMOGs will say they hate these troublesome players (also known as *griefers* or *PKers* [from "player kill"])—but by the same token when they sit around and tell their war stories, what do they invariably talk about? "Once I was riding from Trinsic to Britain, and a group of eight PKers jumped out of nowhere and tried to gank me. They chased me halfway across the continent, but eventually I lured them within range of the city guards, and let the idiots catch me. WHAP! The second I got tagged by the first PKer sword, guards came swarming in from everywhere and not a single one of those jerks escaped!"

Illustration by Ben Bourbon

Be careful about allowing players to have "police powers." It might just make them more powerful criminals.

Like it or not, the style of play from griefers can be entertaining. The trick is to build a system such that the griefers have *appropriate* opportunities to do their thing, but can't do it *everywhere*—while the "victims" have some compelling reason to put themselves in harm's way, but don't *have* to. Another take on this is that some developers feel that griefers provide some interesting game balance and additional "challenges" akin to the unpredictability and "injustices" faced in the real world. If everyone played by the rules all the time, Earth would be a sterile place. Either way, it's possible to make griefers work *for* you, rather than *against* you, if you work at it.

Some MMOGs have tried to deal with griefers by creating PvP (player vs. player) *optional* servers or areas. But this only works to a limited degree. Having a server filled with nothing but bullies is no fun. There are no natural victims, because there's no compelling reason for victims to be there. Similarly, the servers where PvP doesn't exist are less fun, because it's simply not as dangerous to wander the countryside. Dangerous player killers provide an element of tension that's exciting. It's useful, as long as the victim can't be attacked relentlessly to the point of harassment.

Courtesy NCsoft

Some of the most fun in MMOGs (*Lineage II,* shown) comes from huge player vs. player battles.

World of Warcraft has a different system where you can turn on a flag that makes you *eligible* to attack or be attacked by other players. Although this is more flexible than having dedicated PvP areas, it still prevents any real danger or excitement, because most people just keep the flag turned off the majority of time for the sake of safety. (But consider the notion that "safety" is less exciting than "dangerous.")

Similarly, *World of Warcraft* and *Guild Wars* have *instances*, or virtual copies of a quest map, so that only you and your party can exist in a private copy of the map where important quest objectives reside. In this way, grief players can't step in and *spoil* the quest. This can be a great solution to *spoilers*, but it only addresses that one kind of troublesome player.

Courtesy NCsoft

Quest map from *Guild Wars*. Each shield marks a quest location in the game.

Typically, designers wind up having multiple solutions to multiple kinds of troublesome players. However, if we recognize the potential value of troublesome players, they can add to the entertainment of the game by virtue of them being more dangerous and unpredictable than computer-controlled opponents. But are there more systemic solutions that can save the good parts and squelch the bad parts of this kind of player?

The trick will be to find a way to allow aggressive players to wreak their havoc more or less at random (but not constantly against a single target), while also allowing players to be placed in that sort of danger (without subjecting them to being ritually harassed by one or multiple players in succession).

In a perfect virtual world, players will feel like they're taking a risk when they cross through the forest on a dark, moonless night—but they'll have a compelling reason to want to chance it. Most of the time, they'll get through unscathed. When a PKer occasionally whacks them, they won't be victimized or chronically abused. Maybe they'll even have a chance to give a little payback to their attackers when they least expect it. Again, this is something to discuss in a design brainstorm. For now, it's a constraint that we need to recognize and put some thought into.

Sacred Cows

Sacred cows can be defined as what is considered to be "conventional wisdom" in game development. There are an awful lot of statements in the MMOG development community that begin with "*You can't do that in an MMOG, because...*" For example, one popular sacred cow was that "crafting and housing" are *required* in MMOGs. Why? Because these systems were included in early MMOGs—so somehow it was assumed that without them, an MMOG simply couldn't be fun. This is utter nonsense, especially in light of the fact that most systems for housing and crafting are *uncommonly boring*. They do serve a purpose, but that purpose can be accomplished in other ways besides housing and crafting.

First, let's look at the purposes of housing and crafting (I call features like this "enhancement features"): *Housing* allows players to permanently change the map. In essence, they can leave their mark on the world. *Crafting* allows players to control their ability to get cool stuff that they'd otherwise have to hunt and fight for. It lets them make things that will cause others to seek them out so they can acquire those things. Crafters have feelings of importance and self-determinism.

The question is: Can we convey these feelings (ability to leave your mark, a feeling of importance, and self-determinism) onto the player in ways other than housing or crafting? Of course we can. All we have to do is to know what feeling we want to impress upon the player, and then choose from the countless methods of achieving it; forcing ourselves to use the same tired old mechanism as every MMORPG before it? That is *truly* limiting.

We didn't have enough room in the schedule to implement a combat system, but you can make a KILLER two-story style house with AWESOME landscaping in the backyard!

Illustration by Ben Bourbon

"Enhancement features" are exactly that. Things like housing and crafting can make a good game better, but they can't *replace* actual game play. In point of fact, contrary to popular belief, they are *not* necessary to an MMOG at all.

Another MMOG-specific sacred cow is: "In MMOGs, player characters can't die permanently. Players have a huge investment in their characters—and if you kill any, those players will quit rather than start over." While the philosophy of this statement makes sense, the statement itself is misleading. What you shouldn't do in an MMOG is permanently erase those achievements that the player finds most valuable or useful. But "achievement" doesn't necessarily have to be a "character." Let's suppose that the goal of your game is to create a family dynasty of some sort. For fun, let's say it's a Mafia family—and you've decided to make the *family itself* important, rather than one of the individual members. Maybe you have lots of characters, and one of them is Vincenzo the Seven-Fingered Assassin. Through his efforts, much of the competition has been wiped out. Vincenzo is a valuable operative who has made the family very powerful. But if Vincenzo is killed, that doesn't destroy your family or its accomplishments. You still have your "business interests," your reputation, and your bank account, among other things. In fact, in this instance, Vincenzo is more like a "magic sword" than a character. Losing him may be a shock to the player, but it won't ruin his crime family. He has other operatives, and other ways of intimidating the competitors. Losing Vincenzo is just a setback. It's completely possible to kill off a character, and not have it force the player to start over from the beginning. The ability to permanently kill a character introduces a level of tension and drama that is much more compelling than knowing that no matter how badly you screw up, you can just resurrect your character and try again.

We have to be careful with sacred cows. Sometimes "conventional wisdom" is outright wrong, and sometimes it's misleading enough that it might obscure genuinely interesting possibilities if we accept it blindly. So the constraint here is: Whenever you hear conventional wisdom, especially when it starts out as an absolute statement like "you can't do that in MMOGs…" you should challenge it. Treat it as a problem that simply hasn't been solved yet. It's not really a sacred cow, so don't treat it like one. Assume there's a way to do it, and attack. A sacred cow should act as a bright, shining beacon, pulling you toward unexplored territory. You may have noticed that, ironically, this section on sacred cows contains a few sacred cows of its own. By all means, challenge these assumptions. Perhaps they're just problems that haven't been resolved yet!

Virtual Economy

The presence of a *virtual economy* is another commonly recognized constraint in MMOGs. The way it works is this: You kill an opponent, who then drops some form of money or item that can be sold. A few minutes later, a new opponent respawns to take the place of the old one. The new opponent also has money or items that can be sold. So if you think about it, that money has to come from somewhere. Where? Well, the game system *creates* it. Every time an opponent or enemy creature spawns, the system effectively creates more money.

Used with permission of Sony Online Entertainment

The *EverQuest II* live team keeps a close eye on all resources.

As any student of economics can tell you: If you continuously create money, it will quickly cause inflation. This is because as more and more money is added to a system, that money becomes devalued. A real economy is a closed system. Printing new money is done only on a very limited basis. Occasionally, say when there's a war, the government will resort to this—and the result is always huge inflation.

Inflation in an MMOG causes a problem—especially to new players who haven't been in the game very long and haven't accumulated much money. Items that were cheaper when the game first started now become astronomically expensive. For example, when *Ultima Online* first launched, you could buy a house for 40,000 gold pieces. Four years later, that same house could cost 200,000 gold pieces or more simply because there was so much more gold in the system. New players just couldn't afford a house, so they became a luxury for the more veteran players.

Player-Run Economies

Though it's received a lot of negative press and had a tumultuous life, I think some of the most innovative design I've ever seen in the MMOG world took place in the original *Star Wars Galaxies* game. While not the first game to do it, I don't think I've seen a better implementation of a player-run economy in any game except perhaps *EVE Online*. Almost every in-game item, from clothing and weapons to housing and vehicles, was created by players through crafting systems—which were complex and increased in difficulty as the player progressed but rewarded players with a deep, multi-textured and satisfying experience. It may not have been very *Star Wars*-y to be a tailor on Tatooine, but it sure was a lot of fun.

—Milan Petrovich (Associate Dean of Academic Affairs, Art Institute of California—San Francisco)

To offset this problem you need to do three things:

- Create "*gold sinks.*" These are basically ways to take money back out of the system. NPC vendors that sell items (especially consumable items that can be used only a limited number of times) are one way. Selling titles, special status, guild charters, etc. are other mechanisms. *World of Warcraft* charges a percentage for using the Auction House to sell the items you find out in the field. There are many, many different ways to create gold sinks. The key here, though, is that there must be a set of items or services that can *only* be obtained through NPCs. If players can make all of these consumables, then the money won't be removed from the system. It will simply change hands from one player to another.
- *Integrate a system of metrics.* Make sure you build ways into your system to measure the amount of gold per active character that is in the world. By constantly measuring this, you will have a better idea of when you need to make adjustments.
- *Create automated price adjustment systems.* Creating such systems is important to regulate inflation. Some early MMOGs included systems that automatically adjusted the prices NPCs charged for items, depending on fluctuating player demand.
- *Make your system expandable.* An expandable system allows for the addition of consumable items to NPC inventories whenever needed. This is done quite commonly. As developers learn about the economy of their own game, they use patch updates to constantly add new items for sale within the system. By controlling the quantity and types of inventory that are for sale, developers are, in a way, able to regulate the economy.

If you build your game systems with the ability to measure and adjust the supply of money in the world, it's not hard to keep this issue from getting out of control. As a general rule, you should assume that once the game is "mature" (say, 20–30% of the characters have reached maximum level), you should expect to be removing money from the system as fast as you're introducing it.

Cultural Considerations

In the United States, we tend to have a self-centered view of the world. Somehow, we always seem to think only of a U.S. audience when we design games. We either fail to recognize that other cultures have different tastes and sensibilities, or we just don't care because the U.S. market is "big enough." This is absurd, of course. There's utterly no reason to discount foreign markets. Especially when it comes to MMOGs, a global market is a distinct possibility. *Ultima Online* drew half of its subscribers from outside the continental United States. Likewise, a huge portion of *World of Warcraft* subscribers is also from outside the country. The market is absolutely out there, so ignoring it is foolish.

Courtesy of Blizzard Entertainment, Inc.

World of Warcraft is equally popular in multiple regions around the world, with large subscriber bases in several countries.

But if we're to address this constraint, we need to understand how other cultures differ from our own in a functional sense. If we can do so, we may find that it's entirely possible to devise a cross-cultural game that will be well received in *many* countries, not just the United States. (If you think that's impossible, look at practically any game made by Blizzard!)

Before we go any further, keep in mind that no cultural difference is inherently superior or inferior. They are what they are. When you begin work on an MMOG, take the time to investigate the major regions where your game is likely to sell in the long haul. Understand how those players play their games, what they like, and what they don't like. Understand what art styles appeal to them, and what styles don't. Consider music, sound effects, and even fonts. If you don't provide for an ability to make your character's name in Kanji (Chinese characters), for instance, you're doing a disservice to your potential Japanese market. You'd be surprised at how some databases just don't work well with double byte strings when you don't build them for that.

When I was the producer for *Ultima Online* live, I had the privilege of working closely with a very strong Japanese group led by JB Shoda. As we developed game systems and art assets, they provided us with an invaluable wealth of feedback about how these things would be received by the Japanese audience. We observed some profound differences between what would be acceptable to a Japanese audience as opposed to a U.S. one, and we were able (with a great deal of work) to find some happy neutral ground on many aesthetic issues. Along the way, having seen audience reactions to *Ultima Online* in Japan, Europe, South Korea, and Australia, quite a number of distinct cultural differences in taste became apparent. We noted that South Korean audiences prefer much more challenging games than Americans. South Koreans also have the majority of their MMOG players in game rooms. The Japanese audiences seemed to be much more social than most cultures, and were generally far more effective in managing teams and guilds. Membership in groups was extremely important to them. Europeans, on the other hand, seemed much more likely to take advantage of *role playing* (as opposed to just methodically mowing down monsters in order to advance and collect loot). Americans were by far the most prolific collectors of rare or difficult-to-obtain objects. Americans seemed the most obsessed with absolutely maximizing the power of their characters as individuals (as opposed to, say, the Japanese, who might be more interested in maximizing their character for group utility).

—*Rick Hall*

Assume that it's possible to craft a game that will appeal to multiple cultures, and make the effort to build it that way from the start. Decisions you make at the beginning (such as art style) can't be changed once you get into development. Don't make the mistake of choosing concepts and styles that will hamper your potential success worldwide, when it's perfectly possible to satisfy a wider audience with a bit more effort. (Include in that effort consultants from the regions you're trying to satisfy. Don't assume that a cursory examination of a given culture will make you an expert.)

Quantifying Ourselves

The presence of other players is a theme that permeates most MMOG design constraints in one way or another. It affects us in several direct ways, as we've seen in the virtual economy, cultural, community, and troublesome player constraints, especially. But one rather *indirect* way we are affected by crowds is that they offer us a *limelight* to stand in.

It might sound ridiculously obvious to state that one major reason we humans enjoy competition so much is that we like to win, but it's surprising how often we treat that concept in a superficial way. We don't think about *why* we like to win. What is it that drives us to engage (and hopefully overcome) other humans? Why is it so much more fun to beat a human opponent than a computer-controlled one? The answer is because, honestly, we like to show off. Winning is fun because then we get to run around and *tell* everyone we won. We want to be the general riding around in the ticker tape parade in New York after winning the war. We want to be the hero who everyone looks up to. We all want our 15 minutes of fame. And that's the primary reason it's more fun to

Electronic Arts, Inc.

In *Dark Age of Camelot*, killing other players in RvR combat is a *lot* more fun than killing computer-controlled monsters.

beat another human. When we beat a computer opponent, there isn't usually anyone around to witness it. Even when there are witnesses, they usually say, "Yeah, you won because the program isn't very smart. If I'd been controlling that monster, I'd have dodged your attack, rolled up behind you, and caved your skull in."

When we beat another human, we've been able to quantify ourselves in front of witnesses (at the very least, the person we defeated). Like it or not, the defeated party has to admit that at least this last time, you were better. We not only get the victory, we get built-in acknowledgement. We get to show off. But the next day we may tell a bunch of our friends about our astounding feat, and they may be skeptical. They may doubt we beat that tough PKer or the ancient red dragon. What we need is *proof*. And that's where the constraint comes in.

We need to think about how important it is for players to be able to *quantify* themselves in some concrete way. This is especially true if each player can do so in a way that is difficult for others to replicate. The more unique the form of quantification, the more difficult it should be for others to acquire, and the more they will enjoy having it. Spend some time to really think about that. Rewards help quantify players, but we can't overuse them. If it's too easy to get them, they cease to have meaning, and they don't say the player *achieved* anything. When everybody can get the reward it's an expectation, not a reward. It won't advertise the player's achievements.

Then again, some designers worry that if a reward is too hard to obtain, then too few people will achieve it and it won't have meaning for the rest of the players. In addition, as game developers, we like to think that as many people as possible can enjoy the fruits of our labors. If we make an especially cool-looking sword, or particle effect, we want everyone to desire it.

But those are both dangerous thoughts. We have to remember that the more people achieve something, the more that accomplishment is devalued. Not only must we accept the fact that certain accomplishments will be obtained by only a small percentage of the players, we have to embrace that idea. We have to realize that even if a player is unable to accomplish something, the fact that he sees someone else who did will *still* affect him in a positive way. Don't just hand out "unique" rewards like they grow on trees. Don't make the mistake of trying to create a special reward for every player, either. That's akin to giving every participant in a footrace a trophy (first place, best shoes, best effort, best sportsmanship, etc.). Not only does each individual trophy have no meaning in an instance like that, even the *winner* feels like he or she accomplished nothing.

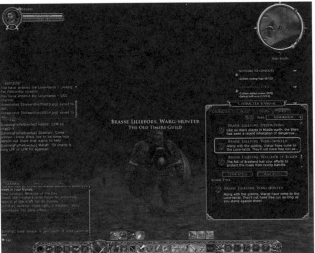

Copyright 2007 Turbine, Inc.

Being able to show off your rank in an MMOG is a common way for players to quantify themselves. Everyone they come near in the game world can see what they've accomplished (*The Lord of the Rings Online*, shown).

By the same token, don't take all of this to mean that we should create only a half-dozen extremely unique rewards for our player base of 200,000 people. There has to be a balance. Feel free to be liberal in dishing out rewards, but just make sure they're honestly *earned.* Try to think of interesting quantifications. The easiest (and by far the most overused) reward winds up being a powerful magic sword or ring, or neutron blaster, or something similar. Not only does that allow us to quantify ourselves, it's also functional. It increases our ability to achieve even higher rewards. It's also boring and cliché.

Consider some of the more interesting forms of quantification that have been introduced. How about those systems that reward players with a military rank (accompanied by a visual title and powers of command in group battles)? We've also seen personal particle effects, clothing, trophies, and even permanent tributes on the world map. Maybe players can be rewarded with their own theme music when they enter a scene, or maybe NPCs can recognize the player's achievements (á la *Fable*). *World of Warcraft* rewards players with price breaks, access to special vendor items, unusual mounts, and immunity to attack from allied creature types.

There are unlimited ways to reward players for their accomplishments, so be creative. Don't just give them 100 gold pieces or a fancy sword. Those are fine, but nothing special. Players will move mountains to get special status, rewards, or other forms of quantification that set them apart from their peers. The more creatively you quantify your players, the more they'll want to accomplish your goals. And the more those quantifications set players apart from the masses, the more valuable they'll be perceived.

::::: Player Rewards in *The Lord of the Rings Online*

Well, I am biased, of course—but I feel that *The Lord of the Rings Online* contains some of the most innovative features in the market today. My personal favorite innovation is the Deed System, which constantly rewards players for exploring the world and completing various tasks.

—Jeff Anderson
(President & CEO, Turbine, Inc.)

This chapter has introduced you to the various issues involved in developing an MMOG. It's important to get exposure to the scope and scale of this sort of undertaking. An MMOG is a huge project that must be considered from many different angles if it is to be successful. In this chapter, we've seen how financial models, technology, performance, support issues, and massive numbers of players can all affect the decisions you'll make and the approach you'll take. It's essential to sit down before you start actually developing your game and identify as many different kinds of constraints as possible. These will be the major issues that you want to address, so keep your list someplace highly visible. As you work your way through the brainstorming process, constantly ask yourself if you've addressed any of your constraints yet, or if it's possible to address any of them by adapting some of your evolving features. Keep in mind that you want to think about constraints on a high level. These are concepts (or even philosophies)—not features. Try to treat your constraints in a functional manner. For example, don't ask, "Are we addressing the revenue model?" That doesn't tell you anything. Instead ask, "Will this design provide a style of pacing that will entertain players for a thousand hours?" That's functional, and something against which you can measure.

Finally, the way you address your constraints should be systemic, not feature driven. For example, if you're trying to provide a solution for grief players, don't think about a PvP flag. That's a feature that simply throws out the good with the bad, and shows you didn't understand the problem in the first place. Try to think of a way to change people's perceptions or adapt their style of play. Don't fight against human nature. Try to use it to your advantage. You can only maximize the effectiveness of your solutions if you fully understand the problem and how it's affecting the game. Take the time to do so. It's worth the effort. This may seem like a huge undertaking, and in truth it is. To consider it all, you'll need to put together a team with a programmer, designer, and artist, at least. In the next chapter, we'll learn how to do that, as well as organize a schedule, and learn what the overall development lifecycle of an MMOG looks like. With good planning and organization, even the most complicated project can be undertaken successfully. Knowing what you're up against from the beginning is the first step to making a great game.

:::CHAPTER REVIEW:::

1. What are some monetization models for MMOGs and how does each model contribute to business constraints?

2. What are some unique issues faced by MMOG developers with regard to artificial intelligence performance?

3. What are a few techniques for dealing with troublesome MMOG players? How are virtual economies and in-game culture affected by such players?

CHAPTER

3

Organization
make a plan before you start

Key Chapter Questions

■ What is the most important step in the *development process*?

■ Why is it essential to get a *server* up and running as early as possible?

■ What is the single biggest *mistake* that MMOG developers make?

■ Why are *expansion packs* so important for MMOGs?

■ Where does most of the MMOG *revenue* come from?

In this chapter, we will provide an overview of the structure of the development process, discuss the goals of pre-production, explore the formation of a development team, and show the overall timing and expectations of the various phases of development. You'll learn why organization is of paramount importance to MMOG development and how to get the project off the ground properly from the beginning.

By now, you should realize that MMOGs are not like other games. The scale and complexity of an MMOG are such that proper organization from the start is critical. If you don't begin the development process with a thorough plan, you may wind up wasting years of effort and millions of dollars. With that in mind, let's look at the project from an initial 100,000-foot view. We'll start by examining the development process.

Pre-Production

In a typical game project, the *pre-production* phase is where you employ a small team of your brightest developers to craft your overall vision for the game. This is where you decide what the game will be, what it will look like, what it will feel like, what your major technological focus will be, and try to get a solid idea about the schedule and budget for the rest of the development process. In this phase, it's tempting to just take an educated guess at all of these items without really giving them the time and thought that they deserve. That's a mistake that most developers have made at some point, and one some continue to make game after game. Pre-production is not a phase to be taken lightly. The best games will often take 1/4 to 1/3 of their entire development schedule in pre-production—sometimes longer.

Diagram by Per Olin

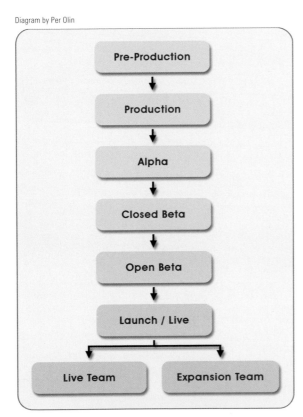

Phases in the online game development cycle

Most of the points we discussed in Chapter 2 are considered during this phase, as well as all of the concept work, sketches, scheduling, and design. This is the phase where you must decide what technology you can implement, what your overall scope will be, and what your staffing plan will look like. By the time you exit the pre-production phase, you should have: all of your pipelines built (pipelines are software tools that allow artists and designers to get content into the game without having to resort to programmer effort); a functional prototype (running on a server); and the final look and feel; and completed game design. If you plan on creating more design or artistic concepts in the production phase, you are following the wrong approach—and there's an overwhelming likelihood that you will create insurmountable problems for the remainder of the project. We take a deeper look at this phase a little later. The following cannot be emphasized strongly enough: Pre-production is the lynchpin of the development process. It can make or break your game. Don't short-change the pre-production phase.

Now that we have a reasonable outline of what the whole development process looks like, let's take a more detailed look at the pre-production phase. This initial phase should be reasonably expected to consume somewhere between 25% and 33% of your entire development schedule. That would be 9–12 months out of a three-year development cycle.

Some people will think this is excessive. They'll tell you that they can't afford an entire year out of the schedule just dreaming up blue sky design ideas. Clearly, such people are entirely missing the point of pre-production. Try to patiently explain it to them. Start by putting it this way. There are nine main goals for the pre-production phase:

1. Craft a razor statement.
2. Identify the core game mechanic.
3. Establish the core visual.
4. Write the game design document (GDD).
5. Write the technical design document (TDD).
6. Assess and acquire key engine components.
7. Create and iterate a game prototype.
8. Establish the asset pipelines.
9. Draft a project schedule.

With any luck, using game industry jargon will make it seem like you know what you're talking about, and they'll back off. If that fails, however, it's best to understand exactly what each of these goals mean.

Razor Statement

A *razor statement* establishes the project vision. It is a single, simple declaration that epitomizes the essence of the game. It's not a catchy slogan or a marketing tag line. It is a functional tool for aligning the development team. It is meaningful and descriptive, clear yet concise, and intended to set the project focus. It is not intended to give precise information about design details, but rather to provide high-level direction. Let's look at a few examples:

Good razor statements:

- This game is about lightning-fast, tactical combat in a politically charged cyberpunk universe.
- The movie *Wall Street* meets the game *Railroad Tycoon* in the 22nd century.
- Strategic decision making in a humorous, Looney Tunes version of an urban single's club.
- Accumulating reputation and star status in a predatory Hollywood atmosphere.

Bad razor statements:

- Become a hero in a medieval fantasy world.
- Build the greatest MMOG ever.
- Create a world where vampires and vampire hunters engage each other in a series of dramatic confrontations, with one side armed with supernatural skills and abilities, and the other side armed with numerical superiority and a variety of classic anti-vampire weapons.
- An MMOFPS set in the universe of the movie *Pitch Black*.

What makes items on the first list good, and those on the second list bad? Think about it. The razors on the first list give you a pretty strong idea of what the game is about. Regardless of whether you like those particular ideas, the razor should give you a clear image. The ideas provide a feel for the atmosphere, the fundamental kind of gameplay to expect, and even some thoughts about fiction. They're also simple. Read them once, close your eyes, and you can probably repeat them word for word.

The razors in the second list are each bad for a different reason. The first one tells us absolutely nothing about gameplay. The second tells us nothing at all about the entire game. The third is far too complex and difficult to remember. And the fourth, while it tells us about the atmosphere (envision the movie *Pitch Black*) and the gameplay (most FPS games have a basic set of similarities), it gives us no unique element that will distinguish our game from any other game. The fourth razor might just as well say "A standard FPS that depends on a Hollywood intellectual property to generate its sales."

Keep in mind that a razor isn't intended to convey every detail or feature in your design. We should assume that every genre of game has its expected features and MMOGs are no different. The razor simply defines where you will focus your attention and what makes your game unique.

Although the concept of a razor statement is not uncommon for development of single-player games, one could argue that it is even more vital for MMOGs. In MMOG development, designers are often eager to view the game as an artificial world and hence make it the everything game. They find it difficult to resist the temptation of "kitchen sink" design (throwing in every feature they can possibly think of, whether it fits the core game idea or not). You will often hear this referred to as "scope bombing." Use the razor statement to help alleviate this problem. You should pursue a policy of ruthlessly trimming every feature that doesn't contribute to the razor—at least early in the pre-production phase.

The term "razor statement" almost defines itself. It is a declaration that describes the fundamental concept of the game in such a way that we can measure our aesthetic style and all of our key features against it. Any proposed feature that doesn't fit the spirit of the razor should be cut from the design, regardless of how cool we think that feature is. If it doesn't fit the razor, it doesn't belong in the game.

Core Game Mechanic

Once we understand the razor, we can begin work on the core game mechanic. Sometimes referred to as the gameplay target, this is simply the main activity in which the player will engage. It is what the players will spend the majority of their time doing. By definition, that makes it the most important part of the design.

Strange as it may sound, many developers don't have a firm grasp of this concept. They tend to view the game as a whole, with every part contributing an equal share to the entertainment. This just isn't true. Every feature will have its own amount of usage. For example, in *World of Warcraft*, players generally spend a great deal more time fighting than they do at the Auction House. (This is not to say that the Auction House isn't an important feature.) We have to consider where players spend the majority of their time, and work on that first. If fighting is what players will do most, then we have to be absolutely sure fighting is fun. It is the core of our game. As such, we should invest as much effort and iteration during the pre-production phase as necessary to ensure that fighting is fun. There's no point in designing ancillary features if the activity in which players spend most of their time is boring.

Again, this concept is often considered important in single-player games, but it is even more important with MMOGs. It is hoped that MMOG players will subscribe to a game for a year or more. They simply won't do this if the core game mechanic is dull. No amount of flashy graphics or engrossing storylines can cover for a bad design or implementation in this area. It is essential to do this properly.

When you think you've got a pretty good prototype, here's a good test to see where you stand. A couple of hours after you submit it to the testers, sneak into the QA area and observe the scene. If any of them are throwing Nerf toys at each other, yawning, talking on the phone, or playing *StarCraft*, your prototype isn't any fun. Stick it back in the development oven, let it cook a little longer, and try again.

Core Visual

Much like the core game mechanic, you will need a core visual (often referred to as a visual target). Games are a visual medium. The things you see onscreen make up a large part of your immersion. Bad graphics make it difficult for players to become engrossed in a world, and banish the hope that they will become addicted to it.

Many people may think that the core visual is simply a set of concept sketches and illustrations. While this is a great place to start, it is by no means adequate. A better approach would be to let your team of pre-production artists really go to town in the beginning. Let them create a short cinematic scene that shows exciting or immersive action in all its animated glory. Let them go hog wild with special effects, animations, and high-poly models. Let them create a scene that is exciting, evocative, and fascinating. That will become your target. The challenge from there will be to see just how closely your pre-production prototype matches the scene your artists dreamed up.

You might be surprised to discover just how effective this technique can be. Not only will it provide a concrete direction for the entire team, but it also invariably gives rise to new design ideas and features. It also exposes flaws in your thinking early in the process, and helps prioritize where you'll want to spend your development time.

Game Design Document

This part of pre-production is unmitigated drudgery, and yet extremely important. After you've built a prototype, your design team must methodically document the functionality of the rest of the game, from the core mechanic to the lowliest UI screen. Note that the phrase "after you've built a prototype" is important. You should never try to design fine details until you're happy with the core game mechanic. The core game mechanic is built in an iterative fashion. It changes often, sometimes dramatically, during pre-production. Since the finer details will work to enhance the core game mechanic, it makes no sense to design them while the core mechanic is in a state of flux. The best approach is to wait until after the prototype is built and feels fun, and only then try to brainstorm the rest of the details of the game.

Once this is done, the details of the game must be documented clearly and completely, so that you can create a reasonably accurate project schedule. Remember that when you go into the production phase, you'll throw an army of developers onto the team to mass produce content. If you want them to get up to speed quickly and produce content that meets your gameplay targets, then you need to provide them with a highly detailed set of instructions. They need to know exactly how to each feature is supposed to work to write code or build art for it. If you are ambiguous about something, it will probably wind up being implemented in a haphazard manner.

> ## The *Live* Plan
>
> MMOG development faces scope issues that most non-MMOGs don't have to deal with. You must not only have a plan for delivering the content that comprises your release product, but you must also be prepared with your *live* plan—which allows for a constant stream of content. MMOGs are not games with expected play times in the 8–20 hour range. Rather, players of MMOGs expect hundreds and even thousands of hours of content.
>
> —*Graeme Bayless*
> *(President, Kush Games—a division of 2K Sports)*

Technical Design Document

Once you have a set of GDDs to work with, you need to hand them off to the programming team. Their job is to evaluate each feature and document how they will implement it. Again, many developers balk at this step because it is tedious and typically uninteresting, but you have to do it. The process will not only ensure that your features are technically feasible—but as part of the TDDs, you'll want your programmers to estimate how long it will take them to code each feature they document. It's a lot easier to estimate schedules once a programmer has documented their implementation methodology. Again, this is more important with MMOGs than single-player games. MMOGs are far more complex to build—so the more time you spend planning this stage, the more accurate your schedules will be and the less likely you'll encounter impossible coding tasks deep in the production phase.

At this stage, you should also plan to have a set of target performance benchmarks to which you want to adhere. For example, make a point of specifying the maximum bandwidth you want any given player to be using, maximum RAM usage for maps, target frame rates, and estimates on how many players can be onscreen at once. Try to plan for worst-case scenarios and what kind of performance you want in those instances. Think about contingency plans for when player load exceeds the worst-case scenario. For instance, if you decide that no more than 200 players can be in a given place simultaneously, what will your system do when player 201 wanders into the scene? This is a serious architectural issue, and it deserves some thought at this early stage.

Game Prototype

When developing an MMOG, it's extremely important to get something, anything, up and running onscreen as quickly as possible. The name of the game is iteration, and you can't iterate until you have a starting point. Do not attempt to design and plan every detail on paper before you start implementing. The nature of details is that they will change during pre-production. Instead, just design the core mechanic, and build to a level of quality that feels finished before designing the rest of the details.

One of the primary goals of pre-production is to have a functional prototype at the end of the phase. This prototype should be what some people call a vertical slice of the game. It may be only one level or one room. There may only be one kind of main character, and a few different creatures and weapons. But whatever you can see or do should look and feel like a finished product.

That's the goal of the prototype. If you achieve this goal, then everything else you do during the production phase will have a model to be measured against. And at the risk of sounding like a broken record, this too is more important in MMOGs than single-player games.

MMOGs are invariably content heavy. There are far more characters, creatures, and maps/levels, items, missions, etc. than in a single-player game. Let's say you build a few stand-in assets during pre-production, but they don't look like the finished product. What will happen? You'll ramp up the team size during production, and they'll look at the sample levels and characters, see that they're not finished, and have no choice but to interpret what they might look like when the game is done. Everyone will build something slightly different, and the end result will be a Frankenstein mess. But there will be so much content that you won't have time to go back and fix it all, so you'll have to live with it.

Save yourself the mess, and spend the time to build a prototype that looks, feels, and acts like the finished product (at least the core aspects of the finished product). Not only will this help provide everyone on the development team with a unified vision from which to work, but it will also help you schedule more accurately. It's better to know how long it takes to build finished, polished game assets than to know how long it takes to build a useless stand-in asset.

It's also important to remember what was stated earlier: you need a fully functional server to go with the prototype. Many times, MMOG development teams have attempted to build a test box or light server to operate the prototype. While this might be a good way to get up and moving early in the pre-production phase, before you go into production your server must be using the final hardware and operating servers that you want at launch. If you attempt to get away with something less, you'll be building on an incomplete understanding of how the final server architecture will affect your game. You'll be building on assumptions rather than definite knowledge, and that's extremely dangerous.

Asset Pipelines

As mentioned earlier, MMOGs are generally content heavy. There will be dozens of characters, scores of level maps, hundreds of creatures and NPCs, and countless weapons, missions, and objects in the world. There will be sound effects, music, and map triggers around every corner. Designers will want to change the amount of damage a laser blaster inflicts and the running speed of an orc every 15 seconds.

This is the type of data that you don't want your highly paid programmers recompiling 50 times a day while they take a nap. During the pre-production phase, you want to identify every type of asset that will be regularly introduced (or iterated on) during the production phase. Once you have a list, do everything possible to automate the process of getting these assets into the game. This automation process, where a designer or an artist can put his or her own assets into the game without having to wake up the programmer is called a *pipeline*.

Let's take a look at a typical art pipeline as an example:

1. *Description*—text describing character
2. *Concept drawing*—pencil sketch of character
3. *Storyboard (Cinematics)*—pencil sketch panels showing character firing a gun in a scene
4. *Placeholder art*—human model with no textures (FPO)
5. *Modeling and animation rigging*—human wireframe with 1K skeleton
6. *Texturing*—textured human model
7. *Shading*—shaded model
8. *Lighting*—lit model
9. *Animation*—moving model with constraints
10. *Effects*—flames/smoke particles added

Diagram by Per Olin

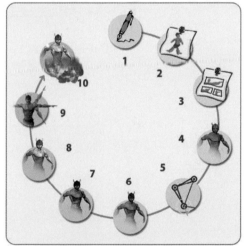

A typical art production pipeline showing the various stages for the creation of an object in the game as described in this section.

There's an obvious balance to strike. Will it cost more programmer time to build a pipeline tool or to have a programmer manually insert the given asset into the game as often as needed? Assume that most assets will be introduced half a dozen times as they are constantly tweaked and polished. If it turns out the asset type in question will be high enough volume, you'll probably want to schedule some programmer time to build the pipeline tool.

Keep in mind that once you hit the production phase, you'll be throwing a small army of developers at content. If your pipeline tools aren't built (and debugged) when your production army begins to march, let's just say the traffic jam will get ugly.

Project Schedule

By now, you should have a pretty good idea of what goes into a schedule. By the end of pre-production, you'll know what assets you have to build and what features you'll have to implement. You'll have design documentation, technical documentation, and a working prototype. You'll have built each type of asset at least once or twice (to a polished, finished-looking quality level) so you'll have an idea how long they'll take to build en masse.

At this stage you'll add up the hours needed to implement your grand design. This calculation might be tedious and complex, but it will tell you how many people you'll have to hire to complete the project by the deadline mandated by the executive powers that be.

This will be followed by a short but loud outburst of violent opposition from the suits, followed by a period of intense haggling where you beg for more resources and time. The suits will respond by slashing away at your feature list, accusing you of padding your schedule, and demanding that everyone work overtime for the next two years. Somewhere along the way, you'll sort it all out and settle on a schedule that everyone can live with.

Reprinted with permission from Microsoft Corporation

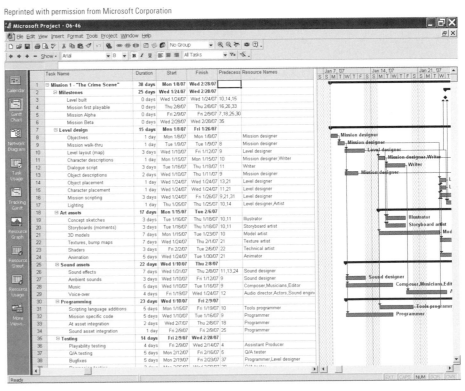

The project schedule describes the milestones, tasks, staffing, and dependencies throughout the project. This is an example from Microsoft Project for a single mission in a game.

Production

When you're satisfied that you know exactly where your game is going and how you're going to get there, it's time to ramp up the team to the size of a small army and crank it all out. Contrary to what you might intuitively think, the *production* phase shouldn't utterly dominate the project's development schedule. It should take somewhere near 30–50% of the time between initial concept and game launch.

It's important to understand that the production phase is expensive (expect to ramp up your team to perhaps three or four times the size it was in pre-production)—and, although a lot of work is accomplished here, it should be cookie-cutter work. By the time you have reached the production phase, you should have your art style established, your game design completed, and your pipelines in place. Your developers should simply be churning out content according to an established set of well-documented guidelines. Ideally, you want to have an environment where even your least creative developers can produce work that fits your high-quality standards.

During production, you should be implementing 100% of your work on a server, which became operational during pre-production. It's a catastrophic mistake to enter into the production phase without having a full-fledged server that has the capacity you expect at launch. If you try to develop on a system that can only handle a few dozen players, you'll probably find that everything blows up in your face when you finally do implement a launch server.

The Importance of Scale

As you work on MMOGs, you will quickly find that issues of scale create unique problems. Experience has shown conclusively that the problems you encounter with 100 players are completely different from the problems you will encounter with 1,000 players. Similarly, you'll encounter yet a new crop of issues when you try to support 10,000 players. With each order of magnitude that your number of players increases, you'll discover a whole new set of problems. Bank on it. This will happen.

By the time you hit the production phase, you're ready to move quickly. You have a gameplay focus, a visual target, full documentation of the intended features and how they will be implemented, a working prototype, and a functional server. You'll have a pretty good idea how long it will take to build each type of asset, so you'll have a schedule you can have faith in. You'll know how many programmers, modelers, level builders, and animators you will need. It is hoped that you'll be able to assemble your development army and go into battle. You must prepare for two main things before this happens: staffing and communication. Keep in mind that this will probably be a large team. It's not at all uncommon for an MMOG development team to consist of 40–70 people. As much as you'd like to, you won't be able to wave a magic wand and make them appear. You have to start acquiring your team before the production phase begins. More often than not, at least some of these people are working on other projects within your company and just waiting to be transferred onto the MMOG team. Others will have to be hired. Either way, it can sometimes take literally months to ramp up the team from the size of pre-production, say 8–12 people, to production. Be prepared for this and start the process before the production phase begins. Know where your team members are coming from and when to expect them to be available.

> Your production plan completely depends on what scale you are going for. To compete with the big boys at Sony, Blizzard, and NCsoft you need teams of 50+ and budgets in the tens of millions and at least three years to build and balance.
>
> —*Starr Long*
> *(Producer, NCsoft)*

Communication is the other critical issue with teams of this size. You'll need to make sure you have adequate systems in place so that everyone is on the same page, sees the vision of the project clearly, understands the chain of command, and knows the submission and approval process for their work. It will be difficult to check in with every member of the development team every day. You have to provide a communication framework so that they can operate without micromanagement.

> Team size depends on the development team and publisher. For core ideas and design, no more than two or three. For implementation, as many creatives as you can afford to manage!!
>
> —*David Javelosa*
> *(Professor, Santa Monica College)*

Assuming all goes smoothly and your team ramps up as it should, you'll begin rapidly adding features and content. The production phase will hit full stride, and the game will really start to take shape. It sounds like you can relax a little and put the ship on autopilot. Unfortunately, you can't. You need to put things in motion so that the next phase can commence seamlessly after production is complete.

MMOG Development Can't Be Small-Scale

The ideal MMOG project would involve one person developing for free in his or her spare time. Sadly, we don't have the tools and assets available for one person to build anything all that substantial yet (or, if you want to be nostalgic, any more). . . . The biggest problem I've had to overcome in MMOG development? Getting the financing together.

—*Dr. Richard Bartle*
(Visiting Professor in Computer Game Design, University of Essex)

Mario "ThunderBear" Orsini on Team Size, Development Budget, & Schedule :::::

In the early 1990s, Mario Orsini founded Team Orbit—a group of artists, programmers, and filmmakers. They gained notoriety by releasing their content through the Internet, holding the number one download slot at FilePlanet for weeks at a time. Mario now directs Team Orbit in the cross-development of commercial games and films—providing technical support for Unreal Engine licensees. Its members have worked with Blizzard, Disney, EA, ICT, Epic Games, and Silicon Knights. Mario is now developing *Orbit Wars,* an IP that spans three feature films, a five-year episodic television series, and a five-year MMOG. Until recently, Mario was the Executive Director of the Academy of Game Entertainment Technology (AGET). He is on the Board of Directors at Studio Arts, the famed academy for film effects. His personal skill sets include CAD engineering, audio engineering/mastering, film effects, compositing/post-production, 3D modeling, animation, programming, level design, game design, sound design, and cross-platform production (video games and film). Mario Orsini is an established leader and a pioneer in the emerging field of cross-media development.

Mario Orsini
(Executive Producer,
Team Orbit/
Academy of Game
Entertainment
Technology [AGET])

Team size, development budget, and schedule are, of course, affected by the scope of the intended MMOG itself. For example, normal mapped models can require over 100 hours of development—whereas a standard model is finished in a quarter of that time. If you are making a large, top-of-the-line game with normal mapped models, you can expect to spend roughly $10–12 million on content and 18–24 months in development time. You should be running initially with 1–2 concept artists, 3–5 texture artists, 1 media artist, 4–7 3D modelers, 2–3 animators, and 4–8 level designers. At least three of those level designers should be finishers that are at the top of their craft. Content from the media artist is used for promotional purposes and not in-game. Your programmers will vary—depending on the game engine you choose. Implementing a turnkey solution like Epic's Unreal Engine can cut down both on time and cost dramatically. Once the game is completed, you will need to keep a crew on hand for content updates, as well as infrastructure support. By this time, you've made your release—and its multiple revenue streams should be more than enough to cover the continuing support. Without new content being created and updated on a regular basis, your MMOG will put you in the history books by losing its clientele in record time.

Alpha

Most developers define *alpha* as "feature complete, but not bug-free; playable from start to finish." That definition works reasonably well for MMOGs. By the time you reach alpha, your world should be complete. All of the maps, characters, creatures, objects, sounds, and features should be constructed.

You should expect to spend this phase fixing bugs and balancing gameplay. You should not add new content during alpha. If you're still adding new content, then you're still in the production phase. The point at which you draw that line in the sand and stop implementing new features, adding new maps, adding sound effects, music, special effects, or anything else is when you enter alpha.

We've already said that the alpha phase is defined as "content complete, but not bug-free." The team has implemented every feature, every model, every map, every UI screen, every cinematic. There are still lots of bugs at the start of this phase and the code won't yet be optimized. The goal is to locate and eliminate the bugs and ensure that the code is efficient enough to handle a large number of players without breaking down.

The first part of this process, locating and eliminating bugs, is a fairly well-known condition in game development, and we needn't describe it. Instead, it's important to recognize how the alpha phase is different for MMOGs. Clearly, the difference in this phase comes from the existence of the server, and the large number of players you should expect to see when the game launches.

The two most dominant kinds of bugs you can expect to see in MMOGs come from bandwidth and CPU load. Things that aren't an issue when an individual or small group is playing can balloon to significant problems when the number of players starts reaching into the thousands. It's very difficult to predict what kinds of problems you'll see when that vast number of people begins stressing the system. You won't know until it happens.

You don't want to wait until the game is in beta to identify these problems. Ideally, you'll eliminate as many of them as you can before you unveil the game to the outside world. How do you accomplish this? It's simple: simulate volume by automation.

Alpha: Get Everyone to Play!

It's advisable during the alpha phase to have designers and other internal developers (in addition to your testing staff) play the game as much as possible. Set aside some time in your schedules to make this happen. Your internal developers will be your first line of defense in polishing and balancing the game. No one else knows better how the game was intended to be played.

A great method for finding load-based bugs is to build a series of bot programs that can allow an individual client system to log into the server dozens of times at once, simulating a larger volume of players. By running these bot programs on the development team's systems in off-hours, you can create loads that simulate the activity of many hundreds of players under controlled conditions. It will help you identify, isolate, and resolve many issues long before you get into the closed beta phase.

Similarly, you can use bots to simulate stress on your login servers, memory usage, and database servers. You can also use several different commercially available tools to simulate various network conditions, such as latency variations and packet loss, which is invaluable in understanding how better network connections can affect game balance.

While you're busy solving bugs and trying to simulate heavy server loads, you want to start preparing for closed beta. That phase is where you open up the game to anywhere from a few hundred to a few thousand real players. The phase is called *closed beta* because you'll limit the number of people you'll allow into the game. It won't be open to just anyone.

You might have just asked "Okay, if not everyone, then who will we invite into the game?" You want to identify a group of people who you think will be representative of your target audience. Consider this carefully. If you're building an MMOG for the mass-market sci-fi fan, then the feedback you'll get from a group of hard-core medieval fantasy MMOG players may not be appropriate. Different demographics of people have different expectations and tastes. Your closed beta players will give you feedback that you'll use to polish and adjust the game. They'll help you further tune your game to appeal to your target audience. Be certain they represent that audience accurately.

That means you have a lot of work to do. Long before you reach closed beta, you need to have located this group of players, contacted them, ensured that they have adequate client hardware to run the game, probably had them sign non-disclosure agreements, received their contact information, and have appropriate means to monitor their activities and allow them to easily report bugs and contribute suggestions. You need to be able to communicate with them en masse as well as individually. The infrastructure to do all of this must be in place before you get to the closed beta phase. This is a significant organizational task, and likely will need the dedication of one or two full-time employees for several months.

Closed Beta

Up to this point, most of the process should be familiar to developers of single-player games. But *beta* is where the development process starts to diverge significantly for MMOG projects.

In single-player games, the beta phase is usually defined as "content complete; 100% bug free." At this stage, single-player game developers submit the game to publishers and/or platform vendors for final verification and approval. The process generally only lasts a few weeks for single-player games.

With MMOGs, however, the *closed beta* phase (we have broken beta into closed beta and open beta) is when the game is opened up to a limited set of real-world players. At some point before this phase begins, you'll have identified a few hundred to a few thousand (rarely more than a few thousand) players who will get copies of the game for evaluation. You should have a comprehensive feedback system so that each player can report bugs, provide suggestions, and give you their general impressions of the game.

It's important during this phase to have implemented a set of automatic metric-gathering features. Embedded within your code base should be systems that monitor what features the players use most often, how much time they spend in particular areas of the game, which challenges are most difficult, etc. The reason for this is that although players can give lots of feedback, sometimes you get the most valuable information observing how they play the game. If you find features that are rarely used, consider revising or removing them. If you find features that are used extremely often, they may be too powerful, or overshadow a lot of content that you'd like players to experience, so consider toning them down.

"Shadowing" During Closed Beta

It's not a bad idea to have an invisible character that you can use to follow closed beta players, so that when they find cheats and exploits, you know about them. You'll find that some beta players will try to identify exploits during this phase, but won't report them in hopes that they can use them to get an early advantage when the game goes live. Players can be pretty sneaky, so you have to outsmart them and gather all the data they don't want you to find.

The closed beta phase will consist mostly of this kind of observation for balancing and bug fixing. In addition, you'll probably uncover several new scale issues during closed beta. Your goal should be to tie everything up in a nice, neat package so that by the end of closed beta, your game is complete.

With a few thousand players now happily exploring the world, you should focus on the issues of game balance and network load. No matter how good a job you might have done building bots to simulate traffic; there will still be a percentage of problems that are created by real players. They'll find ways to stress the system that you couldn't possibly think of or simulate.

The main trick here is to make sure that you have at least one complete launch-quality server, and that it is filled to capacity. That will dictate, in part, how many players you want in closed beta. If your server can handle 2,000 players simultaneously, then you might want a total of 4,000 or 5,000 players participating in closed beta. The idea is to max out that single server so you can understand the edge cases of network usage. Later when you launch the finished product, you'll add new servers, but you won't stress any of them any harder than at this stage, so you should be able to see and overcome your worst-case scenarios here.

You will also want to scrutinize your game balance at this stage. As mentioned earlier, it's easiest to do this if you've built a lot of metrics-gathering tools into your game. You should have these tools implemented and in the game before the closed beta phase begins.

As always, during this phase you should be preparing for the next phase, open beta, in which you will open up the game to as many players as you can. In some cases, this might involve hundreds of thousands. This is when your marketing will kick into high gear, getting the word out to everyone. Plan to support the marketing department with screen shots, demos for reviewers, video capture, websites, and whatever else they need. Also keep in mind that to support all of those players, you'll need a lot of servers and you'll want to start hiring customer support representatives. The last couple of months of closed beta are an exercise in building infrastructure.

Open Beta

Recall the last sentence of our closed beta phase definition: Your goal should be to tie everything up in a nice, neat package, so that by the end of closed beta, your game is complete. That's vitally important, and arguably the single biggest mistake MMOG developers make is not meeting this goal. When they enter the *open beta* phase, they still have bugs, problems, and game balance issues.

This begs two significant questions:

1. Why do so many MMOG developers make this mistake?
2. If the game is complete, what is the point of open beta?

The chronic mistake made in Question 1 happens because most developers don't know the answer to Question 2, so let's answer that first. What is the purpose of an open beta? Open beta is purely a marketing vehicle. The point of this phase is to put the game in front of the public and get a word-of-mouth marketing campaign kicked into high gear.

You have to understand that this will be the first official look the public at large gets of your game. (The thousand players or so that you had during closed beta should have been under a non-disclosure agreement, so details should still be sketchy to the general public.) The saying "you never get a second chance to make a first impression" should be in the forefront of your thinking.

You hope that the open beta will introduce a large number of players—say 10–20% of your expected first year total—to the game. The goal of open beta is to impress these players sufficiently that they will start a firestorm of chatter on message forums and convince the rest of the world that your incredible game is worth buying and playing. You want them to generate positive momentum that will assist the rest of your marketing campaign, not work against it.

This is why it's so vital that your game be complete before open beta begins. Countless examples exist of games that entered open beta in an incomplete fashion, and the results are invariably the same. A lot of people looked at the game and found lots of bugs, game-balance issues, and things they didn't like. They summarily proclaimed the game bad, and this became a titanic barrier for the marketing team to overcome. Often, they didn't, and the game was relegated to mediocrity before it was even launched.

Don't Buy Time with Open Beta

Avoid the temptation to use open beta as a means to get extra time to finish the game, or to use a large group of players as bug testers. If you show the world something that is buggy, unbalanced, or incomplete, you will create a negative impression that you may find impossible to overcome, no matter how many subsequent improvements you make.

By definition, the open beta phase should be relatively short. Don't plan on it lasting more than a few months at longest. Realize that if your open beta phase lasts a long time, even some players who genuinely like the game may become bored with it by the time it launches. This will needlessly cost you subscribers at the critical point when you launch the game and want to generate momentum and make money.

If someone tells you that MMOGs are useful because you can launch them with bugs, and to have no concerns because an MMOG's online nature allows you to patch it later, don't listen. This statement can only be made by someone who understands absolutely nothing about MMOGs. It shows a complete lack of understanding of how momentum works in a subscription-based game.

Denis Papp on the Open Beta Phase :::::

Denis Papp has been with TimeGate Studios since 1999, during which time it has earned awards for RTS of the Year, Strategy Game of the Year, and Expansion of the Year. Denis started in the game industry professionally at BioWare in 1996, taking over as Lead Programmer for *Shattered Steel*. Following that, he developed one of the first strong poker AIs, *Loki*, for his M.Sc. thesis with the University of Alberta Game Research Group. Denis' interests in game programming include engine architecture, AI, next generation production pipelines, and anything related to programming. His favorite game is *NetHack*.

Denis Papp
(Chief Technology Officer, TimeGate Studios)

Depending on your budget, open beta would last until the game is stamped ready. Unfortunately, development budgets and other economic requirements will force a game to be rushed out. However, I believe that it is very possible for a well-designed and well-balanced game to minimize the amount of open beta time needed.

Can Open Beta Compromise the Game?

Open beta should never last more than two weeks, which is more than enough time for your team to find what does and does not work. That being said, I generally do not care for open beta; it can compromise the game in the eyes of the gamer before its time. This is like eating a meal before it's even cooked. Often, the engine is not even properly implemented at this time, and it leaves the prospective clients with an inaccurate (and all too often bad) impression. Your QA team should be solid enough to test your product stringently. That being said, open betas beyond the gameplay, infrastructure and latency tests should also be closely monitored for openings that can be taken advantage of by cheaters. Two weeks is more than enough time to determine this.

—Mario "Thunderbear" Orsini
(Executive Producer, Team Orbit/Academy of Game Entertainment Technology [AGET])

Do the "Heavy Lifting" Early On

The length of open beta is more dependent on how much you are able to achieve before it. In other words, much of the heavy lifting needs to take place during the closed beta phase. If you run a closed beta well for about six months, then an open beta can last as little as 2–3 months.

—Jeff Anderson
(President & CEO, Turbine)

By the time you have reached open beta, the game should be essentially done. All of the content should have been completed months ago, the bugs removed, and the game polished and balanced. Now is the time when you want a large group of people to be able to see it.

As mentioned earlier, open beta is necessary as a form of marketing and as a means of seeding the subscriber base. If one understands the momentum driven nature of MMOGs, it is clear why it is so important that the game be completely finished before open beta commences.

From a marketing perspective, the game itself becomes a form of advertisement. The idea of open beta is to expose the game to as large a base of people as humanly possible. Making it free maximizes the size of that audience. People will come in large numbers just to check out the game for themselves. And as they come, the word will spread in a viral, word-of-mouth fashion—and exposure will be maximized.

This is yet another key distinction between MMOGs and single-player games. An MMOG has a different revenue model. The lion's share of the income it generates comes from monthly subscriptions. A single-player game usually only has 20–40 hours of gameplay, so if you give away demo versions of the game, say versions that allow for 4–5 hours of gameplay, you're effectively giving away a big chunk of the potential entertainment value. With MMOGs, however, it's more like setting the hook in fishing. Allowing players to see the game for themselves does not damage the promise of many months of extended gameplay and content. Instead, that promise is strengthened.

The idea of seeding is the second justification for open beta. By most viewpoints, an MMOG needs to feel like a thriving, virtual world. That means every server should be as densely populated as possible from the first day. Players will enjoy the game a lot more if there are many, many other players of varying levels wandering around with them. The world will feel full and vibrant.

By providing an open beta period, this goal will be accomplished. On the first official day of launch, you should have a respectable number of servers already filled up, and new incoming players won't feel like they're wandering around a ghost town. The atmosphere will feel busy, interesting, and entertaining.

With these two points well understood, it should be easy to understand why open beta must be undertaken with a clean, bug-free, well-balanced, polished game. If the goal is to act as a marketing vehicle, then obvious problems will detract from the ability to meet that goal. Bugs and unbalanced systems will give players a negative impression of the game, and a percentage of them will pass final judgment on it and never become subscribers.

Finally, it's a good idea to keep the open beta period relatively short. This phase should not last longer than two or three months. It should be just long enough to achieve a critical mass of players and advertisement, but not so long that players get tired of the game. If one understands the point of the open beta phase, this logic is self-evident.

Live Team

After surviving the first month after launch, you'll probably want to take some Prozac and then divide your team into two groups: a live team and an expansion team.

The *live team* is a group of programmers, artists, and designers who will be in charge of day-to-day operation of the game. Typically, this team is a producer, a few design-ers, a lot of programmers, and an artist or two. Their job is to solve bugs that arise, make periodic small content patches, eliminate exploits (small loopholes in the code or design that allow unscrupulous players to unbalance the game in their favor), monitor the game servers, and ensure smooth day-to-day operation.

It's appropriate to require that the original developers be on the live team for the first 6–12 months after launch. Their critical knowledge in solving problems and keeping a smooth-running ship is necessary and it's also a useful experience for them to see how their ideas function in a real world. One of the worst things you can do is let prima Donnas throw their game over the wall to some poor live team, and then let those prima donnas make the same errors on their next development effort. Seeing an MMOG operate firsthand is the best way to learn, and you should learn from every game you make.

Courtesy NCsoft

Jon Jones, Ian Weyna, and Jamie Gibbs—live team for *Dungeon Runners* at NCsoft

Expansion Team

Happily, the work never ends. Just because your game goes live doesn't mean your work is done. It's only just beginning. You should plan on shipping an expansion pack within the first 9–18 months after launch. An expansion pack is usually just a box with a lot of new content that can be played only within the original game software. Aside from being a form of job security, there are three main reasons to make MMOG expansion packs—managed by an *expansion team*: 1) Within a short time after launch, most of your veteran players will have experienced the majority of what your MMOG has to offer. You'll need to keep them engaged so they continue subscribing to the game. That means they need a regular and healthy supply of new content; 2) Expansion packs provide a convenient marketing boost to attract new players to the game and keep the game constantly in the public eye; and 3) As the number of retail units sold diminishes over time, retailers will want to remove the title from the shelves and replace it with something that generates more volume. New players as well as veterans will buy expansion packs, so this sales volume will attract retailers' attention, and they'll keep your game on the shelves.

Courtesy NCsoft

Steve Nichols and Mark Tucker are the expansion team for
Dungeon Runners at NCsoft

Separate the Teams

Make a point of keeping the live team distinct from the expansion team. A live team's responsibilities are unpredictable. You can't know what sorts of problems will arise, or how much effort will be needed to resolve them. This makes it difficult to schedule things. Since your expansion team will be on a standard project schedule, trying to make one team serve both duties will create scheduling conflicts. Either the live service will suffer, or the expansion pack will fail to meet its schedule. Live teams need to be a completely separate entity from expansion teams.

Launch/Live

Let the havoc commence! No matter how well you have planned and executed your MMOG, the day it launches will initiate utter pandemonium. Be prepared for this. Why will this happen? Because the day the game hits the shelves, a massive mob of people will rush out to buy it. They'll all race home, install it, and start playing immediately. Your login servers will be inundated with tens of thousands of people all trying to get in at practically the same time. Your game servers will be flooded with a staggering number of people all milling around in the same few starting game maps. Customer support lines will be jammed with thousands of people experiencing installation problems. Scale issues you hadn't considered will leap out and start crashing servers left and right. Lag will be awful. Everything will spike at the same time. Your database will experience a meltdown. It's the nature of the beast. Your work of art will blow up in your face and you'll probably want to crawl into a cave and stay there. Try not to panic. Usually within a few weeks after launch, things start settling down. Players start spreading out to different areas of the world. They stop logging in every day and playing for 10 hours at a stretch. You should be able to solve the worst of the unexpected bugs. The first tidal wave of installations will end and customer support can breathe a little. The big tip here is to not let the development team run off on vacation for at least a month after the game goes live. Launch phase should be "all hands on deck, battle stations"!

Post-Launch Planning

What are your plans for the game a year after launch? Three years? Five years? How much *wiggle room* do those plans leave for unexpected responses from the user base? What are your contingencies for personnel turnover or infrastructure changes? These kinds of considerations aren't fundamental in creating standalone games, but they are pivotal for MMOG development.

—Bryan Walker
(Senior Producer, Retro Studios)

Understand that over time your players will drop out of the game. This is as inevitable as death and taxes, and is known as *veteran churn*. In order to combat this phenomenon, you have to attract as many new players as you lose each month. If your game is removed from retail shelves, your ability to carry on this struggle will be hamstrung, and subscriptions will nosedive. The corporate suits, never very courageous under adversity, will get nervous and bolt for cover like a herd of stampeding wildebeasts, and soon you'll start hearing about layoffs and cost reductions. Trust me, you just don't want to go there. Avoid all the fuss and plan to put an expansion pack on the shelves soon after launch, and at least once a year thereafter as long as your game is live.

It is hoped that by reading this chapter you have found a common theme. Everything depends on planning. During each phase of the development process, you must be thoroughly planning for the needs of the next phase. The entire effort is an exercise in strategic thinking. If you keep the big picture firmly in mind at all times, however, it is quite manageable. The big picture is a collage of game design, infrastructure, technology, psychology, and marketing. Don't think of an MMOG as a game. Think of it as a start-up business. Always keep in mind that, unlike single-player games, your job is not done once the game is in a box on the shelves. In fact, at that point, your business has only just begun.

chapter 3

:::CHAPTER REVIEW:::

1. How do GDDs or TDDs created for MMOGs differ from those created for other games? Create a rough outline of a GDD or TDD for an original MMOG.

2. How does the MMOG development cycle differ from that used in developing other games? What is the significance of closed versus open beta phases?

3. What is the function and importance of live and expansion teams in MMOG development?

Part II:
Design & Marketing

CHAPTER

Content

a structural approach

Key Chapter Questions

- Why is a *second-order idea* more interesting than a *first-order idea*?

- How do *tone words* influence a design?

- What is the *core mechanic* and why is it important?

- What are some games that were damaged by having poor *production value*?

- What is the *uncanny valley*, and how can it create problems?

This chapter will discuss a fundamental, structural approach to game design—and will provide a set of tools that will focus and enhance the creative process. It will show game developers where to start in the design process, how creativity is enhanced through narrowing scope, and what parts of the game to emphasize. We will introduce the concept of production value and demonstrate through numerous examples the power of this underappreciated concept.

MMOG Design Considerations

Now we come to the part of the process for which nearly all developers seem to live and breathe: design. By virtue of the fact that you have read this far, let's assume that you are at least partially obsessive-compulsive about games. If you follow the norm, you play every game that you can lay your hands on, and it is thus likely that at some point in your life you made a comment such as, "I play tons of games, and I know what is fun and what isn't—so I think I'm the perfect sort of person to help design them."

This comment is always fascinating; in many ways, it devalues the art of game design. If you were to say "I've been driving cars for 27 years, and I know what makes for a good ride; therefore, I feel I'm perfectly qualified to design the next Ferrari," we could all get a good chuckle. It's a ridiculous assumption to believe that experience using a product gives you any skill whatsoever in building that product. It reminds me of a particular episode of *The Simpsons* ("Oh Brother, Where Art Thou?"), in which Homer tries to design a car for his half-brother's company. The result, of course, is a monstrosity that costs $82,000 per unit and drives the company into bankruptcy.

But when this is pointed out, the response is often, "That's true, but game design is far more subjective than building a car. You need an engineering degree to build a car." Sure. But the results are no different in subjective pursuits. Just because you like to read doesn't mean you can write like Hemingway. You might enjoy art and film—but you might not become a painter or director.

The difference, perhaps, lies in two main thoughts:

1. There is no established body of knowledge surrounding game design. Where writing has norms for structure and form, symbolism and allegory, and art has composition, anatomy, and color theory, no one has come up with a theoretical framework for game design that has been accepted academically. Thus, everybody feels they have a right to an opinion, even if it is based on nothing more than a gut feel.

2. It's expensive to build a game. It costs millions of dollars, and requires the efforts of dozens of people, sometimes for years at a stretch. Unfortunately, up until the time the game hits the shelves and sales figures start rolling in, it's difficult to tell whether the design is any good. Unlike writing a book or painting a portrait (which you can make by yourself in a few months) it's much too costly to experiment with game designs. Thus, the average person can go through life believing that they have genuine talent designing games, and no one can prove they don't.

As time passes, many game designers have developed an intuitive grasp of their art. Experience has given them a nebulous feel for game design, but often they don't have a methodological approach. They don't have words to describe how they make a good design, and they can't always be certain why it's fun. As a result, we tend to chalk this up to inherent talent and treat it like a sort of magic. It's not measurable, so you either have the skill or you don't. The game designer's output is ill defined, poorly understood, and often inconsistent.

What am I doing? I'm designing the game. What does it look like I'm doing?

Illustration by Ben Bourbon

With an MMOG, the problem is magnified. This is mostly because the game genre is so different from single-player games that there hasn't even been much time for designers to evolve an intuitive sense. When designing an MMOG for the first time, developers typically fall into three common traps: they simply emulate the model of an established game; they fire blindly in the dark at something completely new; or they try to make a game that literally does everything. In each of these cases, the approach seems dubious given the major investments that are required.

Even turning to books has little value. The majority of books that deal with the subject of game design aren't very good. More often than not, they are simply lists: this is a good idea, and this is not. There is rarely a systematic methodology. And even in the rare instances where a logical approach is attempted, authors usually do so from a distinctly single-player perspective, which is only marginally helpful for MMOGs.

As we've already noted, organization is essential in building an MMOG. There is little margin for error, so it's important to zero in on good design ideas as quickly as possible. In this chapter, we attempt to understand a conceptual framework for design thinking. We look at a set of tools for clarifying creative thought, and try to understand the fundamentals of game design in general, before embarking specifically on MMOG thinking.

Realize that so-called white page design is dangerous for MMOGs. You should never just sit down and start brainstorming specific game features at the beginning. You need to start with a plan to create a framework, carefully establish that framework, and then start considering features. You will want your game features to feel like they all belong together. They should each contribute to and enhance a central theme. To do that, let's start by understanding some fundamentals of entertainment.

Bill Louden on MMOG Genres :::::

Bill Louden
(Professor, Austin
Community College;
Founder & President,
GEnie)

Bill Louden is one of the early pioneers in the online, Internet, and computer massively multiplayer online game (MMOG) industries. He was a founding member of CompuServe and Founder and President of GEnie at the General Electric Company from 1985–1991. Bill designed and developed *MegaWars*, the first commercial multiplayer game, in 1982 while at CompuServe. *MegaWars* was a science fiction, space exploration game based on multi-player teams. The game ran continuously for over 18 years until it was retired in 2000. Bill was also instrumental in the production, licensing, and publishing of over two dozen multiplayer games that helped to launch Mythic Entertainment, Kesmai, and Simultronics. Bill teaches game computer industry courses at Austin Community College and graduate business courses at the University of Phoenix Online—where he is lead faculty for the college of Graduate Business and Management.

RPGs work as MMOGs because you are creating persistent, virtual worlds—alternate realities if you will—that one can enter at any time to the familiar environmental state when you left it, yet that world continued when you were away so it is always both familiar and new. Other genres are very difficult to apply to MMOGs for this reason; especially those genres that have discrete starting points or endings. One genre that I think could be applied is simulations—especially the emerging crop of games that focus on educational aspects such as triage simulations, medical procedures, hostage crisis simulations, etc.

Central Theme

When you were an infant, there was probably a stage of your life when your mom got right up in your face a few hundred times each day and said the word, "mama." Eventually, you repeated the word, and she made some pleasant sound and danced around excitedly. Maybe she gave you a cookie or some juice. You got positive reinforcement, and the cycle of learning was off at a gallop. You had learned the magic of pattern recognition and association. On that momentous day, you fell into the established cycle of observation, speculation, and validation.

From the day we are born, humans are conditioned to this pattern. We observe the world around us. We look for known patterns or parts of patterns. When we find those patterns, we naturally look for associations, much like that first association of the sound your mom made ("mama") and the sight of her face. When we think we've found a correlation between two things, we experiment. We speculate. When she puts her face in front of us, we mimic the "mama" sound. And when we are right, we are accustomed to receiving some sort of reward. We arc validated.

This Pavlovian cycle is conditioned into us from the start, and the process becomes permanently hardwired into our brains. Everything we do is a reflection of it. In a sense, we live for this simple cycle. It seems that a big percentage of what makes us human is our innate desire to form associations between ideas. We can't help it. It's what we do. We associate as a way of life. If you're going to learn how to design games, this fundamental understanding of human nature is a good place to start.

Ah, but if you're paying attention, the immediate question that comes to mind is, "So what? What good does that do us?" That's a good question. Academic-sounding observations are valueless unless they can be applied in some meaningful way. So what value can we get out of the notion that people are hardwired to gravitate toward the OSV (observation, speculation, validation) pattern?

Let's look at how this concept can be applied. Mystery movies and books provide great examples. The viewer (or reader) is provided with countless clues, some obvious and some subtle, some meaningful, some not. The audience must observe details about the environment, other characters, behaviors, words, objects, or virtually anything they see or hear. They must look for patterns or inconsistencies (anti-patterns, if you will) and try to extrapolate their meaning.

Humans are hard-wired from birth to look for patterns and associations.

Illustration by Ben Bourbon

The classic private detective exemplifies associative thinking techniques

Content: a structural approach   chapter 4

After observing enough details, the audience will begin to speculate about what's going on, who the killer is, or what the answer to the mystery is. Often, there are numerous possibilities, but the clues that have been provided, if skillfully done, make more sense with one particular conclusion over any other. Regardless, when the story reaches its climax, the audience's speculations are validated. And as audience members, are we not most pleased and entertained when we have the feeling that we unraveled the mystery, especially if we've done so before anyone else? Of course we are.

> It's the RPG part of MMORPG that makes them compelling in a way that no other form of leisure activity can match—not the MMO part.
>
> —Dr. Richard Bartle
> (Visiting Professor in Computer Game Design, University of Essex)

Jeff Anderson on the MMOFPS Market :::::

Jeff Anderson
(President & CEO, Turbine, Inc.)

Jeff Anderson joined Turbine, Inc. in 2001—bringing a diversified background in game development, business management, and law to the company. Under his leadership, Turbine implemented a new corporate strategy transforming the company from a single-franchise, contract-game developer into a premier publisher and operator of online subscription entertainment. Prior to joining Turbine, Jeff was the vice president and executive in charge of production for Origin Systems, a subsidiary of Electronic Arts, where he managed the *Ultima Online* franchise. Prior to Origin, he was the executive director for the consumer products division of Viacom—managing Paramount Pictures' worldwide interactive licensing, merchandising, and business development. Before Viacom, Jeff was Vice President of Operations at Mission Studios Corporation, a game developer. Jeff also practiced law at the firm of Holleb & Coff in Chicago, Illinois—where he concentrated in both intellectual property and corporate litigation. He graduated summa cum laude from the University of Illinois with a bachelor's degree in economics and received his J.D. from University of Chicago Law School.

MMOFPSs continue to be a big success in Asia and will likely transition into the North American market. Why this success? It most likely goes to the type of players who are interested in FPS titles. There is a definite sense of competition and community around these players that make the FPS genre well-suited for the online world.

The exact same concept applies to puzzle games. We observe. We speculate. We solve and are validated. We are entertained. In fact, if you think about it, games of strategy also bring out the OSV cycle, as we try to understand how various mechanics work together to form the basis for a larger plan, or we try to identify our opponent's patterns of play, and then exploit flaws in their thinking. Many games include strategic elements, from RTS games to RPGs, sports games, and countless others.

But this concept can be used in a broader sense than just solving puzzles and mysteries, or playing strategic games. Remember, the OSV cycle is pretty fundamental to who we are. Nearly anything can trigger it. Specific styles of music are known to create consistent imagery. We can associate music with geographic locations, ethnicity, emotion, machinery, activity, and groups of people. Artistic styles are commonly used to convey a desired tone in a game world. Sound effects can clearly be used to establish a desired atmosphere. There are myriad mechanisms for eliciting specific kinds of responses from an audience.

> There's a lot of potential for action games or shooters to be very successful and popular as MMOGs. However, most shooter players are accustomed to getting the online multiplayer play for free, so this would require a lot of added value.
>
> —Denis Papp
> (Chief Technology Officer,
> TimeGate Studios, Inc.)

In all of these cases, we play off of recognizable patterns that have been imprinted into the audience's mind for their entire lives. People have been taught to associate anything they can see, hear, smell, taste, or touch with consistent categories of concepts.

We hope you get the picture. In any game design, you must first decide what sorts of concepts and imagery you want to put in the minds of your players, and then start figuring out how you can trigger the desired responses. It's like reverse-engineering the association. For example, if you want your player to experience tension, then you want to focus on features, visuals, and sounds that evoke that response. What causes tension? You can use this as a clear direction for focusing your thoughts. In other words, it should be treated as a central theme.

Validation

Providing details for people to observe is great, but they can't be too obvious, or what we might call *cliché*. Why? Something cliché is, by definition, something we've seen many, many times in the past. There is nothing to speculate about and hence no form of validation is required. And without the ability to speculate and be rewarded with validation, we find the subject matter boring. It doesn't appeal to our inherent attraction to the OSV cycle. The techniques and tools in the next few sections will help us learn to avoid this sort of pitfall.

Mindmap

A *mindmap* is a tool for clarifying, unifying, and focusing our thoughts. The basic idea is to start with a simple central concept, and begin by charting everything we know about that concept. The reasons for this will be made clear momentarily.

In the accompanying diagram, we started with the well-used idea of dragons. Although the example is rather oversimplified, it demonstrates the kinds of results people typically have when they first try to make a mindmap. We arrive at some superficial, uninteresting, standard properties of dragons. If we stopped here, we'd decide that the results are unimpressive and conclude that they provide no value to the game design process.

Diagram by Per Olin

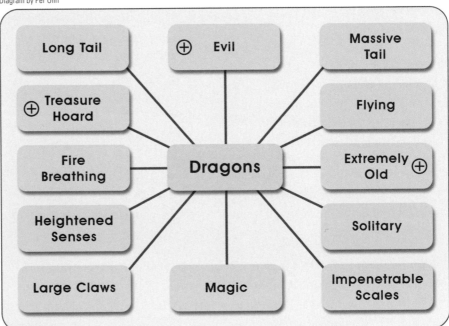

Typical results from a first pass at a mindmap

Before you throw in the towel on mindmaps, try to understand how they operate. Their job is to assist in creative thinking. Creative people are somehow able to form associations between disparate concepts, and come up with an unusual spin on existing ideas. For those of us who aren't so creative, the numbers of associations that are available to us are small. We have trouble keeping a large number of them in our heads all at once. The mindmap is a way of putting them in front of us visually. By being able to see everything at once, we have an opportunity to expand on any given idea without having to juggle all of the possible associations simultaneously. Let's see what happens when we take the first pass of our mindmap and try expanding on a couple of the ideas.

Diagram by Per Olin

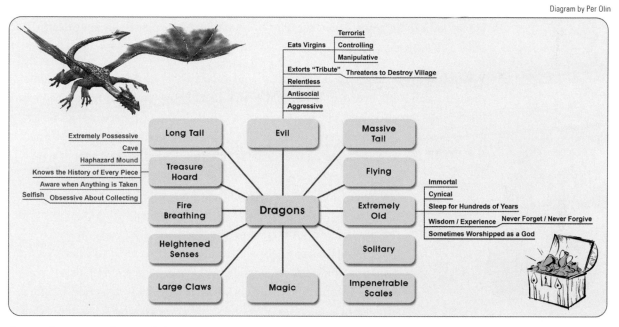

A second pass at our dragon mindmap

In the mindmap example, we haven't expanded on every possible concept from our first pass (although we certainly could have). However, by zeroing in on specific items, we've been able to take them deeper. I tried this exact example with a couple of students at school, and during the brainstorming session we recalled dragon-related books, movies, games, and comics that we'd seen in the past. Anything and everything is fair game when brainstorming, and if you let yourself have fun with it, a mindmapping session can span many hours.

—Rick Hall

Initially, we saw a couple of examples of second-order ideas. Although each of the new entries tracks back to the central concept of dragons, they are one step removed. This is important. If we recall the previous section about the OSV cycle, we get an interesting view of the speculation and validation properties. First-order ideas (dragons breathe fire, fly, are big, etc.) aren't interesting specifically because they're cliché. We all know these things and have seen them hundreds of times. But the second-order ideas often make us think, even if just for a moment. They fit in with the idea of a dragon, but not as stereotypically as the first-order ideas. And it's that moment of thought that makes them a bit more interesting.

From here we could explore outward to another level, which we might label our third-order ideas. Keep in mind that going out to that level is difficult for most people to do in their heads. Why? It's hard to keep that entire picture in your head all at once. But with a mindmap, it's easy.

When you use words such as "obsessive" and "possessive" to describe the dragon's thoughts about his hoard, and you realize that he is hyper-aware of the location and history of each and every piece of treasure, it reminds you of a person with obsessive compulsive disorder (OCD)—the type who wants everything to be ordered and predictable. It's an interesting view of a dragon—consistent with stereotypical behavior, but not something that is commonly pointed out explicitly. It's possible that something like the USA television series *Monk* could be created with this exact process. If you made a mindmap of private detectives, you'd soon realize that the very traits of observation that they need to solve crimes are similar to the traits of people who have obsessive-compulsive disorders. The character Adrian Monk is a brilliant detective, but he is plagued by a plethora of phobias and compulsions—a combination that gives the show a unique charm.

Illustration by Ben Bourbon

Germs
Bugs
Residue
Disease
Dirt
Dust
Grime
Disorder
Sludge

The 'defective detective' is an idea that could easily have evolved from a mindmap.

So what if we took that as a spin on our game about dragons? What if we thought about game features, characters, and environment that were specifically designed to accentuate a dragon's obsessive-compulsive nature? Our dragon might be slightly mentally unbalanced, and our game mechanic could have features that are designed to play off of his obsessive compulsions. It's at least an intrinsically more interesting starting point than trying to figure out how many hit points of damage a dragon's fire breath inflicts.

If the obsessive-compulsive disorder didn't attract us, we could talk about viewing our dragon through the evil node. Looking at the notes in that section, our dragon appears rather like a terrorist. After all, by extorting villages into giving up their money and/or daughters under threat of having their homes incinerated, a dragon is running the medieval equivalent of a protection racket. That sounds like another possible theme to explore in our game design. What kinds of game mechanics come to mind when we view our dragon as a sort of medieval mobster? That's certainly not a stereotypical depiction of a dragon, but it is nonetheless thematically consistent with their established behavior in many previous books and movies.

Of course, in a full design, we would want to treat our mindmaps more thoroughly than we have here. Ideally, we could explore every first-order concept fully, and may wind up creating several ancillary mindmaps for second- and third-order thinking. Ultimately, we'd want to choose one or two ideas of the second or third order to work with. These concepts will act as filters for all of our future thinking. They will help us eliminate the extraneous ideas and zero in on those that contribute to an established theme.

A 'mobster dragon' is probably more interesting than a standard fire-breathing cliché.

Illustration by Ben Bourbon

Tone Words

A *tone word* is designed to evoke a specific emotional response or create a specific impression in the minds of the audience. It is another filter, similar to the kind that was established by the mindmaps, and its purpose is to further narrow and refine our design thinking. Let's continue our example with the dragon.

Assume we've decided that we want to view our dragon as a creature that is obsessive-compulsive in nature, and he runs the equivalent of a medieval protection racket on the local villagers. While this probably gives us some immediate ideas to consider, it might still be too broad of a topic to work with reliably. We can further narrow our focus by considering the tone that we want our game to have.

Let your mind dream about our OCD dragon mobster for a moment. What image comes to mind? Can you think of an adjective to describe him? Perhaps predatory? Ruthless? Selfish? Vicious? These are all fine adjectives that might describe a stereotypical mobster, but before we rush off in that direction, let's play around a little. What if we used the adjective incompetent instead? How about lazy? Perhaps we could think about words like bored, sadistic, industrious, narcissistic, disinterested, jovial, or sarcastic. Any of these words could be used instead of predatory, and if we considered them as filters they would definitely send us off in totally different design directions. A lazy and sarcastic OCD mobster will probably approach life quite differently from a predatory and ruthless OCD mobster. This difference will clearly affect the kinds of features that come to mind for our game, but it will do so in a positive, creative, and non-stereotypical way.

Although our mindmaps and tone words have created filters that technically eliminate many, many potential ideas, this doesn't impose a limitation on us. On the contrary, when provided with such a narrowing set of restrictions, most people are inspired with more ideas, not less. Even looking at the preceding examples, it should be obvious that tone words and mindmaps enable creative thought rather than limit it.

But the idea of tone words is even more powerful than simply providing a solid foundation for dreaming up game mechanics. Again, think about the tone words mentioned earlier with respect to things such as music, art style, dialogue, and animation style. Each of these will be profoundly affected by the tone words. For example, music that conveys a predatory environment would sound very different from music that we'd expect to hear in a world that is occupied by an incompetent main character. In the same manner, our art style, animations, and dialogue would all be similarly affected. In a sense, every facet of the design can be made to reflect the desired tone. The idea of creating tone words to act as filters is very powerful. These words can become pervasive in the way that we think about the entire game. Without them, our ideas will probably tend to lack thematic consistency and focus. The game and the world it is set in will have elements that feel random or like they don't belong, and the audience will become confused.

Remember: People live for the OSV cycle. They want all of the ideas, theme, tone, and environment to feel logical and consistent. As they absorb the environment, they'll begin to notice patterns as well as see things that don't belong. They'll fixate on those details and try to figure out where they fit in. If the inconsistencies eventually reveal their purpose, it's all well and good. However, if the audience arrives at the conclusion that they don't fit, then there is no validation, and hence no reward. It doesn't feel right, and they become frustrated. Eventually, if there are enough inconsistencies, the audience will conclude that they simply don't like our world, and we'll lose them. Tone words are a good tool for helping to avoid this kind of thematic inconsistency. They clarify our thinking and provide a clear direction for the game design.

Core Mechanic

Although this topic was discussed briefly in the previous chapter, it is worth discussing again in greater detail. Among the game-designing community you will hear the phrase *core mechanic* tossed around on a regular basis. It's a well-used part of the game designer's dictionary. But as mentioned in Chapter 3, it is odd that it isn't well understood.

Let's review functional definition first. The *core mechanic* is "the fundamental interaction that the player will spend the majority of his or her time performing." This is a critical component of the design of any MMOG, and as such, it is worth investing a considerable portion of your preproduction time to get it right.

::::: Team Play in *City of Heroes* & *City of Villains*

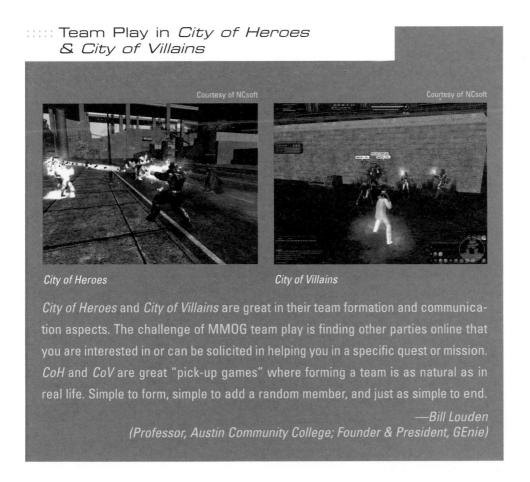

Courtesy of NCsoft   Courtesy of NCsoft

City of Heroes   *City of Villains*

City of Heroes and *City of Villains* are great in their team formation and communication aspects. The challenge of MMOG team play is finding other parties online that you are interested in or can be solicited in helping you in a specific quest or mission. *CoH* and *CoV* are great "pick-up games" where forming a team is as natural as in real life. Simple to form, simple to add a random member, and just as simple to end.

—Bill Louden
(Professor, Austin Community College; Founder & President, GEnie)

Thinking strategically, we cannot fail to realize that the core mechanic is something that a typical player may spend 50–75% of the time doing. It has to be fun. In *City of Heroes*, the player easily spends 50–75% or more of the time in combat. If combat isn't fun, then the quality of all of the other features becomes irrelevant. In an MMOG, in which you expect people to spend hundreds or even thousands of hours, it is unrealistic to expect that we could get away with a boring or unbalanced core mechanic. Who wants to spend hundreds of hours doing something boring? Ironically, the core mechanic itself might comprise a relatively small percentage of the total game code and assets. Yet upon this small set of features rests the fate of your entire game.

Avoid "Complete Design" Before Implementation

Many development teams prefer to have a sweeping, all-encompassing, complete design before they start implementing the game. Unfortunately, to put it bluntly, this idea is simply wrong-headed. Ancillary features are often highly dependent on the core mechanic and they should be constructed to enhance it. As a result, it is pointless to waste much time designing anything else until at least a prototype of the core mechanic has been built and everyone agrees that it is fun. We know the core mechanic will change and evolve throughout the early stages of development, and when it does, the features that depend on it will follow suit. Why waste time documenting features that are practically guaranteed to change before we ever start implementing them?

It is, however, inadequate to use an ambiguous and broad term such as *combat* to describe the core mechanic of most games. Combat can come in many flavors and often depends on a game's primary genre. A core mechanic requires further clarification to be meaningful. When we design a game, we need to understand what differentiates our core mechanic from that of other games. And clearly, there must be a differentiator. If the core mechanic is no different from the competitors' core mechanics, then there is no reason to expect that our game will be successful. Clones or wannabes don't tend to attract much attention from consumers.

Courtesy of NCsoft

Courtesy of Lockpick

The combat in a game such as *Auto Assault* is dramatically different from the combat that exists in *Dreamlords*.

There is a point worth mentioning here. A core mechanic should almost never be a direct result of fiction. If you find yourself saying "Our combat is different because everyone else does medieval fantasy games, and ours is cyberpunk," you are deluding yourself. Functionally, the only difference between a fireball and a handheld rocket launcher is a particle effect and a sound effect. The fiction is just a label and by itself it doesn't constitute a differentiator. If your core mechanic is to be truly different, this difference must be a substantive difference.

To illustrate the point, let's consider a few examples. In a game like *Splinter Cell*, the core mechanic revolves around using the environment to accomplish objectives through stealth. In Will Wright's *Spore*, the core mechanic is about playing God by influencing evolution. *Need for Speed Underground* boasts a standard racing core mechanic, but it differentiates itself by going to great lengths to give the player an overwhelming sense of speed. The various incarnations of the game *Commandos* have as a core mechanic the concept of navigating a complex web of enemy patrol movements. In each case, if we consider the games carefully, we will see a highly polished core mechanical theme that the developer clearly devoted a great deal of time to perfecting. We will also see that many of the ancillary game features build upon this core, enhancing and extending it tremendously.

Eidos Interactive Ltd.

Commandos: Beyond the Call of Duty contains a core mechanic of navigating a path through a complex web of enemy patrol movements. Here, the highlighted enemy's line of sight is indicated by the green arc (which is interrupted by the rockpile near the bottom of the screen).

Only after the core mechanic has been designed, prototyped, iterated upon, and the development team agrees that it is fun on its own should we begin to seriously consider additional features of the game. When you follow this approach, you will find that your ancillary features will build upon a foundation that is already fun, and will serve to enhance it. Once you can actually see the game in action, ideas will come to mind that might not otherwise have presented themselves.

Understand that games must be experienced to be truly understood. Many ideas that look good on paper don't turn out to be fun when they are implemented. Our minds play tricks on us when we write down a design. It is easy to romanticize an idea because we are viewing it through our own personal experience, which is usually accompanied by many factors that aren't incorporated into the game.

When we design a combat system for our science fiction fantasy game, perhaps we are remembering a movie such as *Star Wars*. In our minds, the movie was so much fun to watch that we don't even notice that generating a random number to determine if we hit a target, and then generating another random number to represent damage isn't anywhere near as much fun as watching a Jedi warrior use his shimmering lightsaber to slice through an armor-clad bounty hunter whom we've come to hate. We confuse the context of a story with the mechanics of a combat system, and it never dawns on us that the combat system itself has no real entertainment value.

Production Value

Before we discuss why *production value* is so important, let's first take a moment to define it. Production value is an expansive concept, encompassing everything from the quality of the 3D models, to animation, sound effects, camera work, music, particle effects, and a myriad of small details. Production value is the set of details that creates immersion. That's the short definition. It encompasses all of the polish that combines to make a world seem alive and believable.

To achieve good production value, it is important to have attention to detail and the patience to craft it into every aspect of the game. To be clear, this does not mean that things have to look real. On the contrary, any world can define its own reality. It means that things must be consistent with the expectations of the audience.

For example, if you pay attention to the X-wings and tie fighters in the movie *Star Wars*, you will note that they don't have a realistic flight model. In space there is no friction. Ships in space should move according to the vector of thrust, and when they turn, that vector still exists. Real space ships fly sideways or even backward and sort of skid when they turn. George Lucas realized that this wouldn't look right to an audience who had little exposure to real space physics. He opted instead to give his fighters a flight model that his audience could understand. Thus, X-wings and tie fighters fly more like a World War II fighter plane than a real space ship. It doesn't matter that this was unrealistic. It catered to people's expectations, and was therefore more easily accepted.

> When teaching my students at the university about game development, one of the first notions that I try to drive home to them is traditionally met with skepticism and disappointment. The last thing any aspiring game designer wants to hear is me telling him or her that a game's production value is three to four times more important than the actual design. Unfortunately, in my experience, this is definitely the case.
>
> —*Rick Hall*

:::::*EVE Online*: An Engineering Approach

> *EVE Online* is very well-designed. It has an almost engineering approach: everything is there for a purpose, it has multiple checks and balances, and no part of its vision is ever compromised. It's clear what the design is saying, and you never get a muddled message. I'm very impressed by it.
>
> —*Dr. Richard Bartle*
> *(Visiting Professor in Computer Game Design, University of Essex)*

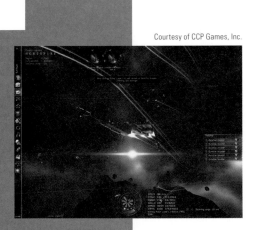

Courtesy of CCP Games, Inc.

Similarly, consider the numerous games that populate the fictional genre of high fantasy (medieval fantasy). Some enjoy great success, and some are catastrophic failures. While there can be many reasons for success or failure, one that immediately catches my attention is brought about when developers have the desire to be too creative.

Designers often scoff at traditional high fantasy canon. If you suggest to some designers that they should have dwarves and elves and orcs and goblins in their fictional world, they act like you are insulting their mother. "Never!" they shout. "I'm more creative than that! I can easily invent 10 completely new fantasy races before the end of the day." And so they do.

Character races in *EverQuest II* include most of the traditional fantasy races (Dark Elf pictured here), plus several newer races.

But what these designers fail to realize is that they are creating what is known in psychology circles as *cognitive dissonance,* resulting from an inconsistency between one's beliefs and actions. The fact is that back in the 1920s and 1930s, Robert E. Howard (creator of *Conan the Barbarian*) and J.R.R. Tolkien (creator of *The Hobbit*) indelibly etched into our minds our perception of reality in high fantasy. They established an image that is so well known and accepted by audiences worldwide that if someone wants to join that genre, they must work within it, not try to reinvent it.

When game designers decide they simply must be creative and toss out the entire established canon, they unwittingly defy their audience's unvoiced expectations. The audience expects high fantasy and they get something else. It's like when you reach for the soda can, believing it's Pepsi, only to discover that it's Mountain Dew. It doesn't matter if you like Mountain Dew or not. When you first taste it with the expectation that it's Pepsi, you're likely to spit it on the ground. Your reaction is invariably negative.

The same holds true to an even greater degree with a fictional genre. If people expect high fantasy, you should give it to them. It's fine to put your own spin on it, but you need to ground players in enough of their expected reality that they feel a certain level of comfort and familiarity. We can even relate this back to our OSV cycle. Armed with a traditional high-fantasy pattern, we can see the differences clearly when a developer merely spins it. We'll be able to focus on these differences, and if they're sufficiently thought provoking, logical, and consistent, we'll find ourselves understanding the environment, and this will be perceived as enjoyable.

But when everything about the high-fantasy world feels alien, the audience loses their grounding. There is nothing specific for them to focus on because everything is new. They end up floundering with an information overload, trying desperately to memorize alien-sounding words and deciphering incomprehensible behaviors, cultures, and lore. They must spend far too much time just orienting themselves to the basic patterns of the world, and there is no time left to focus on specific concepts on which they can speculate. Remember, people love to speculate, especially if there is a chance they can be right. It makes us feel smart, and we want to see more.

In the end, all of this wraps back around to the concept of production value. The virtual world that you create must be, at least in large part, exactly what the audience expects. People should give the world 90% tradition, and 10% invention. The tradition gives the audience a foundation upon which they can feel comfortable in exploring and speculating on your inventions.

Myst Online: Uru Live does a good job of mixing familiar elements (such as the stone pavement) with the fantastic (the odd lights).

These two components, traditional expectations and creative inventions, will consume a large portion of your development time if you're doing it right. They require a staggering attention to detail, and often a substantial investment in time and resources. However, if done properly, they are well worth the effort. Consider just a few examples of good production value.

The game *Diddy Kong Racing* brings to mind an easy example. Look at the cars when they back up. They don't just move backward. The tail lights come on when the car moves in reverse, just like a real car. The driver turns his head around and even rests his arm on the back of the passenger seat, just like a real driver. The car even behaves correctly, with the steering axis remaining on the front wheels, producing the characteristic behavior of a car moving in reverse. The designers of this game didn't have to pay attention to these details. They could have made the car simply move backward with far less effort. But the fact that they went the extra mile has a strong, yet subliminal effect on the player. It feels right. Often the player isn't even consciously aware of why it feels right. It just does, and they like it.

Another great example comes from *The Prince of Persia: The Sands of Time*. The detail in the Prince's animations is incredible. Almost anything the character is able to do has its own animation. When he walks along a narrow ledge, his arms spread wide as he hugs the wall. If he steps too close to an edge, he'll stumble, sometimes even catching himself when his hand touches the ground and he regains his balance. He walks toe-to-heel with his arms spread wide as he tightrope walks across a narrow beam. He leans into his turns as he runs around corners. He swings his sword in multiple ways in combat, and

Realistically leaping a gap in *Prince of Persia: The Sands of Time*

is even thrown tumbling across the floor when he is hit. His hands and feet are correctly placed when he ascends a ladder, or he can grab the side rails and slide down daringly. Every motion has its own characteristic animation, and every animation is crafted with skill. The result is a breathtakingly real character movement, which never fails to generate a positive response from the audience.

Electronic Arts, Inc.

Audio and graphics production values in *SSX Tricky* make the game highly immersive.

How about the sports broadcast style of audio treatment in *SSX Tricky*? The voice-acting talent, dialogue, music, and general atmosphere created by this audio background are incredibly immersive. The sound creates excitement and atmosphere, mimicking (possibly even exceeding) a color commentator in an extreme sports event. Comments are relevant to the action onscreen, unlike many games where the comments are seemingly random, often making no sense whatsoever when one considers the current situation in the game. Again, the result is that the production value transports the player directly into the world of extreme snowboarding. It feels authentic.

World of Warcraft also has some strong production values. Consider the different character races, and what Blizzard has done with them. Many of the races have their own specific theme, and their behavior, quests, and even the accents of their spoken words reflect that theme. The dwarves are patterned after hard-drinking Scottish highlanders. The Tauren are patterned after Native Americans. The humans are basically Americans. Trolls speak with a distinctly Jamaican accent. By patterning different character races after real nationalities, Blizzard has given the players an easy way to identify each character race with a specific image, as well as creating a model for them to draw upon for their character's behavior, quests, and even dances.

As you can see, many things must be considered to create a logical, immersive, believable environment. None of these things could be considered necessary in terms of the actual game mechanic (i.e., whether the dwarves have a Scottish accent

Courtesy of Blizzard Entertainment, Inc.

Diverse character races in *World of Warcraft* heighten the game's production value.

or not doesn't impact the gameplay one bit), but they are all powerful in terms of making the environment immersive.

If we try to look at this section on production value in its totality, it's sweeping in scope, but simple in concept. It is also often fraught with controversy. Many developers underrate the need for production value in a game. They are desperate to pack their game full of as many features as humanly possible. Although they can understand the concept of immersion, and even place value on it, when the time comes to draft a schedule, they see production value as a drain that reduces the number of features they can put into the game.

The tricky part is recognizing the need for production value. It's different from a game feature in one critical area: quantification. We can get a feel for the relative value of a feature simply by implementing it. The more a player uses a particular feature, the better the designer likes it. Ideally, every feature in the game will be specifically used at one time or another and this usage helps us to quantify its value.

But production value isn't used. Often it's not even explicitly noticed. The game just feels better, and players aren't even aware why this is. This makes it difficult to quantify production value, and therefore it often falls low on our list of priorities. When we write out our schedules, anything we can't justify explicitly in terms of its contribution to the game tends to be cut.

Consider production value as a set of features. Recognize that if you want your players to spend a year or more playing your game, then it has to feel more like a world than a game. It has to be consistent, logical, acceptable, and believable. Each bit of detail that you integrate into the game will take you another step closer to the goal of creating a virtual world. If you can decide how much immersion is worth to your game, this will help you decide how much effort to put into the production value details.

Visual References

When you get to the stage when you're trying to decide what goes into your game world, don't work solely from your head. Gather references. Look at films with similar environments. Visit real-world locations (if you can) that are similar to your environment. Is there a location in your game that's set in an opera hall? Visit one. You can visit aircraft carriers, battlefields, crowded cities, and jungle islands. If you can't go there personally, then get several photographic references. You'll be amazed at how many details are present that you'd never have noticed without specifically looking for them. This sort of detail will bring your game to life.

The Uncanny Valley

It should be obvious by now that we need to devote a significant amount of effort to creating audience acceptance for our world. As we've already noted, this doesn't necessarily imply complete realism, and in fact, in some cases too much realism is a bad thing (as it would have been if George Lucas had used a real space flight model in *Star Wars*).

Masahiro Mori, a Japanese roboticist, did a fascinating study on a strongly related subject in 1970. Mori found that as a robot was made more humanlike in its appearance and motion, humans tended to increasingly accept and empathize with it. However, after the appearance and motion reach a critical point, human acceptance drops off dramatically into what Mori calls the *uncanny valley*. Further improvements in the appearance and motion will bring acceptance back in line.

The explanation for this phenomenon is that at early stages, when a robot is sufficiently humanlike, we tend to focus our attention on its human qualities. They stand out, so we pay attention to them. If they're done well, we accept them. However, as the appearance and motion continue to improve, at some critical juncture when it appears nearly human, the non-humanlike features will be what we fixate on. In other words, if the robot becomes sufficiently humanlike, then we expect it to be so—and we'll notice the small details that aren't right. At that point, the robot becomes creepy. Perhaps it has a flat, dead expression on its face, moves with a wooden motion, or has unblinking eyes. It doesn't matter that it has perfectly proportioned features, lifelike hair, and perfect skin. There's just something unnatural about it, and our acceptance plummets.

Diagram by Per Olin

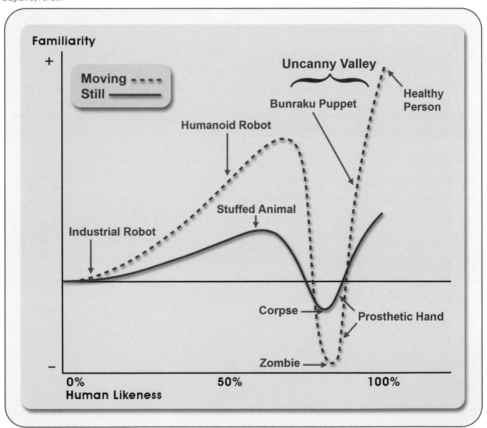

Masahiro Mori's uncanny valley

If you study the accompanying diagram carefully, you'll note that the movement quality has an even more pronounced effect on human acceptance than physical appearance. Something can look perfectly human, but if it moves with an awkward, mechanical shuffle instead of a lively step, the audience won't like it (unless it's actually supposed to be a zombie, or we're making a specific point that it's not human).

We can take Mori's conclusions a step further with games. Appearance and animation are important, but so is behavior. You can make a perfectly lifelike human character model and move it with a staggering array of flawless motion-captured animations, and yet nothing will say "I'm not real" like having the character make idiotic, illogical decisions in response to player actions. If anything, the uncanny valley curve for AI would be even more pronounced than the curve for motion.

This phenomenon has powerful implications. In games, we strive to make our world as acceptable as possible to our audiences. It's interesting to see that a well-animated talking dog would be far more acceptable to an audience than a nearly real 3D human model that has some small-but-fatal imperfection. Without naming names, a recent MMORPG suffered from this problem. Despite the tens of thousands of polygons-per-character model, high-resolution photorealistic textures, intricate skeletal structures, and plethora of animations, the characters didn't seem real. They had a waxy look to their skin, expressionless faces, dead eyes, and mechanical-looking animations. The result was unfortunate. Had they paid attention to the uncanny valley, perhaps they'd have made different choices and been more successful.

Courtesy of Blizzard Entertainment, Inc.

Who cares if he's not perfect? He's just plain cool!

As a final noteworthy point, consider the art style for *World of Warcraft*. The character models have exaggerated proportions, simplified texture maps, oversaturated colors, and stylized, exaggerated animations. The developers at Blizzard aimed at a distinctly cartoon-like aesthetic, and the game has far better acceptance among MMOG players than any competitor with a photorealistic look. This is partially because with a photorealistic look we expect everything to look perfect and life-like. Any little flaw stands out like a sore thumb. But if the whole style is more like a cartoon, we simply don't fixate on imperfections because it's not supposed to look perfect. In other words, *World of Warcraft* can get away with flaws more easily because the game's art style de-emphasizes them.

Thinking back to what we learned in Chapter 1, recall a fundamental tenet of MMOGs: They are more than just a game. They're a lifestyle. If we remember this simple concept, it's easy to understand why production value is so vitally important. If you want people to live in your virtual world for an extended period of time, it has to feel like home. It has to feel vibrant, alive, and consistent. It has to have a style and focused theme. It must be a place that makes players think and wonder and dream. Atmosphere is critical, perhaps even a touch more than content, although they run neck and neck.

When you begin the pre-production process, don't just start writing down design features and details in a furious stream-of-consciousness babble. Start with a plan. Create a narrow focus for your thinking, sketch it out, and build a prototype. This is your fundamental player interaction, your core mechanic. Iterate on that core mechanic relentlessly. Take as much time as you can to ensure that it's fun. Only after you're happy with it should you expend any effort fleshing out the rest of the design.

Similarly, use the same process for your production value features. Don't start off building the entire world at once. Focus on building one tiny section and a couple of characters. Breathe life into them. Give them personality and style. Make that tiny corner of the world really feel good. When you're done, and you have an acre of land, a hero, and a villain, and they all look and feel like you want the rest of the world to feel, that's when you can start to map out the rest of the world. Don't make the same mistake so many other developers make when they try to write a 2,000-page design document before building anything. It's a titanic waste of time. Focus all of your early attention on establishing your gameplay and visual benchmarks. Do them as well as you can. Get them to a finished level of quality before wasting time thinking about the rest of the game. You may just be shocked at how profoundly these two things will impact the remainder of your project.

:::CHAPTER REVIEW:::

1. Conduct a mindmapping session for an original MMOG idea. Discuss your experience and results, focusing on your central theme.

2. What is the importance of a core mechanic and how does it relate specifically to an MMOG?

3. What are some techniques for avoiding the uncanny valley, and why is this phenomenon particularly problematic for MMOGs?

CHAPTER

5

Gameplay
multiplayer expectations

Key Chapter Questions

- How did *level grinding* emerge, and why is it a problem?

- What are the four basic *player types* in MMOGs?

- What methods are used to achieve *balance*?

- How is *feedback* different in an MMOG as opposed to single-player games?

- How are *player groups* like double-edged swords?

Designing an MMOG is vastly different from designing a single-player game. This chapter will show how to undertake the design first by understanding who the players are and what they expect from the game. It will show how several early MMOGs didn't completely compensate for understanding the player, which resulted in some flawed design thinking. This chapter will also explore some basic tools for understanding game design in general and how these tools apply to the massively multiplayer environment in particular.

Understanding the Audience

For the past 20 years, MMOG developers have devoted nearly all of their energy to seeking new landscapes. While we understand at some instinctive level that MMOGs have the potential to be something truly unique, we have not yet opened our eyes to the world of possibilities. We've been drawn backward into the history of what was and unable to look forward into a future that might be.

If we think back to the history of MMOGs (discussed in Chapter 1), we can see a clear genealogy. Text-based adventure games were the great grandfather of the whole clan. With the simple technology of the day, they established a family of games that were goal-oriented, finite experiences, often based on solving puzzles or leveling characters through combat.

Text-based adventures soon gave birth to text-based multi-user dungeons (MUDs). This was nothing more than a reaction to the limitations of the computer. Computers couldn't (and still can't) make compelling opponents, nor could they make terribly useful allies. Artificial

> The real voyage of discovery lies not in seeking new landscapes but in seeing with new eyes.
>
> —*Marcel Proust*

intelligence (AI) has not reached the point where it can accurately model human behavior. Fortunately, the solution to this dilemma was easy: lacking the ability to simulate humans, we simply brought in real ones. Text-based MUDs soon evolved into graphical MUDs; this seemed like the next logical step, since computers were able to display reasonable animated images. Why tell players what's happening when you can show them?

As technology continued to march on, we invented new techniques for network programming and found that we could put more than just a handful of people into a tiny village; we could put thousands of people into a giant world. The dynasty of the MMOG had begun. Unfortunately, this accumulation of small changes over time has culminated in an innovation that isn't well understood at the highest levels. All we ever noticed along the journey were the individual changes. We haven't stepped back to look at the big picture and realize the fundamentally new entity that MMOGs now represent. We're still paying homage to the great clan patriarch, even if we dress him in new clothes and give him fancy high-tech gadgetry.

Electronic Arts, Inc.

Repeated spellcasting and skill improvements in *Ultima Online*

Why is this the case? Even in the most popular MMOG on the planet, *World of Warcraft*, we still have nearly inexplicable throwbacks to text-based MUDs. Despite the fact that we can see swords swinging and blood spattering, and explosions, and damage points flying off the characters and monsters, someone still felt it was necessary to have a text window scrolling the damage numbers. There are even some current MMOGs that scroll completely useless messages like "it is dark" or "it begins to rain" despite the fact that the sky contains a slowly moving, bright, full moon or the rain falls in torrents, leaving ripples in every pond, stream, and puddle. If we can't bring ourselves to part with our treasured text descriptions, it should surprise no one that we are equally unable to let go of legacy design thinking. This is a problem of far greater significance.

The ancient predecessors to MMOGs were originally intended to be 20–30 hour experiences. Players would be presented with a series of puzzles and challenges, each of which was individually custom-built by the developers. Completion of each goal was rewarded with higher character levels and better equipment. It was a nice, simple form.

Spellcasting in *EverQuest II*

When MMOGs entered the scene, that form became distorted. We know from the revenue model that the vast majority of money comes from subscription fees, rather than box sales. This means that we want the customer to spend several thousand hours playing our games, a number that is a couple of orders of magnitude greater than previous games.

We don't need a calculator to see the problem. If a 30-hour game requires the efforts of a 15-person team for 18 months, then a 3,000-hour game requires a 750-person team for three years! At least that's what it would take if you wanted a proportional amount of content with the same level of quality. This would fix the development budget at something like $225 million. Obviously, some alternative had to be found.

So what did developers do? Since brute force was out of the question, they took the path of least resistance. If you can't generate a hundred times the content, then make the content you do build last a hundred times longer. Sounds simple, doesn't it?

They broke out the calculators, drew some curves, and created a timeline of progression for players. They decided how long it should take for characters to reach each level in succession, and tried to work it out so that it would take many, many months to reach the top level. As a result, in MMORPGs, you might have to kill 10 monsters to reach level two, then 20 to reach level three, 50 to reach level four, and so on. By the time you reach level 60, you've killed literally hundreds of thousands of mindless, computer-controlled bad guys. Often as you approach the maximum level, your character winds up facing the same small handful of monsters over and over, as you struggle to earn enough experience to reach that top level. Players have coined a phrase for this phenomenon: they call it "level grinding," and yes, it's every bit as tedious and boring as the name suggests.

Many MMOG developers recognize the problem with level grinding, but rather than solve it, they simply spend an enormous amount of time attempting to justify it. They realize that they need to stretch out the length of the player's experience, and they admit that it's literally impossible to create sufficient custom-built content. They feel forced into the level-grinding trap because they have failed to completely understand the MMOG as a fundamentally new paradigm.

Comedy Central's *South Park* pokes fun at level grinding in the episode, "Make Love, Not Warcraft," when the boys have to kill 65 million boars in *World of Warcraft*.

Developers will point out that given the tedious nature of level grinding, players need a large number of interim goals to motivate them to continue playing day after day. They'll tell you that each new character level is being used as a carrot. "Just kill 50 more monsters to make level 32. Yeah, it sucks, but it's not far to go." That's what keeps bringing the player back for more pain and boredom. It's always the next level, the next cool sword.

This leads to further complications. Somewhere it has to end. Whether the maximum level is arbitrarily fixed at 50, 70, 100, or whatever, sooner or later players will reach it. Then what? Without the lure of the next level, what is there to bring the players back for more? The typical solution has been to create a PvP (player vs. player) combat system, or some other substitute, commonly known as an *elder game*.

Illustration by Ben Bourbon

Courtesy of Comedy Central

Gameplay: multiplayer expectations   chapter 5

This kind of thinking is what programmers call a *hack*. It's a totally new kind of functionality that's effectively bolted onto the existing game system. If you think about it, this solution is nonsensical. Why would you want to create a game that leads the player through hundreds of hours of one kind of gameplay, only to force him or her to do something completely different thereafter?

The hope is that this elder game will provide the player with an endless supply of entertainment, because the level grind is no longer his or her primary play experience. Elder games are usually built with maximum replayability in mind. One can't help but ask: If the elder game accomplishes this goal of infinite replayability, then why make the player suffer through the first few hundred hours of level grinding before getting to the fun part?

The answer lies mostly with legacy design thinking. We do it because that's the way we've always done it. It's what we're familiar with, and even though it's far from perfect, we at least understand the strengths and weaknesses of building level-based, content-driven games. Oh, and by the way, if you've been paying attention, this should sound familiar. The discussion in Chapter 2 on the notion of sacred cows addresses this exact problem from a slightly different direction.

If we're going to think about a fundamentally different kind of MMOG design, the first thing we need to do is figure out, in an abstract sense, what players like about MMOGs and what they want from them. Strip away things like fiction and specific game features for a moment, and try to consider the problem from the hundred-thousand-foot view. What is the player getting out of this kind of game?

Fortunately, Dr. Richard A. Bartle, noted game researcher and co-developer of the first MUD, has already given us quite a bit of insight into this question. Paraphrasing from Dr. Bartle's website, the four dominant things that players liked about MUDs (which we'll equate to MMOGs for the time being) were the following:

- *Achievers*: Players take on as many of the game's goals as possible. They are relentless in their pursuit of acquiring everything from the most powerful equipment to being at the top of any existing leader board. Anything that can be quantified is what they fixate on. It is important to note that achievements that aren't readily visible to other players are less valuable.
- *Explorers*: Perhaps a more accurate word for this type of player might be *maven*. These players will seek every scrap of information they can find. They live to explore and learn, and then enjoys disseminating this knowledge to other players. Information that is obscure or difficult to obtain is highly prized by the explorer. This can be anything from mapping the topography of the world to knowing the minute details of the game's mechanics.

- *Socializers*: For socializers, the game itself is nothing more than a backdrop, a common ground where things happen. These type of players enjoy camaraderie more than anything else. They like to talk, role-play, observe, form clubs or guilds, and help other players achieve their goals. They like to know who everyone is and what's going on from a social perspective.

- *Killers*: For the killer, nothing less than a human opponent will do. The fun comes from knowing they've bested a real person, which is viewed as infinitely more difficult than exploiting the quirks in the AI programming of computer opponents. It's about bragging rights and measuring themselves in the virtual world's hierarchy. They enjoy a predatory environment, whether it is as a lone wolf or as part of the pack.

Dr. Bartle goes on to say that while most players exhibit various levels of each of these four categories, they also tend to have a dominant play style that favors one particular category over the other three. Almost by definition, these four categories of MMOG players have a basic commonality. All of them require interaction with other players. Whether this takes the form of showing off, socializing, victimizing, or measuring themselves, it stands to reason that MMOG players' interests leverage the network.

You might find this observation to be rather obvious. All you have to do is play a few MMOGs for a while, and these four categories of players are readily apparent. However, it's important to explicitly define them. If you're going to design an MMOG, you have to clearly recognize each player type for what it is, and tailor your feature set to accommodate each type accordingly.

Diagram by Per Olin

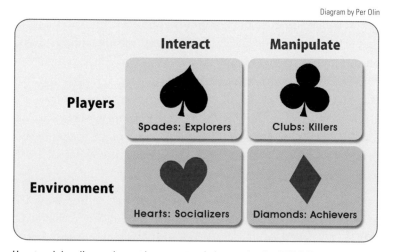

Hearts, clubs, diamonds, spades—types of players that "suit" MUDs.

Dr. Richard Bartle
(Visiting Professor
in Computer Game
Design, University
of Essex)

Dr. Richard Bartle co-wrote the first virtual world, *MUD* (multi-user dungeon), in 1978 and has thus been at the forefront of the online game industry from its inception. A former lecturer in artificial intelligence and current Visiting Professor in Computer Game Design at the University of Essex (U.K.), he is an influential writer on all aspects of virtual world design, development, and management. As an independent consultant, he has worked with most of the major online game companies in the United Kingdom and the United States for more than 20 years. His 2003 book, *Designing Virtual Worlds*, has established itself as a foundation text for researchers and developers of virtual worlds.

My theory has developed since I first proposed it. As it stood originally, it had four problematical elements to it:

1. There were two types of killer.
2. It didn't explain how players gradually changed type over time.
3. It didn't account for one of the oft-cited reasons that players give when asked to explain "fun," namely "I like immersion."
4. It was all observational, with no connection to existing theoretical works.

The two types of killer were "griefers" and "politicians": one who tries to dominate others slyly and selfishly, and the other who tries to do so openly and selflessly. I could also see, though, that there were subtle differences in other types, too. For example, explorers who explored to expand the breadth of their knowledge did so in a scientific fashion, yet those who explored to expand the depth of their knowledge were more like computer gurus who "just knew" how things should work. I added an extra dimension to capture this distinction, which I called "implicit/explicit": implicit actions were not reasoned out in advance but were done unthinkingly; explicit actions were considered and thought through. Griefers do not think about why they do what they do (although they may think about how they do it); politicians do give thought to their motivations and rationalize them in terms of helping the game. Explorers working scientifically will consider what they're doing as if it were an experiment, testing the boundaries of their theories; gurus wouldn't bother, since they already know the world so well that they understand it implicitly.

Adding the extra dimension gave me eight types instead of four and solved one of the problems. I was then able to use the new 3D model to trace how players changed behavior over time. The most common development path I observed was evident in the four-type, 2D graph: killer to explorer to achiever to socializer. Some other paths seemed to oscillate between two types, though—for example, killer to socializer to socializer to killer. With the new model, I could place them in particular subtypes of killer or socializer or whatever and, as a result, I found that all four of the paths I'd observed empirically followed the same basic course of action: implicit to explicit to explicit to implicit, along a track the shape of a reversed Alpha.

With this, I was able to account for immersion—which is how far you are along the track at any one moment. The farther you are along, the more you understand the virtual world; therefore, the more a part of it you are able to feel, and (crucially) the closer you are to being yourself. Immersion is basically a reflection of how close to self-understanding you are playing in the world. Virtual worlds were always about freedom and identity (MUD1 was specifically designed for both), and a sense of immersion is how progress in this regard manifests itself.

Finally, I could link the theory to other, existing theories from other disciplines. The player development tracks that players of virtual worlds follow the "hero's journey" narrative that was discovered by Joseph Campbell in the 1940s. His theory was that all myths and folk tales followed the same basic pattern, because in understanding that pattern people were able to understand themselves and their place in the world. Players of virtual worlds follow the same journey, but instead of experiencing it secondhand through the eyes of a protagonist, they can undertake it themselves. This is why virtual worlds are so compelling: they enable people to be, and to become, themselves. The "hero's journey" links to many other areas of academic study, in particular psychology, so at last my player types model could be anchored in other work supported by other tried-and-trusted theories. *[Author Note: The hero's journey will be discussed in more detail in Chapter 4.]*

Basically, you play a virtual world to have "fun"—which is whatever you can do now that will advance you along your hero's journey. You can have a virtual world that can be relatively stable, attracting mainly players who are socializers or achievers—but they need a continuous stream of newbies to keep them going. Balanced worlds don't shed players as much, so they don't suffer so much if the newbie flow is reduced.

Choosing a Mechanical Theme

One all-too-common problem that MMOG designers have is relying too much on the idea of inflicting damage. Back in the early 1970s, when pen-and-paper role-playing games were all the rage, the innovation of hit points was introduced. Before that time, game mechanics tended to be rather binary in nature. If your piece on the game board attacked another piece, it resulted in either a capture or destruction of the opponent's piece. Everything was either on the board or off. There were no in-between states, so game mechanics relied on skill, luck, or strategy.

The idea of hit points transformed games. Everything went from being black and white to shades of gray. At the time it was quite interesting, and it worked well as the backbone of RPG combat systems, where luck, skill, and strategy took a backseat to role

Chris Brooks (www.chrisbrooks.org)

Dungeons & Dragons being played during GenCon (annual gamers' convention)

playing. Hit points were a simple way to statistically resolve combat, leaving gamers free to play the bulk of the game where it was intended to be played, in their imaginations.

As it turns out, the idea was so widely reproduced that now it's become the game designer's knee-jerk reaction to everything. Don't get the wrong idea. There's nothing intrinsically wrong with hit points, but it does create an unusual problem. Designers have become so fixated on them that they have lost sight of virtually anything else. Ask most designers to start work on an MMOG, and they immediately start talking about how much damage a fireball does, the rate of fire of a crossbow, how much damage a character's armor can absorb, etc. The vast majority of their system will inevitably be reduced to a variety of ways to inflict, absorb, restore, or avoid damage.

The problem isn't limited to RPGs, either. Hit points are widely used in fighting games, strategy games, simulations, card games, and even some sports and racing games. One might even say that hit points have become the 800-pound gorilla of game design.

Functionally, starting off without the hit-point crutch drives the designer to think in terms of a mechanical theme. Since they can't base their design on inflicting damage, they are freed to think of alternatives. In other words, this technique removes a common barrier to creative thought. This is a great starting point for any MMOG design.

When you begin crafting your mechanical theme, try to start off with a narrow scope. Don't try to design the entire game all at once. Initially, just try to work with a specific

> One of the first exercises I give to new students is to design a game without being allowed to use hit points. This never fails to generate an entire roomful of blank stares. Happily, after overcoming their initial difficulties, I've found that students dream up far more interesting designs when they begin with this constraint. Later, I tell them they can go ahead and add hit points back in if they really want to. The point was simply to keep them from being blinded to all other possibilities.
>
> —*Rick Hall*

aspect of the game. You can worry about expanding the game design later, but your mechanical theme will become the foundation for the core mechanic. The possibilities are limitless, but in the next section, we'll look at several potential categories. We'll look at each in isolation, but you should understand that any of the following themes can be combined with other themes in many different ways.

Skill Mechanic

Skill mechanics are methods of accomplishing a goal that usually involve little decision making, luck, or trade-offs. Instead, they depend on hand-eye coordination, pattern recognition, or memorization. A skill is something that can be trained, practiced, memorized, or understood. Games of skill can be broken into three main subcategories: physical, mental, and emergence.

Physical

The *physical* skill mechanic is represented by such genres as: first-person shooters, platformers, fighting games, space flight simulators, driving simulators, and arcade games such as *Pac Man* and *Space Invaders*. This is a difficult kind of mechanic to turn into an MMOG, mainly because of inconsistent network latencies. If you plan on building a game with a physical skill mechanic, you'll probably have to implement at least some of it on the client side to cut down on this problem. This means you'll either need to obfuscate your client-side code to discourage hacking, or validate the results on the server side.

Mental

Genres of games that require *mental* skill include: memory games (*You Don't Know Jack*); logic games; word games (*Scrabble*, *Literati*); pattern-recognition games (*Tetris*); comprehension games (this is mostly the result of some early work in educational titles); and puzzle games (including adventure games with puzzle elements such as *Day of the Tentacle* or *Full Throttle*). It is interesting that while there are some large trivia games online, we don't traditionally consider these to be MMOGs. These games have many thousands of simultaneous players, but the lack of socialization and immersion probably help contribute to this perception. Nonetheless, it would be interesting to see someone attempt to create an MMOG based on a mental skill mechanic.

Three Rings

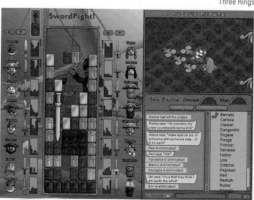

World War II Online focuses on physical skill mechanics such as hand-eye coordination.

Puzzle Pirates involves mental skill mechanics such as pattern-recognition.

Gameplay: multiplayer expectations chapter 5

Emergence

The unusual *emergence* mechanic requires the developer to provide a set of tools that enables players to explore the subject matter in a kind of simulation. It is a special kind of mental skill mechanic that utilizes experimentation and pattern recognition. A

Electronic Arts, Inc.

perfect example of this mechanic is Will Wright's *Spore*, a game that allows players to manipulate evolution. During the course of the game, players create unique species of creatures with distinctive abilities, societies, and behaviors. This is accomplished technically through the use of procedural models, textures, animations, and behavioral verbs. The players aren't really provided with a hard list of specific goals. Instead, they are allowed to set their own goals and use the tools that have been provided to try to achieve them. Although Will Wright describes his game as a massively single-player online game, it could conceivably be turned into an MMOG if that direction were desired.

Spore—a massively *single-player* online game that involves emergence mechanics by allowing players to manipulate evolution.

Strategy Mechanic

A *strategy* is a long-term plan with the goal of indirectly inducing an imbalance between opposing sides that will confer a lasting advantage in one part of the environment, often at a cost somewhere else. Strategies involve the act of observing subtle details, recognizing their significance, and transforming them into tangible, long-term advantages—If you find yourself building specific strategies for the player to find, that's a puzzle game—not a strategy game. In strategy games, you can only build an environment and a set of tools that can allow strategic thought. This could be called a *strategically capable environment*, and the distinction is subtle but important.

Many different factors can allow strategic thinking, but they all rely heavily on decision making by the player. To make each element easier to understand, we've provided examples of games that use elements strategically as a major or minor part of gameplay.

Maneuvering and Mobility

This type of mechanic works off the principles of movement and position, and often depends on the environment itself. For example, different spots on the map may represent cover, defensive advantages, barriers, speed advantages, access to resources, avenues of escape, or better visibility. Many RTS games incorporate elements of a maneuvering mechanic. As mentioned in Chapter 4, the game *Commandos* depends heavily on maneuvering, because the player must guide his or her team of characters through a web of patrolling guards. Chess is another example of

Tabula Rasa

a game that depends on maneuvering and position. Both sides begin the game with the exact same pieces in the exact same configuration. The point of the game is to maneuver your pieces to a position where their potential is maximized, in order to capture the opponent's king.

Formation

Another important aspect of strategy can involve the arrangement of one's forces, referred to in sports and military circles as *formation*. Any student of military history can tell you that the science of battle formations has a profound impact on the outcome of a conflict. With differing types of units, the initial placement determines when, how, or if the given unit can participate. The game *Ancient Art of War* incorporated this concept with great success, not only providing the player with existing troop formations, but allowing them to devise their own. Football, of course, is another good example of the use of formation mechanics. When it's fourth down and goal to go with the ball on the one-yard line, most coaches are going to stack the line.

Dreamlords incorporates strategy mechanics such as formation.

Stealth and Deception

Several games have relied on stealth as their core mechanic, including *Splinter Cell* and the *Thief* series. In both games, combat was an option, but it was largely discouraged. Instead, the games required players to use various tools and the environment itself to discover ways to get around and avoid opponents. It is a surprise that, while several MMORPGs do allow stealth class characters, the insistence on earning experience exclusively through direct combat has ruined what might have been an interesting play style.

Copyright 2007 Turbine Inc.

Copyright 2007 Turbine Inc.

Stealth mode in *The Lord of the Rings Online* can make a player's character nearly invisible.

Deception can come in several forms. One can use visual illusions, disguises, disinformation, turncoats, and feints of many sorts. The point of a deception is usually to lure the opponent into committing himself or herself to the wrong thing, scare him or her away from taking an appropriate action, or camouflage one's location, intent, or direction of travel. Unfortunately, this mechanic is used only sparingly in games for some unknown reason. One can find occasional instances of illusions (the boss monster Jandice, in *World of Warcraft*) and disguises (the spy in *Commandos*), but there don't appear to be many games that take significant advantage of deception as a strategy mechanic.

Courtesy of Blizzard Entertainment, Inc.

Used with permission of Sony Online Entertainment

One of Jandice Borov's multiple copies in *World of Warcraft*

Illusionist (left) and two of her forms (Troll and Ratonga) from *EverQuest II*

Control of Information

Information is power, or so we are told. Whether you know where your opponents are going to strike next, how much money they have available, or what technologies they're researching, the knowledge itself can be leveraged to your advantage. We can find some simple examples of the control of information mechanic in many RTS games. The fog of war in *StarCraft* is one example. This feature makes enemy troops, buildings, and movements invisible if you don't assign specific forces to keep track of them. It requires you to place units in harms' way if you want to see what's going on. The spies in the *Total War* series are a similar example. They allow you to view your opponent's defenses in order to tailor your attack accordingly, but you must dedicate effort and resources, or provide some other trade-off, in order to gather this information.

Stealth mode in *Dungeons & Dragons Online* allows player characters to sneak up and spy.

These are simple and obvious examples, but there are many unused possibilities. Consider the way in which armies will endeavor to cut each others' lines of communication or jam satellites. Preventing allied units from coordinating with each other has interesting implications. How about the way that certain governments are able to bury information that might be damaging to them? What about the impact of insider information in stock trading? Even the concept of blackmail is a clear example of how knowledge imparts advantage.

Economics and Resource Management

It's hard to consider certain business subjects such as logistics, accounting, and allocation, and envision them as fun elements of a game. Yet, despite the superficially dull image, these subjects are clearly demonstrated in a plethora of extremely popular games such as *SimCity*, *Railroad Tycoon*, *Command & Conquer*, *Civilization*, and *Capitalism*. The basic idea is that players have an income (not necessarily money, by the way) that they must spend on elements such as construction, investments, improvements, loan payments, and bribes. Resources are usually limited such that it is impossible to have enough money to buy everything, so choices must be made.

Courtesy of Lockpick

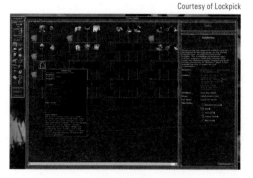

Dreamlords

The opportunities for using this as an MMOG strategy mechanic are enormous. Consider a stock-trading simulation where players could create and control markets. The existence of hundreds of thousands of players all trading in the same world is fascinating. Try to imagine an MMOG set in the 17th century pirate-ridden Caribbean, where players could operate as pirates, navies, traders, or large corporations such as the East India Company. If economics and resource management were used as a main mechanic, the result might be quite different from the majority of combat-heavy products on the market.

Psychology

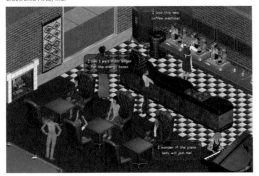

Electronic Arts, Inc.

The Sims Online relies on a psychological mechanic by providing players with the ability to affect the happiness of their Sims.

Even the element of psychology has been used as a mechanical theme. It is commonly used in head-to-head games such as poker. Although the foundation of the game's rules is built on a random distribution of cards, the betting procedure allows players to create tendencies, read other people in various ways, and to bluff. By carefully controlling the amounts and timing of each bet, it is possible to plant assumptions in the minds of our opponents and use them to our advantage. To use this in an MMOG design only requires a simple set of tools that allows us to bluff effectively.

Another kind of game that relies on a psychology mechanic is demonstrated in *The Sims*. In this game, players are provided with a set of tools that allows them to impact the happiness and productivity of a virtual person. It's truly surprising to think that a mental-health simulation was the most popular PC game in history.

Politics

Courtesy of eGenesis

A Tale in the Desert contains one of the most robust political systems in online games. Players may propose, and vote on, just about any proposition—from electing leaders to determining allowable behavior.

From the *Medieval: Total War* series to *Power Politics III* and *Frontrunner*, there are several games that use politics as a major gameplay component. All it requires is a network of autonomous governments or other organizations, each of which has semi-predictable behavior and is armed with an array of abilities to impact the players. Often, these institutions have specific agendas and goals, and sometimes different institutions oppose each other. Stir these ingredients together, and a complex backdrop is produced in which the player must operate.

Luck Mechanic

The mechanics of luck simply involve anything that is random or beyond the player's ability to control or predict reliably. The trend in games seems to be steering away from this element, most probably because things players cannot control often frustrate them.

Gambling

Gambling games give the player the belief that the outcome of any given venture can be at least contained, if not directly controlled. If one knows the statistical probabilities involved, there is the feeling that an educated guess is possible. The betting, then, must take place only after the probabilities can be calculated, and this is the point at which the player feels some control. When the odds are low, the player usually makes modest bets. When the odds improve, bets increase. As noted earlier, adding concepts such as bluffing increase the player's feeling of control, and hence mitigate some of the frustration when the roll goes against him or her.

Used with permission of Sony Online Entertainment

The "Goblin Gamblin' Game" in *EverQuest II* involves luck.

Divination

Divination is the belief that something or someone can tell the future. Games of pure divination were quite popular several hundred years ago. However, the only modern examples that can be found involve Ouija boards and Tarot cards, and these are no longer considered games. With that said, it's not beyond the realm of possibility that the element of guessing or fortune-telling might play at least a small part in a game mechanic.

Divination is a primary element of a Ouija board, which is no longer considered a game.

This section is in no way intended to represent a comprehensive inventory of mechanical themes, or even a particularly deep study of those presented. It is merely a small sampling to illustrate the point that a narrowly focused topic can provide a great deal of gameplay if properly understood. When you embark upon the initial stages of a game design, choose a narrow mechanical theme and learn about it. Study it in detail. Understand how it works, and look for examples in movies, books, and other games. Make mindmaps and tone words, hold brainstorming meetings, and pursue the theme as deeply as you can. Design, like invention, is 10% inspiration and 90% perspiration.

It is entirely possible to use multiple kinds of mechanics in the same game. But the key to making this work is to design one at a time, thoroughly, before moving on to the next. It might be an interesting experiment in an MMORPG to use a different mechanic for each character class, to give them each their own fundamentally different feel. Understand, though, that in doing this, you might be creating difficult match-ups. This may not necessarily be a bad thing, as long as each character class has sufficient utility in an equal number of situations.

Balance

You don't have to be an industry veteran to have heard the phrase *game balance*. Developers talk about it. Reviewers talk about it. Players talk about it. It seems that it's incredibly important, but the million-dollar question is: How do you accomplish it? It's not as straightforward as it sounds. The standard wisdom says that two players will have equal chances if they are given equal tools. Many designers will simply go with that and not give it another thought. We see this approach taken with many RTS games such as *Command & Conquer*, *Age of Empires*, and *Warcraft 2*. In each case, the units might have different names, but they have identical capabilities and numbers. Balance is assured.

Courtesy of NCsoft

Even though MMOGs usually have a wide variety of classes, games such as *Guild Wars* are theoretically balanced because any player can choose any combination of classes for a character. However, designers must still continually focus on maintaining balance among the very diverse set of characters that players create.

Total equality doesn't have to be the only answer. As mentioned earlier, a study of historical games can often provide insight that can be quite useful. To see what is meant here, let's look at a couple of instructive examples.

Fox & Geese

The origin of this game is unknown, but it most probably dates back before the 13th century AD. It was popular not only in Europe, but all over the world, albeit under different names. Versions of this game were found in China (known as *Shap luk kon tseung kwan* or *16 pursue the general*), Japan (*juroku musashi* or *Sixteen Soldiers*), Iceland (*Refskak* or *Fox-Play*), Russia (*Volki i Ovtsy* or *Wolves and Sheep*), Holland (*Schapp en wolf* or *Sheep and Wolf*), and even among Cree and Chippewa Indians (known as *Musinaykahwhanmetowaywin*). Given the game's broad appeal worldwide and the fact that it existed for several hundred years, one can probably make the assumption it was reasonably well balanced. The rules are very simple:

■ One player has a single counter (the fox) and the other player has 13 counters (the geese).

■ At the game's start, the geese are placed on the board, as shown in the following diagram. The fox may be placed on any vacant spot.

■ Both fox and geese can move along any line horizontally or vertically to the next free space (intersection of lines).

■ The fox can capture a goose by jumping over it in any direction to the next free space, and can make multiple jumps if able, as in checkers.

■ The geese cannot capture or jump the fox.

■ The object of the game for the geese is to surround the fox, either with other geese or the edge of the board such that it is impossible for the fox to move. Upon doing so, the geese win.

■ The object of the game for the fox is to capture enough geese that they have insufficient material to prevent the fox from moving.

The obvious question should be: Why is this game balanced? After all, one player has 13 pieces and the other has 1. If this were designed like many of today's RTS games, the result would be a slaughter by the geese, and no one would play the game.

There is a critical difference between the two sides, however: the fox can capture, while the geese must surround. In other words, the units of each side have different capabilities, and it is in this difference that balance is achieved.

Diagram by Per Olin

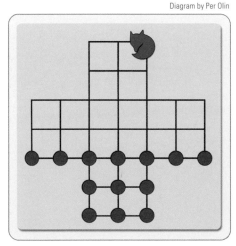

Fox & Geese

Hnefatafl

Hnefatafl was a Viking board game believed to have been invented around the 4th century AD. There are many variations of this game, with different-sized boards and numbers of pieces, but the proportions are always the same, roughly 2-to-1 numerical superiority in favor of the attacker. Again, the following game rules are quite simple.

- The board is arranged as shown in the accompanying diagram, with the attacker having 24 pieces (the black pieces) and the defender having 13 pieces (the white pieces). All pieces are the same except for the one in the center, which is the king. The attacker has no king.

- The object of the game for the attacker is to capture the defender's king. For the defender, it is to get the king to escape by reaching a board corner.

- All pieces move in a straight line along a row or column (no diagonals, similar to the way a rook moves in chess).

- The light squares in the center and corners are called king's squares, and only the king may land on them, although any piece may move over the center square.

- Pieces may not be jumped. Ordinary pieces (but not the king) are captured by being bracketed (called custodial capture) by two enemy pieces across from each other horizontally or vertically. The king's square can also be used (in place of a piece) to capture an attacker or to capture the king. A piece may safely move between two enemy pieces, though; only the moving player may capture.

- The king may be captured by being surrounded on all four sides by enemy pieces or the king's square. The board edge does not count as surrounding a piece; a king that is against a board edge cannot be captured.

- The attacker moves first.

Diagram by Per Olin

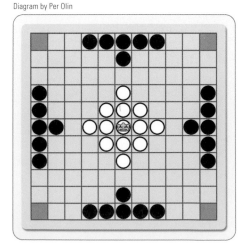

Hnefatafl

In this game, the pieces on both sides (even the king) have the same rules of movement. Yet despite the 2-to-1 numerical advantage enjoyed by the attacking player, the game was balanced enough to have survived for approximately 800 years until it was finally displaced by chess. How can this be?

The answer is quite simple. The two sides have different goals. The defender's goal is to get his or her king to exit the board via one of the corner squares. The attacker's goal is the opposite, to prevent this. Since each side has a different goal, then equal forces are unnecessary. All that is required is for each side to have sufficient forces to achieve the required goal.

These examples are not anomalies. Setting aside the fact that both were popular for several hundred years, there are many other games that had similar notions of balance, where opposing sides had unequal numbers of pieces. These included *Asalto*, *Siege of Paris*, *Cows and Leopards*, and many others.

It may seem unusual to look at centuries-old games to understand modern computer games, but the advantage they give us is the ability to see fundamental concepts demonstrated in a clear and simple manner. From these games, it can be seen that there arc actually three ways to achieve balance in a game:

1. *Equivalence of forces*—The same number of forces, resources, and capabilities on each side.
2. *Differing unit capabilities*—Unequal numbers of units are allowed if the units with the inferior numbers have superior abilities.
3. *Differing goals*—Even with the exact same capabilities, unequal numbers are possible as long as sufficient forces are provided for each side to achieve the desired goal.

Games such as *Dark Age of Camelot* have different classes available to each realm, and further restrict classes for each race within that realm. Maintaining balance in this setting is one of the hardest and most important tasks for the designers.

Looking at it from this perspective, balance doesn't have to be the standard, straight-up equivalence that we see in many games. In fact, one can point to a brightly shining example in the RTS genre: *StarCraft*. In this game, the Zerg can have a great deal more units than the Protoss. Zerg units are cheap and quick to build, but not very powerful. On the other hand, Protoss units are expensive and slow to build, but very difficult to kill. Despite this difference, you won't find many people who will tell you that *StarCraft* is an unbalanced game. Different players have their preferences, but any race can win.

Multiple Genres

When looking for ideas, it isn't necessary to look exclusively at games within the same genre. In fact, this can be a drawback. When you only look at what the competition is doing, you're likely to either unintentionally copy it outright, or simply iterate with a few small twists and changes here and there. Oftentimes, looking at something totally alien to what you're trying to design can lead to much more innovative ideas or approaches.

Feedback

No matter what sort of game you're trying to design, it's important to provide *feedback* to the player. Feedback means letting the player know what's going on. We see this in many simple ways. Sometimes things highlight when you mouse over them. Buttons make noises when pressed. A character reacts when hit. There are hundreds of particle effects, sound effects, flashes, and score changes every time a player presses a button or accomplishes something.

This is all good, but it's only the beginning. Players need to be alerted whenever anything happens in the game, especially the things they can't see. When the home base is attacked and you're currently on the other side of the map, you might get a call on the radio yelling "We're under heavy fire here!" Sometimes your character pulls a lever and hears a grinding sound as a door opens in a room somewhere else. Sometimes they step on a pressure plate and an alarm rings. These are all examples of things that the player might never realize had happened unless you specifically let him or her know.

Even this isn't enough. You will often want to draw attention to things just so that your players can understand the game better. For instance, in some games AI is important. When an NPC character begins the decision-making process, some games will put a small icon over its head, indicating its reasoning process. Without this icon, players may never be able to understand the cause and effect that's taking place, and they may instead assume that the game is either cheating, or acting in a random manner. This is a thought you definitely don't want to be in a player's head.

Courtesy of Flying Lab Software LLC

Pirates of the Burning Seas involves action sequences that incorporate wind-up animation.

A fourth kind of feedback can occur when you want to warn the player that something is about to happen. This is especially useful in games of physical skill. Think about a fighting game like *Soul Caliber*. When your opponent throws a punch, there is a small wind-up animation, and perhaps a graphical effect or a sound. Combined, these effects not only tell you that you're about to be hit, but also tell you how you're going to be hit, giving you a short window within which to react.

Finally, feedback can be used to contribute to the sense of immersion. For example, if a mouse-look feature is being implemented, it would just make the game feel better if the character being controlled turned his or her head and looked in the direction to which the cursor was pointing. (Actually, this feature might be purely aesthetic, or it might be a kind of feedback to opponents. If they see they're being stared at, or perhaps not being stared at, it will very likely influence what they do next.)

To make it easier to think about, let's arrange feedback into five categories: direct action; indirect action; comprehension; foreshadowing; and immersion. During the design process, make a special point to consider feedback in terms of each category. After crafting the core mechanic, go back through it and measure it against each of these five categories. It's important to remember that while you understand every minute aspect of your game, the players will not. Everything must be absolutely crystal clear to them because you won't be able to explain anything to them while they play the game. If they can't figure it out for themselves, they'll either get frustrated or lose interest quickly.

Focus Testing

Have players try your game when the core mechanic is complete. Just ask them to play, and give them no explanations of anything. Then afterward, see how much of it they got, and how much they never realized was happening. It's a great tool for iterating this critical aspect of any game.

Illustration by Ben Bourbon

Remember also that in an MMOG, feedback has two distinct audiences: the player and everyone who can see them. Feedback in an MMOG is a two-way street. It allows the player to better assess his or her own actions, and simultaneously allows others to assess the player. This can have profound gameplay implications. You may find that distributing feedback to anyone within visual range of a given player can create powerful new ideas.

For example, if the player currently has the inventory screen open, perhaps you could show this graphically with him or her pulling out a backpack and rummaging through it. Upon seeing this, perhaps another player realizes he is distracted, and decides to take advantage by attacking. However, learning from this experience, the player then creates a trap where the opens his inventory screen to create the illusion of distraction. You can guess the rest.

That's one simple example. Clearly, there can be many more. When considering the feedback system of any MMOG, give specific thought to treating it as the aforementioned two-way street. You will probably find that this opens up all manner of new ideas for strategy and counter strategy.

Groups & Role Playing

Before you move on to the next section because you think this one is about how to satisfy a roomful of overweight, potato-chip-eating, dateless geeks, take heart. It's not that kind of role playing. The kind of role playing we're discussing isn't about people saying "thee" and "thou" a lot, it's about providing players with specialized functions as members of a team. This is something that is very different from a single-player game. In those, a single-player has only themselves to depend on, so they must be given all the tools that are necessary to be completely self-reliant. But in multiplayer games, especially MMOGs, this isn't completely necessary.

As a designer, you should know that it's important to provide plenty of incentives for players to act in groups instead of as individuals. Why? A player who has friends, allies, teammates, and comrades is far more likely to play your game on a regular basis. This is due primarily to peer pressure. If everyone else is going to the party, you don't want to be left out, so you'll go even if you weren't planning on it. It's a little manipulative, but most MMOG developers want to capitalize on this.

> While it sounds like the businessman's fondest dream to have all of that peer pressure floating around out there forcing players to come back day after day, it is a double-edged sword. While I was producer on *Ultima Online*, we made a point of observing players at great length. We found that even players who were very happy to be members of a guild still spent as much as 70% of their time alone. It was common to hear a player say "I love my guild, but sometimes I just want to come in for half an hour, collect some loot, and head out. I don't want to split it with anybody else, and I don't want to have to go where they need to go. I just want to go anywhere I want and have fun by myself."
>
> —*Rick Hall*

To achieve this, developers have begun giving specific roles to character classes. In MMORPGs, you're probably familiar with many of those classes. A tank is often the character class that gets up close and personal with the opponents. A tank has tools and abilities that are specifically designed to keep the bad guy's attention centered on him. Tanks usually have tough armor and lots of hit points, but they often don't inflict much damage.

A healer is complementary to a tank. The healer inflicts little damage, doesn't have many hit points, and has poor armor, but as long as nothing is beating on the healer, he or she can use healing abilities to keep the tank alive.

Tank (front), caster (right), and healer (left) in *Guild Wars*

Courtesy of NCsoft

A nuker, caster, or DPS (damage per second, i.e., a character that inflicts tremendous damage) usually has poor armor and low hit points, but is able to inflict massive damage. Again, the DPS character is complementary. It needs the tank to keep the bad guys away from him.

Of course, it isn't necessary to think only in terms of hit-point-based MMORPGs. No matter what genre of game you're designing, if you can create specialized roles for each type of character, you're providing incentive for people to operate in teams. The caveat to this is that you must be careful not to make it compulsory to be on a team.

This is a mistake that many MMOG developers make to one degree or another. In their zeal to try to coerce players to act in teams, they come close to making it impossible for them to act alone. Some developers actually go so far as to admit that this is their specific intent. They don't want solo players.

Understand that these people see peer pressure as a negative thing. They may love being a member of a group, but the constant, intense pressure exerted on them by the rest of the group makes the game start to feel more like a job than a game. They eventually rebel, and on a regular basis they cite this on exit interviews as their reason for leaving the game.

Illustration by Ben Bourbon

Social Dynamics in MMOGs

A study by Nicholas Ducheneaut, Nicholas Yee, Eric Nickell, and Robert J. Moore titled: *"Alone Together?" Exploring the Social Dynamics of Massively Multiplayer Online Games* asserted that enforced grouping isn't as useful as many MMOG developers believe. By studying play patterns in *World of Warcraft*, they found that many players join guilds primarily as a result of necessity (i.e., high-level dungeons are impossible for a solo player to explore) than because of an innate desire to be in a group. The study further suggested that level-based games such as *World of Warcraft, Dark Age of Camelot*, or *Everquest* create inherent problems as a result of the inability of characters of differing levels to group together. As a result, the game design in some level-based games can discourage groups. This is true, although it does not have to be the case with level-based MMORPGs. The sidekick feature in *City of Heroes* allows lower-level characters to temporarily operate at a higher level of ability based on their allies' level.

Used with permission of Sony Online Entertainment

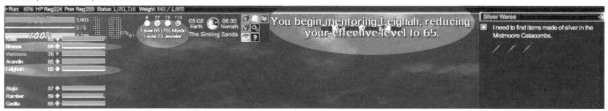

EverQuest II's mentoring system is one the most sophisticated team play systems available. The four highlighted areas near the top of the screen show that Brasse is mentoring Leighah, which reduces Brasse's effective level from 70 to 65 (to match Leighah's Level 65).

The key should be to create an environment where the formation of groups is encouraged, but not forced. That means that although each player should have a specialized function in a group, it should nonetheless be completely possible for him or her to act alone at any time. Perhaps acting alone will make progress slower, make certain locations inaccessible, or make other things more difficult, but as long as the players are always able to make forward progress on his or her own, then he or she will be able to escape the peer pressure when needed. In other words, try to aim for the best of both worlds. Try to encourage groups as much as possible, but don't allow them to become oppressive necessities that drive away the casual players.

Forced Team Mentality

Another notion to avoid is the forced team mentality. It has sometimes been suggested to build MMOGs that require, for instance, a separate player for each position on both sides of a football game. This is a very, very bad idea. Believing that 22 players can be reliably coerced to show up at an exact time, stay online for an entire game, remember all the plays, and act as a team. This is a pipe dream. Don't fool yourself into thinking it's a good idea.

Community

An area where MMOG developers have done an exceptionally good job is promoting a sense of community in their virtual worlds. Like the previous section on promoting groups, this sounds like an extension of the idea, and in fact it is. But promoting groups is usually done on a temporary basis. Players get together to achieve a specific objective, and then they disband.

Communities should have a more permanent feeling. Players should be free to form their own groups and organizations of like-minded individuals, communicate with each other, know when friends are online, and establish a group identity with things such as guild names and insignias.

> Complex puzzle challenges in adventure games won't work in an online multiplayer environment. As soon as the first player solves the puzzles, everyone that logs in afterwards can be told the solution via the chat window.
>
> —*Kenneth C. Finney*
> *(Professor, Art Institute of Toronto)*

Although that sounds like a pretty short list, in fact it can be a great deal of work to develop. You should make a point of reviewing the tools that other MMOGs have created for managing groups, list everything, and get a feel for how much effort will be involved before beginning your production phase.

At that point, you may decide that's enough, and move on to other features. No one would blame you. However, once the game goes live, you may find that it isn't adequate. Some groups will spontaneously form, but some won't last, and many people won't realize the benefit of larger, permanent groups. You might want to make an effort to encourage people to come together.

This can be done in many ways, both in and out of the game. Most MMOG developers have extensive message boards where players can ask questions, meet friends, trade information, or complain about the game. It's all useful information, and as a developer, you'll probably want to watch carefully for what people have to say. Sometimes it's a good source of new ideas.

Inside the game, there are many ways to encourage large groups. Some games allow groups to have goals that individuals cannot, such as control of castles or areas of the map. Players may be able to pool their resources to acquire particularly powerful objects that convey benefits to the entire group. Group vs. group combat is also a common theme.

Used with permission of Sony Online Entertainment

Guild window in *EverQuest II*

The upshot is that if you include tools and features that actively encourage groups (without requiring them, of course), the game is more likely to contain several of them. The more people who belong to a group, the more the world will feel like a collection of virtual neighborhoods, and the more each individual will have a sense of belonging. Create that sense of belonging and maintain it over time, and you'll have loyal players who find it hard to envision themselves playing another game.

These Won't Work in MMOGs

- Saving/reloading
- Pausing
- Cheat codes
- Twitch
- "You are James Bond"
- Bugs
- Bad story arcs

—Dr. Richard Bartle
(Visiting Professor in Computer Game Design, University of Essex)

Customization

For most players, a game world is a place of escape from the monotony of everyday life. When they come home from a long, dreary day of work or school, gameplayers want to enter a world where they feel special. They want to be a heroic warrior, a criminal mastermind, a social rebel, a member of an elite team, or a leader. They want to envision themselves doing things and going places that are otherwise impossible in a real world. The game world is the place where that can happen.

The population of an MMOG provides a wonderful canvas upon which people can paint their own portrait. There are always others who can see the results and, if they like what they can see, to validate them. That's why the crowd is important. After all, to be special implies that there are others who can see and appreciate you. There's no value in being special in an empty room.

However, while it provides the benefit of an audience, the presence of so many others simultaneously creates a problem. The bigger the crowd, the more difficult it is to stand out. A virtual world holds masses of people who are all madly painting self-portraits and shouting for the world to come and take a look.

The process of creating such a self-image in a game is called *customization* (also known as personalization). A customization feature is anything that allows a player to establish a sense of personal identity and uniqueness. Most often, MMOG developers accomplish this primarily through costumes. Character models are constructed in such a way that different bits of clothing or protective gear can be worn piecemeal. In addition, this apparel can often even be colored according to the player's tastes.

Character with stylish gear in *Lineage II*

This simple functionality can get a lot of mileage. Provided with enough different pants, shirts, hats, belts, boots, and gloves, along with the ability to choose one's own colors, it is easy to produce a look that is different from anyone else's.

This look is important. Players want to be able to show up on the scene and have others instantly recognize them through their unique appearance. It's a big part of their ability to create an identity. Imagine if every character in a movie looked exactly the same. The movie would be incredibly difficult to follow and the characters would all lose their distinctive personalities. There is every reason to believe the exact same effect would take place in a virtual world.

Clothing is only one possibility, however. Most MMOGs now allow several different character races, and often have numerous options for head shapes, facial features, hairstyles, and even tattoos. As mentioned in Chapter 1, perhaps the ultimate character customization features exist in the game *City of Heroes*, where it is possible to make your character look like nearly anything with two legs and two arms.

Courtesy of NCsoft

This level of customization is so widespread that it is almost a required feature. With the amount of effort that goes into building all the piecemeal clothing, faces, and body types, it isn't unusual for an MMOG developer to struggle through the process and move on with a sigh of relief. It's a huge effort.

If you want to do nothing more than meet the minimum requirements, then feel free to stop here. If you want your game to stand out from the crowd of other MMOGs, then perhaps this area deserves more thought. It is rich with potential.

Customized character in *City of Heroes*

Consider what makes normal people distinctive. Many athletes have signature moves. Fictional characters in books and movies have trademark lines like "I'll be back" or "It's clobberin' time!" Many actors have become stereotyped by playing a particular type of role over and over. What tools can you provide to the player to allow him customized behavior? People are sometimes made unique by their job title, like surgeon general or president. Some characters have their own distinctive theme music or trademark voice, or unique sound effects associated with them.

There are all kinds of ways that people can distinguish themselves. By providing more than one or two different mechanisms, you will allow people so many different permutations that they can easily set themselves apart in a way that best suits their personality. If you build it right, you might be absolutely shocked at how creatively players will use tools like this to craft highly original and unusual personas.

Tricky Challenges: The Monster in the Closet

Up to this point, the design challenges MMOG developers usually face have been fairly straightforward, and reasonably easy to predict. There are some challenges that are a little trickier. They often lurk in the shadows, waiting until the project is well underway before making their presence known. If you know about them in advance, there will be more options for solutions, so let's look at the most common issues.

Traffic Control

To better explain this problem, we'll start by understanding a little bit about how a server is laid out. Although there are several different choices, the most common two ways to deal with world maps are zones (as in *EverQuest*) or a continuous world (as in *Ultima Online*). When a world uses a zone model, different locations are separated from each other, usually by a mountain pass, city gate, or some other obstacle that requires passing through a narrow portal from one location to another. Passing through this portal causes the client computer to unload the map for the player's current location, and replace it with the destination map.

Players sometimes complain about load times, especially if they are crossing several zones and the load times take more than 10–15 seconds. But working with zones has the advantage that each map location can have unique models and textures, so diversity is easier to achieve.

A continuous world map is one huge map, in which the player can walk from one end to the other without ever having to wait for load times. This is accomplished by having fewer models and textures, thus diminishing the diversity of the world somewhat.

Regardless of whether your world is composed of zones or a continuous map, the server structure is usually similar. To understand how it works, picture your MMOG using a map of the United States, as shown in the following figure.

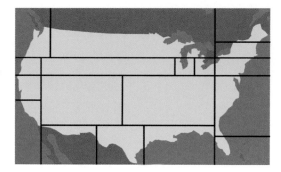

Imaginary server zone map of the United States

Each rectangle in the United States map has its own CPU in the server to manage it. That CPU is responsible for tracking the actions of every player within its boundaries. In the preceding example, there are 18 CPUs in the server box. Note how the smaller rectangles are around major population centers such as New York, Boston, Los Angeles, San Francisco, and Chicago. Larger rectangles represent less densely populated areas. This is because a CPU has finite limits on how many players it can administer. This number will vary greatly depending on the power of the CPU, the amount of overhead the CPU is responsible for tracking per player, and the bandwidth that is required per player, among other things. A reasonable expectation might be that a CPU could administer somewhere between 100 and 500 players. We'll call this a server map.

Regardless of whether your world is continuous or utilizes a zone-based approach, this map applies. The only real difference would be whether a player had to walk through a portal and wait for load times when crossing from one server boundary to the next.

So far, this looks pretty simple, so let's put some players on the map. Assume our server box is composed of 18 CPUs, one controlling each rectangle. Let's further assume that a single CPU can administer no more than 200 players. Simple math tells us that the capacity is 3,600 players at most. However, that assumes the players are evenly distributed, with exactly 200 milling around in each zone.

Unfortunately, there's no guarantee of that. What if there are 200 players in every zone and a player wants to travel from the Boston zone to the New York zone? That would make 199 in Boston and 201 in New York. Our New York zone would be overloaded.

This is an extreme case, but you should be able to see the problem. Whether all the zones are full or not, there's nothing to stop players from showing up in one particular area in numbers that exceed CPU capacity.

The solution to that extreme case is often a kind of brute force. In UO, if too many players showed up around the Britain Bank, the CPU would start randomly teleporting them to alternate cities until the numbers around the bank were back under control. Players call this a *telestorm*, and no one particularly liked it.

Fortunately, it's rare that people randomly congregate in the same place, because the game design encourages them to be disperse. In aggregate, we called these game features *traffic control*. Several traffic control methods are listed in the following sections.

Creature Dispersal

Creatures of similar level are grouped together strategically, so that as a player advances in level, he or she systematically moves from one hunting area to another. It's like dropping a trail of bread crumbs for players to follow. The system of experience points prevents characters from earning anything if they fight creatures too far below their own level, so they don't stay in any one zone for too long. Since players start at different times and progress at different rates, they will disperse naturally over time.

Used with permission of Sony Online Entertainment

The mariner's bell in *EverQuest II* allows the player to travel to another version of the same world, to escape crowds, or to meet friends.

Redundant Services

Obviously players don't spend 100% of their time fighting in an MMOG. There are usually locations that have game services, such as banks, repair shops, auction houses, and vendors. Rather than have all of these located in one centralized place, they are invariably located in many spots in the map. In *World of Warcraft*, for instance, the Alliance has three auction houses, one in Stormwind, one in IronForge, and one in Darnassus. They are all linked together, so when an item is put up for sale in one, visitors to the other auction house can see it. In this way, players won't have to all show up at one auction house to do business, and the zone servers won't have huge crowds focused in a tiny circle in one auction house.

Courtesy of Blizzard Entertainment, Inc.

Auction house in *World of Warcraft,* which has one of the best auction systems available

Instances

Some areas, especially dungeons in an MMORPG, just naturally attract lots of players. This produces two kinds of problems: First, the monsters inhabiting the dungeon are wiped out almost immediately, and then players wind up sitting around waiting in line to kill them when they reappear. This is known as camping for spawn and is considered annoying and tedious. Second, if the developers want to create a quest or mission inside the dungeon, other players will wind up interfering—even if they don't mean to. They'll kill the boss monster or open the treasure chest, or step on the tripwire, and ruin someone else's quest.

Copyright 2007 Turbine, Inc.

A player is about to enter an instance in *Dungeons & Dragons Online* that allows you to play by yourself (or with your party) without interference or crowding from anyone else.

The solution is *instances*. What the developers do is create a copy of the area (usually an enclosed dungeon) called an instance, and only the player and his or her teammates are allowed in that copy. If another group wants to enter the same dungeon at the same time, a fresh copy is made exclusively for them. At any given time, there may be dozens of simultaneous copies of the same dungeon.

Quests or Missions

Have you ever wondered why quests always send your character to some far-flung corner of the game world? Wonder no longer. Aside from being a useful way to introduce players to locations they may not have visited, quests and missions are also a good mechanism for spreading players out and distributing them more evenly across the zones.

Courtesy of Blizzard Entertainment, Inc.

This quest in *World of Warcraft* takes the player to other areas—which is one way to get players away from the most concentrated areas.

Regardless of what kind of MMOG you are building, keeping players evenly distributed is advisable. There are some technology solutions to the problem of overloading zone CPUs, but if the game is designed with the idea of traffic control in mind, it will aid greatly in alleviating this potential problem.

Secure Trading

The funny thing about people in virtual worlds is that when you put them into a situation where they're anonymous, they have a tendency to devolve to almost criminal behavior at times. Unlike real life, in a virtual world there are no repercussions when you break the law. No one knows who you are, and you can invent a new identity any time you want. Even if you're caught, the absolute worst thing that can happen to you is they cancel your account. The victims of virtual crime are helpless to do anything about it, so if they're angry enough about their loss, they may well decide to quit the game. There have been many instances where a single industrious criminal has been responsible for scores of lost accounts. As a developer, this must be viewed as a serious issue.

The easiest area for the criminal element to exploit is usually centered on the trade of items. In online worlds, players have multiple ways of acquiring useful items, some of which they wish to keep and some that they'd rather trade to another player. For years, virtual criminals have found ingenious methods to separate honest players from their gold and items. If they can change an object's name to something more valuable, they'll sell something worthless for a lot of gold. If there are flaws in the trading system, sometimes they can get another player's month without giving him anything in return. There are lots of ways to do it.

Trade user interface in *The Lord of the Rings Online*

When you design your MMOG, you need to take a careful look at every system that allows a player to transfer ownership of anything—money, items, titles, or whatever—and look for ways it can be exploited. Trader is a general title, too, whether you allow players to charge dues for being in a group, pay NPC vendors for items, email items to each other, leave items on the ground, or whatever. Virtual criminals are extremely clever, so make sure you run your designs through as much use-case analysis or focus group testing as possible. Try hard to punch holes in your trading systems before the game is finished, and then figure out how to patch all the holes you find. The last thing you want to do is leave easy methods for people to rip each other off.

The point of this chapter has not been to provide a laundry list of ideas that you can pull out and use when nothing else comes to mind. Rather, as stated at the beginning, the point is to show the reader how to look at things in a new way. Instead of beginning each design as a rush of stream-of-consciousness ideas, take the time to understand what it is you're building. See the project as a series of problems, each with its own set of constraints, strengths, and weaknesses. Look at the big picture, and above all, try not to just design with a me too mentality, limiting yourself to simply mimicking what has been done many times before.

> Every time the number of subscribers changes by another order of magnitude, the entire problem set becomes completely different. A game with 100 people is very different from a game with 1,000 people, and that's very different from 10,000, and so on.
>
> —*Gordon Walton*
> *(Studio Co-Director, BioWare Austin)*

We've seen how the slow evolution of MMOGs has created a new kind of game that is very different from its predecessors. It's not different merely because it has its own set of mechanical features. MMOGs are different because the existence of huge crowds of people changes the way each player thinks and acts. Players can be anything they want. They can do anything they want. They can explore, cooperate, antagonize, and experiment. They will have an overwhelming impact on the gameplay experience of anyone who gets near them.

Single-player games offer a controlled environment where players' actions are predictable, and the game can lead them by a short leash through carefully crafted content at a planned pace. If players find a way to cheat, they can only damage their own experience, not everyone else's. The MMOG, on the other hand, has far less predictability and is much more susceptible to cheating. In such an environment, the nature of the problem virtually demands to be treated differently. Our nice, careful, familiar rules for solo-player game design will break down very quickly when we subject them to the chaos and scale of a massively multiplayer world.

:::CHAPTER REVIEW:::

1. Choose one skill, strategy, and luck mechanic and incorporate them into your original MMOG idea. Discuss which mechanics you chose and how they're particularly relevant to your game.

2. What can we learn about MMOG balance from traditional (and seemingly simple) games such as *Fox and Geese* and *Hnefatafl*? Discuss two balance elements from each game.

3. Describe the four primary methods of maintaining traffic control in MMOGs. Choose two of these methods and discuss how you will incorporate them into your original game.

CHAPTER

Spin

keep community & marketing in mind

Key Chapter Questions

- What is the *demographic* of a typical MMOG player?

- What are some *marketing* techniques that specifically reflect how advertising has changed over the years?

- How do *hardcore* and *casual* gamers contribute to each other's experience in an MMOG?

- What purpose is served by members of a game's *core community*?

- What is the distinction between *conceptual* and *interactive* entertainment?

In this chapter, we will examine the necessity of including both marketing and the community in design decisions. We will seek to understand what role each group serves in the development and advertising processes, how to manage them, and some of the pitfalls that can be expected.

This Isn't Your Grandfather's Market Anymore

The Internet has changed the world forever. This is not an opinion, but a fact of life. It has changed the way we communicate, the way we entertain, the way we learn—and, in a very real sense, it has changed who we are. It's probably safe to say that the Internet has impacted us even more than television, radio, and the telephone combined.

Think about it. Television and radio are static, unidirectional media. You can hear what someone else has to say, but you cannot contribute. You cannot interact or ask questions. On the other hand, the telephone allows you to interact—but only with one person at a time (although a limited number of people can participate in a conference call simultaneously) and only through voice.

Big Stock Photo

Photos.com

Television is a static, unidirectional medium—while the phone allows for interaction (but with a limited number of people—usually only one)!

The Internet, however, allows us to interact with any number of people, anywhere on earth, any time of the day or night, on any subject we want—using sound, text, images, and video. We live in an age of instant communication and instant information. Whether you're interested in quantum physics, Thomas Jefferson's family tree, IBM's 10Q statements from 2002, or a long lost episode of *Star Trek*, it takes only a few minutes to retrieve virtually anything you want.

With such a broadly changed world, we again find that traditional solutions to problems no longer apply. The old tried-and-true methods of advertising aren't as effective as they used to be for everyday products, and they are even less so with regard to products that integrate the Internet as tightly as MMOGs do.

For one thing, there is a distinct trend toward distrust for the old, standard methods of advertisement. Players assume that most screen shots have been digitally altered to look better. They have grown tired of hearing the usual platitudes and are skeptical of anything that labels itself a "faster, better, smarter, prettier" game. They frequently assume that developers have paid off game reviewers to find good things to say about every product they officially review.

> More than once while I worked at Origin in Austin, Texas, something would happen two floors down from me and the first time I'd hear about it was 20 minutes later when there were friends in Seattle or San Francisco sending me Instant Messages wanting to know the juicy details. This is the world we live in now, and it starts with the Internet.
>
> —Rick Hall

In response to this new resistance to traditional advertising forms, interactive entertainment marketers have begun devising new mechanisms for spreading the word about their products. These new methods have evolved in an effort to understand the new game consumer while simultaneously attempting to leverage the power of the medium itself: the Internet.

Demographics

The first step in understanding marketing is to know the customer. Not so many years ago, the customers were almost exclusively early adopters—a group of technophiles that had all of the latest computer hardware. They were predominantly 13–20 year-old North American males who all sported broadband connections, played games obsessively, had somewhat above average IQs, and mostly preferred PC games to console titles.

Illustration by Ben Bourbon

Statistical trends show this outdated demographic has changed quite radically. The average age of a *Second Life* user is 32 years old. Approximately 43% of the players are female and 25% of players come from international markets. Roughly half of the subscribers for *Ultima Online* are from Japan. It is widely accepted that the fastest growing demographic for online mini-games is comprised of women over 50.

Courtesy of Linden Lab

The average *Second Life* user is 32.

Nintendo

The over-50 demographic is alive and well today.

Although the over-50 demographic is alive and well today, it was virtually non-existent 20 years ago. One thing that does *not* seem to be changing is play patterns. Despite the tendency to believe that *World of Warcraft* has broken the mythical casual player barrier, the obsessive nature of play times remains undiminished. In 1999, data showed that the average player put in just over 21 hours per week playing the game. Everyone knew these were hardcore players, and the assumption was that when the casual player was finally attracted into the MMOG market, these numbers would decrease. However, Nick Yee's research focusing on *World of Warcraft* has shown, if anything, the average play times have slightly increased. With over 10 million subscribers worldwide, most industry experts believe that *World of Warcraft* does indeed contain a substantial number of casual gamers, so it would appear that an obsession with the game remains a vital component of the MMOG customer demographic.

> Amusingly, when I was the producer for *Ultima Online*, a PvP contest (player-vs-player combat) was held and the winner was a 63-year-old grandmother from Ohio. Perhaps this really is our grandfather's or grandmother's market.
>
> —*Rick Hall*

Yet another ironic piece of data concerns the technical savvy of the player. Early focus group studies for *Ultima Online* customers showed the average player to be extremely knowledgeable about system hardware. The majority of players knew everything about their hardware and Internet connections. As the market expanded and further studies were made, the technical savvy of the players decreased steadily. By 2004, the average surveyed player couldn't even tell researchers what a 3D accelerator board was—let alone what kind was in their system. (Incidentally, statistics show that nearly twice as many homes are connected to the Internet via broadband than dial-up.)

Electronic Arts, Inc.   Courtesy of Blizzard Entertainment, Inc.

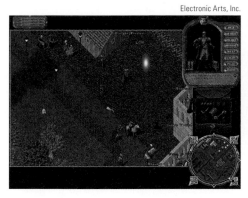

Ultima Online   *World of Warcraft*

However, players appear to be increasingly aware of message forums. Probably due to their decreased technical knowledge, many of the more casual players seek advice on everything from hardware problems to plug-ins to gameplay advice from other players in these forums. Again consulting the work of Nick Yee, studies have shown that over 30% of *World of Warcraft* players consult the message forums on a daily basis, and over 50% consult the forums at least once a week.

A side effect of these message forums is that in addition to technical and gameplay advice, players are also exposed to conversations about other MMOGs, cynicisms about traditional advertising and the evil publishers, rants about rules changes, and discussions on all manner of tangential topics. The result is a thorough immersion into the world of MMOGs in general, not merely the particular MMOG to which the player's forum relates.

The expanded MMOG demographic has thus changed. It seems to be rapidly approaching equality between male and female, 13–45 years old, easily obsessed with the game, socially connected to others through both the game itself and the message forums, broadband connected, and not particularly technically savvy. There has also been data in several places to suggest the notion that casual gamers still make up a unique category of players. They are the type of player who owns and plays just one or two games, as opposed to the hardcore player who tries a wide variety of new products every year. They also are the type of players who are susceptible to trendy fashions and make their appearance as product momentum increases, only to disappear when the game is no longer considered trendy. We'll talk more about them shortly.

Getty Images

The electronic game market is no longer dominated by 12- to 18-year-old boys!

Marketing Is Not the Enemy

Unfortunately, game developers have traditionally perceived marketers to be a sort of corporate enemy. Developers often sneer at any marketer who is not as obsessed with MMOGs as they are, or who is not completely versed in the arcane lore of technology. Developers are often impatient with the constant barrage of requests from their marketing departments for promotional materials, demo versions of the game, screen shots, and detailed information about the game itself. The result is that the two departments often separate into opposing camps, glaring at each other across the divide, each ready to point the finger of blame if anything goes wrong.

Without a doubt this is an unhealthy situation. For a product to be successful, developers and marketers both must work hand in hand. The wealth of data at the fingertips of marketers must be incorporated into the design thinking from day one, while the intricate details of the game itself should be made abundantly clear to the marketers as early as possible. Let's look at how each team can contribute.

Pop Culture

Given the fairly broad demographic, some narrowing is required. To know how to attract a particular type of person, it helps to know what interests that person. What kinds of music does a 32-year-old mother of three listen to? What movies does a 25-year-old Japanese male watch? What art style most appeals to Chinese science fiction fans? The personality of the typical developer is closest to the hardcore early adopter demographic, so they often have no idea what fascinates or immerses the broader population of players. It's a natural human inclination to design games for ourselves, rather than someone we've paid very little attention to.

This is an area where the marketing department can be enormously useful. By identifying the interests and tastes of the broad market that the game should be targeting, the marketing department can significantly impact early design decisions, transforming them into far more appropriate details. Rather than attempt to help design the mechanics of the game, a tendency of some marketers when they can't find ways to get involved, this approach can provide them with a more constructive contribution that may well be more important than the game mechanics anyway.

Market Size

Another concept that developers often fail to appreciate is market size. Simply stated, this is a measure of the maximum potential size of the market as viewed through a particular filter. For example, let's take the PlayStation 2 (PS2) market; note that the number of PS2 units is still much larger than that of next-gen systems. There are 120 million PS2 boxes in existence, so the maximum market size for a PS2 game is 120 million. However, the vast majority of those PS2 owners do not have their consoles connected to the Internet. Thus, for a console-based MMOG on PS2, the total market size would be significantly smaller. This would be further reduced when the game genre (RTS, RPG, FPS, etc.) is introduced. The total market size for a given game will be the overlap of these factors.

Sony Computer Entertainment America

Many other things contribute to market size, including the popularity of the intellectual properties being used, connection type, platform, game genre, the market penetration of various hardware peripherals, and general demographic. By applying all of these filters to the product under development, it is possible to get an idea of the number of subscribers that can be expected. Again, this can provide crucial information when making early decisions. After all, if your maximum market size, after applying all of the appropriate filters, is only 50,000 people worldwide, your game may not be such a good idea.

The market size for a console-based MMOG on a PS2 would be significantly smaller than on a PC.

Design for Marketing

There is just as much that the developers can do for the marketing department. Conventional wisdom used to hold that the marketing and sales departments are your first customers. Understand that if these two groups aren't enthusiastic and knowledgeable about your game, they will not be effective in presenting it to the outside world. It is incredibly important to obtain their buy-in. In a very real sense, you must sell your game to your own company before they can sell it to the public at large.

One of the ways this can be accomplished is by putting yourself, as a developer, in the shoes of the marketer. Try to visualize what your marketing campaign will look like. What will be the main marketing hooks that you'd expect to see on the back of the box? Can you come up with four or five marketing points that present your game in a favorable light in comparison to the rest of the MMOG world?

Often developers respond to this request by saying, "That's not my job. It's the marketer's job." This is just plain silly. If, with your unique knowledge of your own game, you can't give five reasons that compare it favorably to the competition, then what makes you believe a marketer can? Marketers need hooks. If you don't supply them with specific, significant, impressive, unique features to contrast with the competition, they'll wind up either simply inventing them or worse, having nothing at all to say.

You'd be surprised at how often this technique of having the developers come up with their own list of bullet points for the back of the box demonstrates clearly that the product needs more thought before moving out of the pre-production phase. As developers examine the game point by point, they often find that it contains nothing particularly innovative. The vast majority of the features have been done many times before, and there is nothing special to separate their game from the pack. Requiring developers to make this effort often forces them to be just a bit more objective about their designs.

Marketing Assets

Most skilled marketers will tell you that timing is an important concept in advertising. Simply putting out a few screen shots and prints ads for a month or two before a game launches isn't terribly effective. Good marketers endeavor to create a rhythm of interest. They strive to get people talking about some specific aspect of the game for a few weeks—and then, before interest wanes, they introduce something new and even more exciting for people to talk about. Over the course of several months, this roller coaster ride of advertisement systematically ratchets up the hype about the game so that the desired fever pitch is reached at the same time the game hits the shelves. The initial marketing effort can start six months or more before the projected game launch, and must be systematically grown during that entire time.

To accomplish this, the marketer must plan for the types of assets and information that must be released, when they must be released, and how often to sustain and grow public interest. Each new release of information will be strategically planned to reveal a new facet of the game and give customers something new to talk about. Assets might include screen shots, video, soundtracks, design details, action figures, game demo versions, concept art, game reviews, community fan site tools, blogs, print ads, or even television commercials. The order and frequency of the release of these materials is anything but random. It is a carefully planned procedure.

It should be obvious that these assets can't simply materialize out of thin air. Most of them must be provided by the developers. In some cases, such as captured video or screen shots, software functionality might have to be provided directly in the game engine to support the creation of these assets. If you don't have specific staff and schedule dedicated to such marketing purposes, chances are many of these assets won't be made at all, and those that are made will be poorly executed. You can guess the impact on the advertising campaign.

Modern MMOG Marketing

For those who have been paying attention, a question should be forming by now. The preceding information all sounds very traditional, but you should ask yourself if there's anything unusual about marketing an MMOG. Everything noted sounds exactly like the sort of steps to take in an advertising campaign for any game. How are MMOGs different? Let's take a look.

Marketing a Lifestyle

One interesting concept for MMOG advertising is the idea that you shouldn't market the game, but rather you should market the lifestyle. In many ways, this is similar to the advertising campaigns used for AOL and Macintosh.

In the case of AOL, especially in its early days, the service was technically inferior to most of its competitors. This has since changed, but back then bandwidth was limited, its Internet browser wasn't as good as the competition, and email services and web authoring tools were marginal at best. Understanding this, the AOL marketers refused to compare themselves point for point against the competition. Instead, they focused on the users. They portrayed AOL users as mainstream people, not high-tech geeks who didn't want to undertake the technical challenge of installing and deciphering a complex Internet service.

The idea was that everyone wants to be online, and AOL makes it easy. The campaign successfully featured AOL's strengths, ease of use, and an intuitive user interface—and it de-emphasized its weaknesses. They turned the Internet into a lifestyle that the ordinary person could experience without difficulty. If you recall the familiar tag line "You've got mail" you'll know what we mean. Email is nothing special, but AOL turned it into such an unforgettable image that Hollywood even made a movie with that phrase as the title.

Illustration by Ben Bourbon

The Internet isn't a technology; it's a lifestyle.

Similarly, the wave of Macintosh vs. PC commercials used the same approach. They show how simple it is to use a Macintosh, as opposed to a complicated PC, and invite customers to join in. Although clearly the variety of software that is available for the Macintosh is a fraction of that available for the PC, Macintosh marketers don't focus on this. Instead, much like the AOL ad campaign, they focus on inviting John Q. Public to join the 21st century. High-tech is not the wave of the future, they say. It's now, and you can be a part of it. It's easy.

In a similar vein, it is possible to market MMOGs. As we've stated in previous chapters, MMOGs are indeed a lifestyle of their own. Players commit to a huge time investment, make friends, form groups, and depend on each other. Their virtual world is a place where they want to live. It's a place where they can be someone else. They are proud of their virtual accomplishments. In games such as *Second Life*, it's even possible

Courtesy of Intel Dev Zone

Competitors at the Intel Dev Zone Warbot Competition (in *Second Life*) build warbots and pit them against each other in the ring.

to form legitimate businesses in the game world. However, because this kind of time investment can be intimidating to casual players, much as the perceived complexities of the PC and Internet are to typical consumers, marketing the game as a lifestyle that is easy and fun can be a viable approach.

By focusing on the people aspect of an MMOG and less on the game itself, some marketers hope to duplicate the success of products like AOL and Macintosh. It is a proven technique, and the MMOG medium seems appropriate. Focusing on the virtual community and the lifestyle of MMOGs is one clear advertising approach that might be especially effective in attracting casual gamers.

Influencer Targeting

If you have read Malcolm Gladwell's *The Tipping Point: How Little Things Can Make a Big Difference*, you will understand the *influencer targeting* marketing technique. The idea works from the notion that certain influential people, like those whom Gladwell labels mavens and connectors, have a large impact on a product's popularity.

Those remotely familiar with the MMOG industry will have noticed that certain individuals are extremely well known on the message forums. A handful of them seem to know just about every game currently on the market, and most that are under development. These individuals are usually prolific message posters, and often have their own blogs and even their own followings of fans. In some respects, these individuals have a bigger impact on the success of many MMOGs than they realize. If just a handful of these influential people form a consistent opinion about a yet-to-be-released game—and, especially if they decide to post about it relentlessly, a significant following will adopt their opinion.

Marketers have begun to recognize the value of these individuals. They realize that these influencers should be seriously courted. Relationships should be established and the influencers should be invited into the inner circle. Often their opinions at early stages of development are solicited, and acted upon. They are invited to private beta showings and tours of the development facilities. They are given inside information and access to screen shots and promotional material before the general public. They are made into VIPs.

The idea, of course, is to leverage the respectability and authority of these people in hopes that they can attract large followings of customers. Naturally, they have to be impressed with the game. Influencers are notoriously cynical people—and, if they walk away with a bad first impression, the marketing efforts can be damaged. However, on the flip side, influencers can be worth their weight in gold if they like what they see.

This is not the only kind of influencer that marketers focus on. A second kind of influencer exists inside the game itself in the form of guild leaders. Often an MMOG will be populated by several large guilds containing several hundred players or more. These guilds are usually kept together through the efforts of a relatively small number of guild leaders. It is not at all uncommon for the guild leaders to decide that they want to change to a different MMOG and become evangelists to bring their entire guild with them.

Obviously, this sort of influencer can be quite valuable in any targeted marketing campaign. Win the leaders of a group and the rest will follow. With this in mind, marketing efforts can sometimes feel like a political campaign, where it is possible to shake virtual hands with civic leaders and try to win them over. Similar to a political campaign, the hope is that if a couple of major guilds decide to give the new MMOG a try en masse, it may start an avalanche. Targeting the leaders of those large guilds specifically with marketing and sales efforts is a well-known tactic.

Viral Marketing

We tend to think of the word "virus" with almost universally negative connotations—unless we're marketers. To a marketer, something viral doesn't carry a microscopic disease and isn't a dangerous piece of software. It isn't something to be treated and removed as soon as possible. It's a technique for propagating a message.

Consider what happens when you catch a cold. You might get up in the morning, sneeze and cough in a convenience store while getting coffee, at the office, at the toll booth, and around your spouse and kids. During the course of a cold, a person may expose hundreds of others to it. And when those people catch the cold themselves, they will each spread it to hundreds of others in an exponential manner. Every person who is exposed and catches it can potentially spread it to many, many others.

When you consider a marketing message, it would be ideal to have it spread in much the same manner. If every person could spread the message to 20 or 30 others, in no time an astronomical number of people could gain awareness—and sales would be likely to improve as a result. This is the general idea behind *viral marketing*.

Illustration by Ben Bourbon

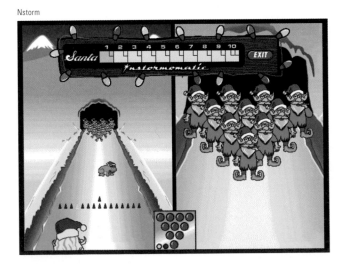

Viral marketing spreads like a cold, but it doesn't make anyone sick.

The trick is to create a vehicle that the target market will voluntarily spread to their friends and acquaintances. It must be entertaining and small. This is an important consideration for a viral technique. If you create a demo version of a game and send it out for free, hoping people will spread it around to their friends, it won't work if it is large. Huge downloads are considered irritating.

An example of a small, successful viral concept was *Elf Bowling*. It was a small application that was sent out via email around Christmas. It had cute little animations and was entertaining and humorous. Many who received it got a good Christmas laugh and a few minutes of entertainment, and summarily passed it on to their friends. Within just a few days of its release, tens of thousands of people had received it.

As it happens, *Elf Bowling* was nothing more than a standalone application. It wasn't intended to market anything else. However, had a marketing message been attached to *Elf Bowling*, it would have reached a huge number of people in a short period of time. In theory, it could have been quite successful.

Nstorm

Elf Bowling

Standalone applications are one vehicle for viral marketing, but by no means the only one. It has been suggested that screen savers, desktop sound themes, cinematic short videos, web sites, songs and jingles, and streaming web radio programs might also all serve the same purpose.

In truth, while producing assets such as those mentioned earlier are obvious examples, even those do not encompass the totality of viral marketing. It's important to remember the technique. All that is required is to get individual people to want to spread a message to multiple friends or acquaintances. Another technique that has been utilized to accomplish this is the use of "plants." Plants are prolific web posters, or people who have a reputation for haunting many different chat groups and posting strong opinions extremely often. There are actually several companies that employ groups of such individuals, and it is their job to blanket the various chat groups, start conversations, and promote a product without seeming to be official spokespersons for that product. The idea, of course, is to start Internet conversations that will propagate beyond the chat groups in which they were started.

Whatever mechanism is used, if it successfully spreads, then any marketing message that is attached to it will propagate as well. The message will reach lots of people, and the hope is they will be encouraged to investigate. Including clickable links, URLs, and email addresses will make it easier for potential customers to discover further information.

Avatar-Based Marketing

Avatar-based marketing is a fairly new concept and the jury is still out on its effectiveness. However, the technique is similar to lifestyle marketing. It differs in one critical way: the interpretation of the player demographic. With lifestyle marketing, we assume that the player is a specific kind of person, based on the fact that he or she is playing an MMOG. We make assumptions about their personality and corresponding assumptions about what sort of marketing message will appeal to them.

Avatar-based marketing seeks instead to target its messages to appeal to the person the player wants to be. There is a startling difference. With a lifestyle marketing approach, we might assume a typical MMOG player to be casual, technology cautious, 18–40 years old, fashion-conscious, middle class—and we would craft a message to appeal to that sort of person. However, with an avatar-based approach, we assume that players want to be someone other than who they are. We instead assume that the player wants to be an adventurous, swashbuckling, uncompromising risk taker. That is the personality type targeted in an avatar-based marketing campaign. Clearly, this is a very different kind of person and, consequently, the marketing message will be different to accommodate this.

Dwarven fan at Sony's FanFaire

No matter which of the preceding techniques the marketing department opts to employ, it is best if you understand each of them at least in principle. While the specific methodology of how the demographics influence the advertising message is beyond the scope of this book, the marketing technique itself will impact some of your design and implementation decisions. Depending on which techniques are chosen, they may affect the kind of assets you build, the order in which they are built, or even some of the features of the game itself. As always, a thorough knowledge of your consumer is valuable in guiding your game development decisions.

The Audience Dynamic

Picture the audience of your MMOG as the set of concentric circles in the accompanying figure. These circles represent an abstraction of the total market of your game, and they comprise three distinct groups of players to whom that game can appeal. Each group will probably react differently to the marketing message, but while the groups are separate and quite unique from each other, they are also strongly interdependent.

Diagram by Per Olin

We've already discussed the notion that casual gamers are most easily attracted to a game when it is trendy. When a critical mass of people are playing it and talking about it, the game becomes the "in" thing and casual gamers are likely to start investigating. Unfortunately, acquiring casual gamers is sort of like trying to become wealthy. It takes money to make money. Casual gamers are unlikely to notice a game until it is already popular. Like wildebeests, they will stampede only with the rest of the herd.

Serious gamers are those individuals who have a fair knowledge of games but have managed to bridge the gap between technophile, obsessive gamers and casual gamers. They know people in both circles. They are serious enough about games to be fairly knowledgeable, but not so obsessive that they will buy every game that comes out, or scour the message boards looking for the next diamond in the rough. They are the type who will be crucial in reaching into the niche world of hardcore and bring the game to the masses.

Hardcore gamers are those who know every detail of every game. They try everything and obtain every plug-in and every mod. They spend countless hours documenting quests and puzzles, making fan sites, and optimizing the best possible configuration of weapons and skills. They are the gameplaying rocket scientists who are so infatuated with their games that they rarely have much in the way of a social life. There just isn't time for it in their worlds.

To market an MMOG, one must start with the innermost circle. This is extremely important. The center, the hardcore gamers, will be the foundation of the game. They will form the community hub, which represents stability and continuity in any virtual world. Without them, most MMOGS would simply disappear in a few months. To understand this, let's review an example.

In the multi-user virtual community, *Second Life*, users have a variety of things to do—but one of the most intriguing activities is using content that has been generated by other users. When someone makes a new doodad that has some hitherto unthought-of behavior, everyone is fascinated by it, and everyone wants to get their own copy. Much of the game's popularity has to do with this flexibility in user-generated content.

Generating content in *Second Life* isn't so simple that just anyone can do it well. Learning the scripting language and the nuances of how objects behave in the game takes some effort. Casual gamers like to use these objects, but very few actually make anything significant on their own. Thus, without the hardcore gamers relentlessly investigating, experimenting, and learning, much of the user-generated content wouldn't exist. Of course, with its disappearance, the casual gamer would probably lose interest quickly and drop out of the game.

Furcadia

Virtually all MMOGs have a hardcore nucleus that provides similar functions. The hardcore players will become the guides, sleuths, content generators, and hard-working community leaders who make the game accessible to other less serious players. They smooth over the rough edges in the game design and lead the way for everyone else to follow. It is to them that your MMOG must initially appeal.

The problem is that many developers recognize only this group. They are abundantly aware of how important the hardcore nucleus is, but they fail to grasp the rest of the dynamic. Appealing exclusively to this group will provide a small total market size, and the resultant subscription levels may not be sufficient to satisfy corporate objectives.

Once a critical mass of hardcore gamers becomes interested, the game must next appeal to somewhat less serious gamers who can act as translators between the innermost and outermost groups. They are the scouts and communicators for the casual gamer world. When they, in turn, reach a critical mass, the next group will be the casual gamer in all their glorious numbers. Only if a game is capable of exhibiting points of interest to all three groups can it be truly successful.

One final point to consider with this subject is the idea that the audience dynamic is bi-directional. We've seen how the casual gamer finds value in the hardcore gamer. Casual gamers are entertained by both the spectacle and knowledge of the hardcore gamer. However, the hardcore gamer finds value in the opposite direction, too. By nature, hardcore gamers need an audience for their efforts. Simply put, it's no fun to accomplish great things if there is no one around to witness them and be amazed. Of course, other hardcore gamers usually aren't impressed by something they can do as well, so who is the audience? It is the casual gamer, of course, who is amazed at the staggering list of accomplishments, titles, information, and magical knick knacks that the hardcore player has obtained. Without this audience to appreciate the hardcore gamer's efforts, the game might be nothing more than an exercise in tedium. In the end, each category of players needs the other.

Intellectual Property

When you mention the term *intellectual property (IP)* to a marketing executive, it's almost guaranteed to generate a positive response. Assuming the IP is a popular one, the reason should be perfectly clear: an existing IP has a built-in audience, and to a degree, a built-in advertising campaign. The marketer gets to kick off a campaign with many thousands of already interested people, rather than having to attract them directly. This leaves the marketer free to concentrate most of the advertising effort simply on getting the word out that the game is under development. With a popular IP, the audience is already biased in favor of the game—and there's some likelihood of them purchasing it.

To marketers, acquiring the rights to a popular IP feels like manna from heaven. In some cases, popular properties such as James Bond or Harry Potter carry with them literally millions of strongly supportive fans—often waiting and hoping for someone to develop a game around their favorite characters or fictional world. So why is it that so many IP-based games are universally panned by critics and players alike?

The reason, unfortunately, is either the ego or inexperience of the development team. Both reasons produce the same result. Some developers despise working on IP-based games because they view themselves as creative people in their own right, and resent being limited by the fictional world that is presented to them. These developers often feel compelled to change major parts of the fiction, create their own storylines, kill off characters that the owners of the IP won't allow to be killed, or interpret the IP in their own unique fashion.

Inexperienced developers, on the other hand, often don't understand what makes the IP popular in the first place, so they completely miss the mark when attempting to re-create the fictional world on the computer screen. Their games are often filled with superficial clichés, labels, and imagery. The game might look and sound like the IP, but it doesn't feel like it.

Did *The Lord of the Rings Online* capture the essence of the intellectual property (IP) or not?

In either case, the problem boils down to one simple principle. When a game is based on an IP, players want the game to feel like that IP. They like the characters and the fiction the way they already are. That's what made it popular in the first place. They will watch sequels on the movie screen, or read about the characters in books—and, as long as the same author, actors, or directors are portraying the IP, it remains consistent and true to its original standards. The last thing a fan of a popular IP wants is for someone to rush off and change anything—and many fans will know every inch of the IP in microscopic detail and they won't hesitate to scream from the top of the highest mountain when you get something wrong. Unfortunately, either through arrogance or ignorance, that's exactly what most developers do when they make a bad IP-based game. They fail to re-create the essence of the existing fictional characters or world. When this happens, the player won't even care if the developer improves on the IP. It's not what they expected, so it's bad. Period.

Thus, the first thing you need to do when you begin work on an IP-based MMOG is to make every effort to truly understand the IP. Watch every movie. Read every book. If possible, talk with the authors, directors, or actors. Read the fan boards. Don't simply try to duplicate the aesthetic. Understand it.

Only after you believe you completely understand the true essence of the IP (and you have a deep understanding of what the fans see in it) should you begin work on the design of the game. As you work through the pre-production process, take the time to actively work with the authors of the IP and the fans. Solicit feedback from them as often as possible. Don't waste time planning hundreds of pages of design, asset lists, and other kinds of documentation. Just focus on a narrow, vertical slice of the game world and iterate on it relentlessly until you get it right.

Keep in mind that you must iterate efficiently. A certain amount of rework during the pre-production process is expected, but you still have to aim toward some eventual hard deadline. This means you have to set a goal for when you want to have your iteration period complete and do everything you must to meet it. In an ideal project, you will build a small, focused slice of the world that looks and feels like the IP by your own self-imposed pre-production deadline. If you work hard and fast, you'll be surprised by how many iterations you can produce in a short time frame. This will be a time of exploration, but every moment is precious. You can't afford to dawdle or waste a single day.

At this stage, many inexperienced developers can make a particularly egregious error in judgment as they plan their design. Especially when working with an existing IP, there will be an overwhelming urge to think in terms of narrative fiction or story arcs. After all, if you're making a game around an IP such as *The Da Vinci Code*, the story is incredibly compelling. Why wouldn't you want to use that same paradigm in designing your game?

The answer has to do with the "conceptual entertainment vs. interactive entertainment" phenomenon. A movie or a film could be considered conceptual entertainment—a static, linear, carefully crafted experience. The author or director makes precise plans to create tension at specific points in time, render a witty line of dialogue at times of irony, and build the action in a well-controlled rhythm leading up to the final climactic scene. It's all very carefully staged and timed to maximize the impact it has on the viewer. Some screenwriters have even been known to read the script with a stopwatch in their hands, in order to know when it's time to insert a car chase, or romantic interlude, or what have you.

This careful precision in timing, dialogue, and action enables the director or author to manipulate the response of the audience in predictable ways, ensuring a positive experience. In other words, the director carefully crafts the entire IP as one giant concept, and everything fuels that concept.

Games, on the other hand, don't work that way. By definition, games are interactive. The player is involved in making decisions and choosing what to do and when to do it. They have an image of their character's motivations in their own mind, and have an overwhelming desire to project part of themselves into that character.

How come the Troll king keeps showing up? I killed him three levels ago!

Illustration by Ben Bourbon

What this means is that there are no guarantees that any major narrative event will happen at a predictable time, for the reasons that the designer envisioned, or even in the order for which the designer might hope. Thus, all of the craft that could go into a static, linear movie or novel will disappear in an interactive environment. Without controlling the pacing and order, good fiction becomes watered down and even nonsensical. The unpredictable, interactive nature of players will invariably wreak havoc with all but the simplest attempts at story-based fiction.

The term "story" refers to a linear, fictional, story arc, where specific events and dialogue are laid out in script-like fashion. Literally anything that requires the player to perform specific actions in specific sequences for the purpose of generating a dramatic effect falls into this category.

There are two main reasons one should avoid this type of thinking in MMOG designs. The first is the fiction will fail to provide entertainment in either one of two ways. Either the random nature of the player's decisions will ruin the emotional impact of the fiction and effectively make for a bad story, or in an effort to control the story, the designers will have to remove so much control from the players that it won't even feel like a game. In either case, the entertainment value will be compromised.

The second reason is that even if the fiction can somehow be made to work, an MMOG has as its target hundreds or even thousands of hours of gameplay. Any author can tell you it's a monumental amount of work just to make a few hours of good fiction. Trying to extend that into months or years of entertainment is simply impossible.

Instead of falling down the rat hole of story arc fiction, MMOG designers need to approach everything differently. Put your efforts into making modular bits of game content that conform to the IP. This might come in the form of missions and quests or dialogue from NPCs, but avoid at all costs the temptation to make cinematic sequences. They just don't work. Instead, think in terms of creating NPCs that behave logically according to the established norms of the IP world. The types of situations, challenges, bad guys, and NPCs should all feel consistent with the IP world. Create short, self-contained parcels of content, where you're absolutely positive that the order in which they are played is unimportant.

The Community

Up to this point, we've talked a lot about how marketing and the developers can work together. Now it's time to discuss the third major contributor to successfully developing an MMOG: the community itself. This is absolutely the most unique aspect of MMOG development, and it is very different from the development process in a single-player game.

We've already established that the hardcore gamers will comprise the lynchpin of any MMOG. Their level of participation is something you must pay particular attention to. You must cultivate their interest in the game, and encourage them to be part of the process sometime after the midpoint of the production phase of the project. When the game goes into live beta, these hardcore players will be your primary source of feedback for testing, balancing, and even advertising the game. After it launches, one of their bragging points will be the ability to call themselves veterans right from day one.

Take note of the part of the preceding paragraph where it states that community participation should begin no earlier than halfway through the production phase. It's probably a bad idea to get them involved earlier, especially during preproduction. This is because the preproduction phase involves a great deal of iteration and experimentation, and the core concept of exactly what the game will be hasn't yet been determined. Introducing a crowd of enthusiastic designer wannabes at this stage will cause nothing but headaches, confusion, and hard feelings.

Without a clear vision of what the game will be, thousands of people will wind up tossing wild suggestions at you every five minutes. The majority of them won't have any cohesive pattern. People will be all over the map. Many of them will become confused and perhaps disenchanted by your preliminary designs.

Aside from the logistical nightmare of trying to sift through this tidal wave of design ideas, when it turns out you have to throw out 99% of them, many potential contributors will be offended that their suggestions weren't accepted. You may lose them as future subscribers. Some of them might even become vocal critics against the game long before it hits the shelves.

Getty Images

By the time you reach the midpoint of the production phase, however, your vision of the game should be much clearer. You can communicate a concise, unambiguous, core mechanic to a select group of community members, as well as show them a polished prototype that accurately demonstrates look and feel. From this, you'll be able to solicit meaningful feedback and suggestions, and get a feel for how the game will ultimately be received when it launches.

Planting the Seed

The point of getting outside people involved at this seemingly early stage has to do with the relative importance of the core community. As discussed earlier, they will eventually provide an important function in your game world. Their efforts will provide stability, leadership, and information for new players once the game launches. They will be the seeds that you plant to grow your eventual community. To do this effectively, well before the game hits the shelves, this core community must be firmly entrenched in the game. They must be ready to form guilds or clubs on the first day, make it easy for newbies to learn how the game works, and essentially be enthusiastic evangelists. If properly prepared, a good core community can make a dramatic difference in the feel of the world.

Clearly, for this group to have all of this knowledge, they need to have access to the game before it launches. They will need time to explore the game world and all of the various game mechanics. The more knowledgeable they are, the better they'll serve in their role as community leaders.

In addition, by including them early enough in the process when they are able to make some contributions to the game features, this group of people will feel much more invested in the game. They will feel like it is at least partly their creation. Their pride in the world will create a feeling of enthusiasm and unflagging interest in the game. This is exactly what you need in a core community: a small army of knowledgeable, fiercely loyal, enthusiastic soldiers.

Organize & Equip

The initial core community should be fairly small—perhaps 100 people. A group of this size will be large enough to provide you with all of the feedback you need, but still small enough to be manageable. You'll need to establish a process for communicating with them, so that their feedback to the team is streamlined and delivered in a timely manner. This responsibility usually falls on a dedicated community manager who will solicit feedback from the players, organize it, deliver it to the development team, and then respond back for the team when changes are made or suggestions are accepted. Avoid allowing the development team to spend too much time communicating directly with the players. Try to route all communication through the community manager, because she or he should be trained in proper methods for diplomacy and consistency. Things can get ugly if members of the development team find themselves in a flame war with the players. It's best to leave the talking to the expert.

As development proceeds, you'll want to slowly add more members to the core community. Larger groups will help you test server performance, as well as accelerate the marketing process. Every new person in the core community will be a potential spokesperson for the game, so it's important to keep them feeling happy and involved.

It might even be a good idea to equip the community with artwork, logos, screen shots, and other materials that they can use to create their own early fan sites. The better equipped they are, the more effective they will be in helping spread the word. They will become, in essence, a powerful viral marketing tool.

As always, there is a caveat to establishing a core community. Although it is vitally necessary, the entire process must be carefully timed. Include them too early and they may get a bad impression of your unpolished, still buggy, less-than-perfect MMOG. This risks turning fans into critics. Include them too late, and they won't feel as invested in the game, and probably won't be as effective in their dual role as evangelists and community leaders.

As you can see, developing an MMOG takes a team that is much broader than a few programmers and artists. By the time the smoke from launch day clears, it shouldn't be surprising to find that several hundred or more people have contributed. Both the core community and the marketing team must be active participants in the process, because their efforts will form the very heart of your game world as well lead the masses to it.

chapter 6

:::CHAPTER REVIEW:::

1. Discuss 3–5 demographics or psychographics you might target for your original MMOG. How would you target these demographics in story and gameplay structure?

2. What marketing techniques are particularly relevant to MMOGs, and how can they best be utilized?

3. How would you design your MMOG so that it caters to different market segments (hardcore, serious, and casual gamers)?

Part III:
Launch &
Beyond

Live!

life after launch

Key Chapter Questions

- What is the significance of *launch* week?

- What are the most important responsibilities for the *live team*?

- What are the purposes of releasing *expansion packs*?

- How might *hacker* activity affect your game?

- Why is there a double-edged sword in *developer-to-player* communication?

This chapter will discuss the structure and responsibilities of a live team. Readers will learn about many of the difficulties they can expect during launch week and beyond. The publishing process for continuous content will be explained, along with some suggestions for common practices and configuration of the live team. Readers will also learn what sorts of security issues they might face, why expansion packs are so significant, and some important rules for interaction between the development team and the community.

D-Day

No matter how much warning you are given, nothing will quite prepare you for the day your game goes live. Despite the years of intensive labor that went into developing it, the utter pandemonium that ensues on that first day is when the battle begins in earnest. No matter how well prepared you think you are, hundreds of thousands of people will assault your game world. It will literally be "under siege." This is not to say that preparation won't help. On the contrary, the more prepared you are, the more likely it is that your game will survive the onslaught.

Usage Numbers

The most important thing you can do at this point is keep the servers operational. This is a lot harder than it sounds. Your open beta testing will have enabled you to see some limited numbers of subscribers. Perhaps a few thousand, or even tens of thousands, will have sporadically tested your server technology during beta. The problem is that beta testing doesn't provide the surge that you'll experience on launch day.

Understand that if your marketers have done their job properly, a huge army of people will be waiting impatiently for the first day the game hits the shelves. On that day, a crowd of people will rush out en masse, purchase the game, and load it up as soon as they get home. They're not going to wait a few days to install it and log in; that's going to happen the minute they get home. You can expect your initial curve of incoming players to look similar to the accompanying diagram.

Diagram by Per Olin

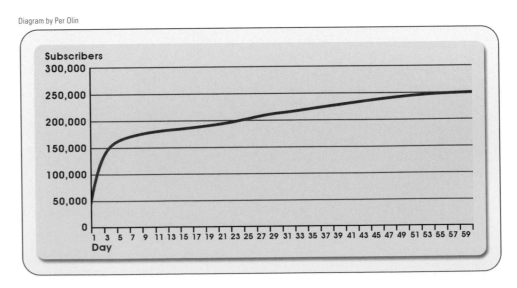

Note that the greatest number of new players occurs in the first couple of weeks, and by the end of the first month you're about 80–90% of the way to a stable subscriber level. In the case of this particular curve, we've modeled a game that reaches 250,000 players. Your game may reach significantly higher or lower numbers—but unless you have a very unconventional marketing model, the curve will have the same general shape.

So why does this curve look unremarkable? The problem (from the standpoint of your network administrators) is that the customers play relentlessly the first few days they own the game. If you're like the typical player, you played your last MMOG for 6–8 hours the first day. The second and third day it was more of the same. It was probably somewhere between Day 3 and Day 7 that you finally cut the grass or got back to the real world for a day or two. You didn't stop playing, but after the first week you weren't completely obsessed. At least this describes the typical player.

As some players decide they don't care for the game and summarily drop out, others will settle into more reasonable play patterns. The result is that, for the first couple of weeks, you should expect a usage spike that will look similar in shape to the accompanying diagram. Usage in this case refers to the peak simultaneous users, or the largest number of players you should expect to see logged in simultaneously at the busiest time of the day.

Diagram by Per Olin

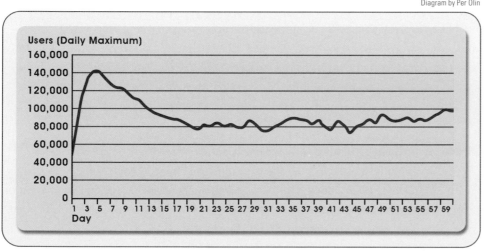

Compare the previous two diagrams, and you might notice something interesting. By the end of the first week, the game reached a subscriber level of roughly 172,000 players. Over the next seven weeks, it steadily increased to 250,000. Yet despite the fact that total subscribers increased by about 45% from the end of Week 1 to the end of Week 7, the peak simultaneous users won't again hit the dizzying heights of the first week. Depending on the game's success, it might take several months or may never happen at all.

In that first week, when the bulk of new players jump in and all play relentlessly, your servers will experience their maximum stress. Your login servers will strain to keep up with people creating new characters and logging into the world. Your databases will be under the same strain. Bandwidth usage will go through the roof because everyone is playing at once. Worse still, recall the server zone map diagram from the "Traffic Control" section in Chapter 5. Every player logging in will start a new character, each in the same starting location. This means that the CPUs that administer starting character areas will shoulder all of the workload for all of the players. It's easy to see how that first week creates the worst-case scenario in terms of server stress, almost by default.

This isn't a simple problem to solve. The corporate suits will balk (and rightly so) at the option of simply buying more server hardware to handle the stress. Why would they want to buy 50% more server hardware if it won't be needed after the second week of operations? That's an inefficient expenditure. You might argue that eventually you'll need it. They'll counter with the argument that maybe you will, and maybe you won't. But even if you do need it later, that might be many months later when hardware costs could be lower. In any event, they'll want to hedge their bets and adopt a wait-and-see attitude.

Fortunately, there are some obvious options:

- **Launch on a Monday**—If you launch during the week, several players who have jobs or busy schedules will wait until the weekend before buying the game. Launching on a Monday will create a somewhat smaller surge that will have four or five days to level out before the next one comes on Friday evening. It's better to have two smaller surges than one huge surge.
- **Give veteran status to open beta players**—It's a common tactic to allow everyone who participates in the open beta to start a new character the week before the game officially hits the shelves. They're going to buy the game anyway, but if they get to keep whatever levels, gold, or items they've earned in that week, it is unlikely they'll be in the newbie areas on Day 1. This spreads the load a little more evenly.

- **Limit supply**—If you think you'll reach 1,000,000 subscribers by the end of the first year, put only 200,000 boxes on the shelves initially. Follow up two weeks later with 100,000 more, and continue to release them incrementally every couple of weeks. Many executives and marketers don't like this plan because it reduces the initial momentum. However, if you limit the number of boxes on the retailer shelves to some maximum number, you're at least guaranteed to know your worst-case scenario in advance.

- **Provide off-peak incentives**—Some developers have discussed the idea of providing rewards for players who create accounts on different days of the week. If the reward is compelling enough, some players will actually wait a few days to obtain an account, thus smoothing out your initial usage spike. Having different rewards for each day of the week might smooth the curve out considerably. This tactic has been discussed but never attempted. The fear is that some players who want to start on that first day will resent the fact that others get a reward for waiting. The backlash from this would most likely not be significant.

Illustration by Ben Bourbon

Other solutions will depend on the particular kind of game you choose to make. The main point to remember is that the usage spike your game will experience in that first couple of weeks will definitely happen and you'll want to address it well in advance of launch day. Every idea you can think of to smooth out that spike is worth considering.

Peak Hour Blues

Life would be much simpler if everyone evenly distributed their gaming time throughout the day. If players worked in shifts, there would be just as many online at 4:00 a.m. as there were at 8:00 p.m. and it would create far less stress on the servers. Unfortunately, the real world of MMOGs creates a daily usage curve that looks more like the diagram on the following page.

It's not hard to predict that there aren't very many people awake and playing an MMOG at 6:00 a.m. In fact, you won't see your first spike until about lunchtime. For the next several hours, things hold steady until players start getting home from school or work. The prime time playing hours are from about 7:00 p.m. to 10:00 p.m.—much like television.

Diagram by Per Olin

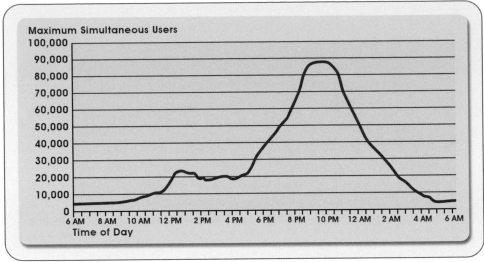

If this is true, then shouldn't the top of the curve happen at around 8:30 p.m. instead of 10:00 p.m.? Yes, but only if it represents a single time zone. The curve actually represents usage across the entire United States. At 10:00 p.m., when people on the East coast are starting to wind down for the evening, it's only 7:00 p.m. on the West coast, when they're just getting started. This tends to make the curve wider and shifts the center a bit to the right. This is significant when you realize that MMOGs require support. The majority of the problems are statistically likely to take place in the center of the bell curve. That means you need network operations people, customer support (CS), and developers available to handle problems. MMOGs don't operate during bankers' hours. When people have problems or the servers crash, you have to fix them now—not tomorrow morning.

Thus, when you're assembling your live team before the game launches, you have to schedule accordingly. Although someone must be available to address problems at any time of the day or night, customer support representatives, game masters, and network operations people have to be represented most strongly during peak hours. This is easily solved and presents problems only if you didn't think about it in advance.

The problem becomes a little more complex if your MMOG has a global audience. In that case, the usage curves can experience numerous spikes throughout the day. However, this problem is usually addressed by establishing local service representation at various global locations. For example, *Ultima Online* had operational support and customer representatives in North America, Europe, and Japan. If your company is large enough to have numerous office locations, this is a viable solution.

Customer Support

Most MMOGs have *customer support* to one degree or another. This can come in the form of phone support to handle billing and technical problems or in-game support to handle game-related issues. The number of CS representatives you'll need depends on the kind of MMOG you make as well as a certain amount of choice.

If you talk to any experienced CS representative about in-game support, they'll probably tell you that 90% of the customer issues they respond to involve the same handful of problems. Players usually have lots of questions about how the game works, they think they've found bugs that they need to report, they get stuck at some location on the map, or they're being harassed by other players.

Courtesy of NCsoft

Lineage II Game Master Luisa Donovan (NCsoft)

There are quite a few things you can implement in terms of game design to address the most common problems. Better in-game help systems and stronger chat features can handle many of the gameplay questions. You can implement automated reporting features to handle bug reports. Several MMOGs have created a button that players can press on the user interface in case they get stuck someplace on the map. Various games have experimented with player justice systems to help players police their own worlds.

The second part of the question of CS staff size is a matter of choice. Due to the unpredictable nature of call volume, you can never guarantee that a CS representative will be available to instantly respond to a problem. Most MMOGs have a queue feature where players submit a request and must then wait until a CS representative becomes available. Clearly, the more CS representatives you have on duty, the faster the customers can be addressed.

However, more CS representation involves more cost to the service, so corporate executives want to limit this. The result in some MMOGs is that they have support queues that last many hours before players get their issues resolved. Others, in an effort to be more customer friendly, live with the expense to field larger CS staffs. It's simply a matter of choice.

To give some indication of the numbers, *Ultima Online* usually had about 8–10 CS representatives on duty in the United States during peak hours in 2001—servicing the roughly 30,000–40,000 players who might be logged in. Response times varied from a few minutes to a half hour but were considered better than most other MMOGs at the time.

Courtesy of NCsoft

Technical customer support team at NCsoft

The *Ultima Online* CS team had some well-established guidelines for dealing with the public. There were rules regarding how to address issues, handle troublesome players, escalate problems up the chain of command, and respond to most questions.

These guidelines require a healthy amount of thought and planning before the game ever goes live. This means that a couple of months before your MMOG launches, you'll have to begin hiring and training CS representatives. Not only must they be familiar with every aspect of the game—but they must learn the communication protocols, rules for dealing with the public, and the mechanics of their own special game clients. A "God client" is a special version of the game that allows the CS representative to appear wherever they are needed in the game world, modify properties of the game world, NPCs, and players, create objects, snoop character backpacks, or stalk the world invisibly to observe unruly players. Take note that if you arm your CS representatives with a God client, it must be planned, scheduled, implemented, and tested accordingly by the development team. Plan your development resources to compensate for this.

Publish Cycle

Once an MMOG has gone live, it becomes a very different animal from the development project it once was. During development, the project was all about content creation and marketing. However, at this stage, your priorities change to two main concerns: continuous content and expansions. We'll consider each separately.

Continuous Content

We define *continuous content* as a constant process of adding small, new features to the live MMOG by patching them across the network. This is an important function of the live team. Understand that no matter how much content you built into the original game, players will burn through it eventually. If we are to judge by history, typical MMOGs see the most hardcore players achieve the highest levels of the game in just a few months. Once they reach the highest levels, or achieve the game's most powerful rewards, you have to maintain their interest level somehow. Continuously adding new content is the most common way to do so.

By adding new features, items, creatures, missions, and locations on a regular basis, you will give the most avid players a constant supply of new things to do. Remember, the goal here is to keep players paying for their subscriptions for as long as humanly possible. Never let that goal out of your sight. In addition, keep in mind that continuous content is defined as something that you patch to the existing game rather than releasing in a box at the retailer. By definition, therefore, continuous content usually involves numerous small additions. The larger content additions will be handled in expansions.

Timing

There are differing opinions on how often a given MMOG should release new content. Most existing MMOGs tend to release new features 3–6 times per year. The frequency is mostly a matter of choice. More frequent addition of content requires more developers, which costs more money. Having less frequent content additions is a cheaper way to run the business but runs the risk of losing players who feel like they've used up all of the existing content. For your MMOG, you'll have to try to strike the proper balance between business efficiency and retaining players for as long as possible.

Team Size and Configuration

The live team's size and configuration will clearly impact its effectiveness. Some smaller MMOGs have tiny live teams, consisting of two or three people. With the smaller live teams, continuous content will be difficult. Standard maintenance will eat up the vast majority of the time on a three- or four-member live team. If you have 6–8 members on the live team, you can probably manage both maintenance and continuous content, but long-term plans for boxed expansions at the retailer will be the next victim. Realistically, you'll probably want at least 10–12 people on the live team if you want any reasonable hope of handling all three functions.

> When I was the producer for *Ultima Online* Live, our team fluctuated in size from roughly 6–20 members. Other MMOGs have larger live teams, reaching sometimes up to 30, 40, or even more.
>
> —*Rick Hall*

Courtesy of Pixel Mine   Used with permission of Sony Online Entertainment

Teams can be small (*Ashen Empires*, left) or huge (*EverQuest II*, right).

It's also a good idea to keep the day-to-day bug fixing and continuous content team separate from the expansion pack team. As you will see, the unpredictable nature of the problems faced by the live team is such that it is extremely difficult to keep to any sort of rigid schedule. Emergencies happen when they happen.

Fixing Bugs and Exploits

While most live teams would enjoy nothing more than to spend all of their time happily dreaming up new features and content for their MMOG, the unfortunate fact of life is that they'll spend far more time addressing problems. With hundreds of thousands of players hammering away at the MMOG 24 hours a day, 7 days a week, it's a guarantee that every tiny bug will be exposed.

There are three kinds of bugs:

- those that create problems to the service
- those that can be exploited to give one player an advantage over another
- things that simply don't work properly

Each kind of bug will be assigned a priority. Clearly, the bugs that can affect the service will be the highest priority. When a bug can cause your servers to crash or significantly affect network performance, this is something that must be addressed immediately—within hours, not days! You must recognize that players are paying a subscription fee because your game is a service. As such, they expect it to remain operational any time they want to play. If players are unable to connect to the game for any significant period of time, anything more than a few hours, the subscription levels will start to drop. It is imperative that someone from the live team be on call 24 hours a day, 7 days a week, especially during holidays when the majority of the subscribers will be free from work or school, and probably playing the game.

The exploit bug definitely shouldn't be taken lightly just because it's been assigned #2 on the priority list. With an exploit, players have found a bug that they can use to gain an in-game advantage. This might be a way to counterfeit gold or items, cheat in order to win fights, or even steal another player's possessions. Regardless, the issue must be addressed promptly.

Game-Secrets.com

Game-Secrets.com web site for exploits

In an MMOG, unlike standalone games, players who take advantage of an exploit can ruin the experience of everyone with whom they come in contact. Serious exploit problems can cost you hundreds or even thousands of subscribers if not squelched quickly. You should plan to resolve exploits within a few days to a week after they are discovered, depending on their severity.

In general, simple bugs where features don't work correctly are the least serious kind of issue. While they eventually must be addressed, it's not unusual for minor problems to remain active for several weeks or sometimes even months. Each should be taken on a case-by-case basis.

Tweaking Game Balance

Yet another function of the live team will be to monitor and tweak game balance. Ideally, a carefully conducted open beta phase will leave the game fairly well balanced. However, the more people who play the game, the more pronounced the imbalances will become. Players have an amazing ability to study every element in minute detail. Given enough time, they will relentlessly zero in on those combinations of weapons, character classes, vehicles, or abilities that provide the optimal functionality.

At some point, specific categories will float to the top of the virtual food chain, and an imbalance will be exposed. If you don't address this imbalance, players will feel like there is no viable reason to choose anything else. The game will lose most of its depth, and the result will again be a decrease in subscribers. You must constantly monitor the game and look for elements such as character classes, objects, and abilities that are overused. It's a good rule that anything that is used by a majority of players is too powerful.

Avoid the temptation, however, of putting too much stock in the complaints of players on the message boards. Players are famous for complaining that their particular choice of character, weapon, or ability is underpowered, while simultaneously pointing at others as overpowered. They generally do this not because something is out of balance, but because they know that if they complain loudly enough, many live teams will cave in and make an adjustment.

Courtesy of Blizzard Entertainment, Inc.

Maintaining balance is one of the most important responsibilities for the live team in *World of Warcraft*.

As well balanced as *World of Warcraft* is, it provides a great example of this phenomenon. Early in the game's life, the paladin class was far too powerful. It wasn't uncommon for a paladin at Level 55 to be able to consistently defeat any other character class at Level 60. Despite this obvious imbalance, Blizzard reacted to virulent complaints from the paladin players on the message boards, and actually increased the paladin's abilities. Eventually, the developer realized this mistake and made further adjustments to even things out, but the point should be clear nonetheless. When you want to see if the game is balanced, look at the metrics with your own eyes. Don't make a knee-jerk reaction based on player complaints.

Testing

After fixing the problems noted earlier, the next step is to get the fixes out to the public. Your game world will undoubtedly consist of many different servers, each with their own copy of the game on them. Most inexperienced live teams make the tragic mistake of rushing a bug fix out to all the servers as soon as it is ready. Especially if the bug is critical, such as a service bug or a potent exploit, this seems like a reasonable response. Fix it and publish it to the world as fast as possible, right? Wrong.

The problem is that when your programmers are tinkering in code where a large problem exists, it's common for them to break something else in the process of fixing the first problem. In extreme cases, a critical bug might get fixed—only to create a far worse one, which is then immediately published to every server in the world. You have to be very careful about this.

Testing is the ally here. Not only do you have to test that the problem has been fixed, but you also must go through the entire game and make sure nothing new has been broken. This is sometimes known as regression testing, which involves the quality assurance (QA) department going through a huge checklist to ensure that at least the obvious, basic functionality of the game remains undisturbed.

Beyond regression testing, it's ideal to have a test server which is your guinea pig for anything you want to publish to the world. It is a special server where players can usually quickly create characters of any level, often equipping them with anything they want so that experimental bug fixes and content patches can be tested.

The idea of a test server is that if the fix creates new problems that QA didn't catch, the few hundred players who haunt the test server will find those problems. It's not a perfect solution, but at least it puts the new software in the hands of a much bigger group than your small QA department.

Assuming your fix passes through QA and the test server, it's still not advisable to publish it to the entire world. Instead, consider a phased deployment, where you take down servers one or two at a time, patch the fix or new content, and then fire them back up. By publishing to servers in small groups, you hope that those servers that were patched early on will find any problems that might still exist, thus at least limiting the new problem to a smaller subset of the entire world.

Naturally, some kinds of emergencies are so important that there isn't time to fix them and test them thoroughly with the process just explained. If it's important enough, you may have no choice but to publish a fix without anything more than a quick pass through QA. Just keep in mind that this is a calculated gamble.

Handling Bugs

To make the whole process clearer, the accompanying diagram shows the usual process of addressing issues in a live environment. Experience has shown that a live team functions most effectively if each block in the diagram has a carefully documented process associated with it. Live team members should have step-by-step instructions for researching, reproducing, fixing, testing, and publishing.

This might sound like overkill, but in truth each step of the process can be quite involved. For instance the final step, phased deployment, is rarely as simple as copying a file onto a server somewhere. A server is a complicated beast. Quite a number of things have to take place there.

Diagram by Per Olin

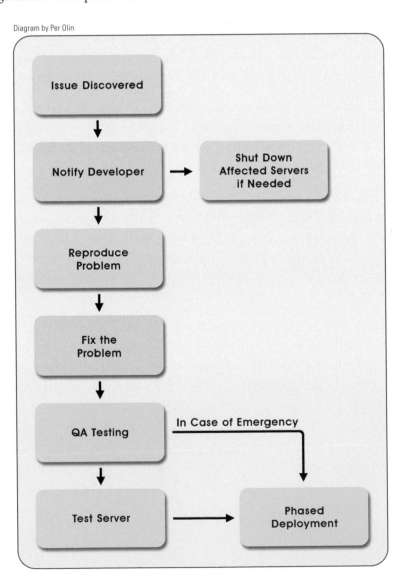

The game itself will be a process running on the server's operating system. This process must be shut down. Perhaps a login server will have to be notified that the server in question is no longer operational. Similarly, a database box might have to be informed. Or perhaps game servers and database boxes can only be shut down in clusters. Network ports may have to be adjusted. Standard security features have to be executed to allow files to be deleted or added. Perhaps configuration files will require adjustment.

When everything is in place, the entire process must be reversed, step by step, until the server is back online. It's not uncommon for the publish process to consist of scores of different steps that must each be executed in the exact order required. You should be aware that the process is so complicated that without documentation and accompanying checklists it is easy to forget something critically important.

As already mentioned, every step in the bug-fixing process should have specific rules for how it will be handled. This is yet another task for the development team to have ironed out before the game is initially launched. That first week is likely to produce some radical problems, so having your emergency response process in place before launch week is crucial.

Expansions

At some point after an MMOG launches, expansion packs begin to appear. Essentially a big batch of new content, an expansion pack usually contains new maps, items, unit types or character classes, abilities, missions or quests, enemy types, or playable races.

All 14 of the *EverQuest* expansions, so far...

If you've never put any thought into it, you probably assume that an expansion pack for an MMOG serves the same purpose as an expansion pack for a standalone game: a way to squeeze more money out of the players. This is the standard assumption from most people. While this is undoubtedly true for standalone games, it's not quite the case for MMOGs. Remember: an MMOG is a service; as such, it earns the majority of its revenues not from box sales—but from subscription fees. What's important is to keep the number of subscribers healthy.

Thus, the expansion pack serves two purposes: it provides a large amount of new content that will keep the veterans happy and, more importantly, it helps maintain what is known as "shelf presence." Neither of these is about generating additional revenues, at least not directly.

To understand shelf presence, you have to think like a retailer. The local game store is usually a pretty small establishment. They carry all kinds of games, and can only devote shelf space to those games that are selling at a good pace. When a game's sales start slowing down, retailers likely want to remove it from the shelves and replace it with something that sells more copies.

Courtesy of Alex Kierkegaard/insomnia.ac

MMOGs are no different from other games in this respect. The majority of sales occurs in the first couple of months, and slows down thereafter. The problem is *churn*—which is the number of existing subscribers who, for whatever reason, decide to terminate their subscription. No matter how entertaining the game is, every month a small percentage of subscribers will bleed away. Typically this is in the range of 1–4% per month.

As long as your game sells enough boxes to create that many new subscribers every month, you'll maintain a stable number of subscribers. Your problems won't start until about a year after the game launches. By this time, sales have slowed considerably on all but the most popular of MMOGs. Retailers will start thinking seriously about pulling your game off the shelves, and giving that shelf space to whatever game has captured the public eye most recently.

When retailers start pulling your MMOG off the shelves, this is when disaster can strike. Without the constant influx of new subscribers every month, churn will quickly become an enormous factor. It only takes 6–12 months to lose as much as half the total subscriber base—and consider that perhaps as much as 80% of an MMOG's revenue comes from subscription fees! Fortunately, the expansion pack can ride to the rescue. As the original game starts fading from the shelves, you can release the expansion pack. From the retailer's perspective, this is like free money. The retailer is smart enough to know that an overwhelming percentage of your existing players are going to buy that expansion pack. They can dust off their calculators and see that if you have hundreds of thousands of subscribers, they're going to sell hundreds of thousands of boxes. They'll happily give the shelf space to the expansion pack.

Courtesy of Michael Fahey

On top of this, the expansion pack serves one more purpose. It gets people talking about the game again. All of your subscribers will be waiting in anticipation for all the new goodies that the expansion pack will bring. They chat excitedly to their friends and relatives, on the message boards, and in email. All of this talk will have the same effects as a viral marketing campaign, and as if by magic, a brand new set of players will come snooping around. Thus, the expansion pack revitalizes the marketing campaign.

Players camped outside GameStop waiting to purchase the *World of Warcraft: Burning Crusade* expansion.

Between this revitalization of the marketing effort, the happy contentment of the veteran players, and the renewed interest of the retailers, your expansion pack will heroically stave off the churn monster for another year or so. With any luck, you can keep producing a new expansion every 9–18 months, and keep the subscriber numbers high indefinitely.

Security

For every 1,000 subscribers your MMOG has, there is probably only one player who has the necessary skills, temperament, and tenacity to become a serious threat to the service. This might not sound too bad, but do a quick calculation and it will immediately dawn on you that your live team of 20–30 people is badly outnumbered. In some extreme cases where subscribers are measured in the millions, the bad guys can outnumber the good guys by 200 to 1 or more. Even in the more modest MMOGs of 200,000 subscribers, the live team is usually outnumbered 10 to 1. This is no trivial matter. Bad guys can hit your service from almost any direction. To make this discussion more easily understood to nontechnical readers, let's look at some oversimplified examples.

Denial of Service Attacks

A *denial of service (DoS) attack* is perhaps the most common form of hacker attack on any online service. The principle is really very simple: The hacker arranges for a large group of remote computers to all bombard the servers with an enormous amount of incoming network traffic all at once. The resultant logjam of data will bring network performance to its knees, sometimes even overloading and crashing the server.

There are numerous ways hackers can cause this effect. Most commonly they will send out a Trojan Horse virus to a large group of players. When they activate it, a huge crowd of computers will begin bombarding the game service with data, often without any of the owners of these computers even realizing what's happening.

Then again, DoS attacks can also take place within the game itself. An entertaining example is from *Ultima Online*. The event is now jokingly referred to as "the purple potion incident," but at the time it was a serious issue. Players figured out that when they threw an explosive purple potion at a target, the explosion calculations that took place on the server were quite CPU-intensive. Normally, this wouldn't have presented a problem. The odd inefficient calculation here or there isn't an issue if the event in question is infrequent. However, when a gang of unruly players became annoyed at Origin one day, they decided to protest.

They assembled a group of several hundred characters outside the Britain Bank and began rapidly throwing hundreds of explosive purple potions at each other all at once. When multiple explosions took place in the same vicinity, it caused the number of radius checks in the server to increase exponentially. The CPU couldn't keep pace with the massive calculations that were required to respond to an event like this, and summarily crashed. The players cheered, and the live team had to work overtime.

Fortunately, problems like these can be controlled at both the hardware level and the software level. There are a number of powerful routers available that can detect and combat DoS attacks. These aren't expensive and are well worth the cost.

Similarly, if your server-side software is written with a DoS attack in consideration, there are several good techniques for filling in the gaps where routers leave openings. By combining software and hardware techniques, it is possible to at least reduce the vulnerability to DoS attacks—although the really clever hackers will still find ways to pull one off.

Account Hacking

No matter how often you tell players not to give out their user IDs or passwords, it never fails that some will do so anyway. The result is never pretty when all of their possessions are mysteriously bequeathed to some other player just before their characters are permanently deleted. It won't matter that this problem is totally the fault of the player. If the player loses everything, there is an overwhelming probability that they will simply quit playing. In other words, their problem becomes your problem, like it or not.

There are several simple methods to alleviate this problem. Backup records of every character can be kept in a database, so when a character gets deleted it can be recovered. Items can be secretly encoded with a serial number so that when the item shows up in another character's inventory, unbeknownst to them they will have left a data trail. The perpetrators can be tracked and caught. Most MMOGs even log the IP address any time a player logs in to his or her account. Should the owner of the account report being hacked, customer support representatives can often track down the responsible individual. In the case of *account hacking*, if you can't prevent it, the next best remedy is to be able to track down and punish the evildoers.

> One of my favorite examples of account hacking comes from a fellow producer. My friend Bryan was enjoying the newly launched *Anarchy Online*. Although he had never given out his account information to anyone, someone managed to get it anyway. He discovered the problem when he logged on one day to find his character standing naked and penniless in an alley. His character's description had been altered to a long string of expletives. Needless to say, he was not a happy camper, even though I personally got a good chuckle from it.
>
> —*Rick Hall*

Used with permission of Sony Online Entertainment

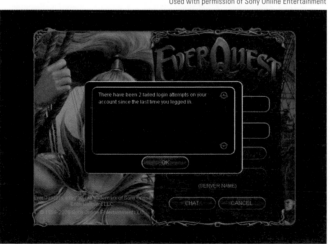

This *EverQuest* warning appears when someone has been trying to access the player's account.

Data Stream Hacking

Another favorite tactic of hackers is to run what's known as a packet sniffer on their computers. This piece of software can monitor all of the network traffic that passes back and forth between the client and the server. With the aid of decryption software and careful analysis, skilled hackers can eventually decipher the data stream. In other words, they'll be able to read the network traffic commands going back and forth between the client and the server.

This ability to read network traffic can be incredibly destructive. Players will take advantage of this knowledge in all manner of ways. They'll write bot software that will play their characters for them. Sometimes they'll be able to change the outcome of combat, teleport themselves or others to remote locations on the map, or gain information about invisible or unseen characters. Knowledge of the data stream can even be useful in carrying on some kinds of DoS attacks.

A few veteran MMOG players may recall a now infamous example of *data stream hacking* that happened several years ago. A rather vindictive player got angry with a rival guild, and when he figured out how to forcibly move characters to a new location, he repeatedly teleported the entire rival guild to the bottom of the ocean! Finding this very entertaining, the hacker began randomly sending entire cities of people to all manner of inhospitable locations, teleporting hordes of powerful monsters into the cities, and even sending hostile guards into the camps of opposing NPCs. The resultant chaos caused an uproar that is still talked about years later.

There are two main ways to combat data stream hacking. The foremost method is to encrypt the data. It sounds simple, but actually involves some tradeoffs. The best encryption is invariably time consuming to decode, and that creates a problem. The player's computer must decode the incoming information in order for the game to be played. If the decoding process takes too long, it will start negatively affecting the frame rate of the game. Thus, the encryption algorithm must be both fast and secure. That's not always easy to achieve.

A second way to combat data stream hacking is to attempt to make it irrelevant. This is accomplished by validating every piece of incoming data from the client. For instance, if the character is traveling at five miles per hour, and suddenly appears a mile away, the server validation software will recognize this as impossible and send a correction back to the player. In other words, your programmers need to make the server smart enough to realize when something impossible has just happened.

A common phrase you'll hear among MMOG developers is "never trust the client." This is a slightly paranoid way of saying that the server should validate any incoming data from the player's computer. No game-critical calculations should ever take place on the player's computer. AI decisions shouldn't run there. Combat results shouldn't be calculated there. Collision checking shouldn't happen there. Absolutely nothing that pertains to the rules of the game can take place on the player's computer.

It also helps if you remember to never send things like invisible data to the client. For instance, if a bad guy is lurking unseen in the shadows nearby, there is no need to send that data to the client if the client can't see the bad guy. Hackers who poke around in the data stream long enough will find this data and they'll be able to see invisible characters and gain an advantage.

Turning the player's computer into nothing more than a screen display and user input device will invalidate many uses for data stream hacking, but it comes with a cost, as almost everything does. When more calculations must be performed on the server side, each server can accommodate fewer players. Naturally, this doesn't appeal to the corporate suits, who want maximum efficiency from the servers. Your programmer's goal, then, will be to streamline the server calculations as much as possible. On the server side, speed is king.

One final point to note about data stream hacking is that once your data stream becomes known, players will begin creating what are known as gray servers—illegal servers that are not under the control of your company. A gray server comes into being when players learn so much about the data stream and the client software that they are able to construct a server that can behave identically to yours. Gray servers are a difficult and serious problem. Players will create them and then either let others play on them for free—or worse, charge a subscription fee for your game. They'll be garnering the revenues that should be legally going to you. It might sound unbelievable that a player could so completely reverse engineer a complex MMOG and duplicate the server-side code, but it's not at all uncommon. Especially in foreign countries where it's difficult to pursue copyright infringement laws, gray servers are rampant. In China, *Ultima Online* was known to have hundreds of gray servers in operation. For every player who plays on a gray server, that's one less paying customer.

Client Hacking

When any game is executed on a computer, all of the game's data resides in that computer's RAM or on the hard drive. Skilled hackers are often able to sift through RAM, figure out where critical game data is stored, and then alter that data through the use of debugging software.

They'll use any scrap of data they can get their hands on. They'll have complete images of every game map in the world, every character model, and every sound effect. If your game includes quest or mission data on the player's hard drive, they'll get all of that as well. Hackers will scrutinize every file in every directory. They'll watch memory to see if game calculations are being made on their side. They'll study every technical detail of the game, searching for anything they can exploit.

At some point several years after *Ultima Online* launched, an enterprising hacker realized that character movement was partially controlled on the client side. The program was using the system tick to determine how fast a character could move. By simply overclocking the CPU, this hacker discovered that it was possible to make a character race around the map at warp speed—giving the character the ability to make drive-by attacks on other players. The character would rush at other player characters from a great distance, attack, and (if it was clear that the fight would be lost) rush off too fast for them to give chase. Needless to say, players were up in arms when this hacker began wreaking havoc in the PvP areas.

Just like data stream hacking, the phrase to remember is "never trust the client." Clearly there is a lot of data that exists on the player's computer. Maps, animations, textures, models, user interface, sound effects, and music are just too large to send over the network. Encrypting these files and obfuscating memory will weed out the "script kiddies" (junior hackers) but the hardcore gearheads will still be able to read them. The best way to keep client hackers under control is to use the exact same tactic used for data stream hackers: validate all data on the server side.

The preceding techniques are merely some of the simpler, more obvious ways that ill-intentioned players can cause problems with an MMOG service. The most talented hackers will always be seeking information. The more they learn, the more dangerous they'll become. The minute they find anything of use, they'll take advantage of it, and the result is always the same. One way or another they'll cause damage that will cost you subscribers.

The point of this discussion is to show not only how destructive hackers can be, but how correspondingly important it is for the live team to remain vigilant against them. As the *Ultima Online* example showed, it might take years for flaws in the game to be discovered. Such discoveries can come at any time. The live team must remain constantly on the alert, ready to detect and combat the myriad different forms that hacking can take. Security is a vital issue in any MMOG, and it will undoubtedly consume a respectable percentage of the live team's time.

Community

There exists a curious relationship between development teams and the player *community*. Players have always been fascinated with game developers. It's one of those art forms that seems like anyone can do it, but somehow very few ever get the opportunity. In a way, it's like playing in a band or writing great fiction. It looks incredibly easy when you're on the outside looking in. As a result, people can identify with the developers of games. They see developers as the artists and writers of a new generation. Television isn't the rage now. The computer is king, and the computer is the stomping ground of today's generation.

Courtesy of Brasse

MMOG fans especially have developed a strong affinity for their developers. This probably has a lot to do with the medium itself, the Internet, which makes developers so accessible. The result is that players get to know developers as individuals. They get inside information about the game as it is being developed and are often allowed to contribute in small ways. It's common for developers to form strong friendships with individual players.

After the game launches, developers often participate in interviews with fan sites, magazines, or even player luncheons—where they get even more exposure to the public. More friendships are formed. It all sounds like a nice, happy, little world—but, in reality, something dangerous is happening. The developers are being transformed from rock stars to pals.

Fan with Jason Roberts at Sony's FanFaire 06 (Programmer, Sony Online Entertainment).

To understand why this is dangerous, think about the rock star analogy. We treat rock stars very differently from our friends. You probably could never see yourself walking up to Eddie Vedder of *Pearl Jam* and saying "Hey Eddie, loan me 10 bucks, will you?" Things change when we're dealing with friends. We routinely ask favors from friends. We take up their time. We sometimes debate, argue, or even fight. We're often willing to step out on the edge for our friends, and do things that aren't exactly nice, or sometimes even illegal.

If you think this isn't a problem, think again. Developers have done all manner of crazy things for their MMOG community friends. Some developers give away powerful in-game items, modify character stats to unfair levels, use God clients to bully other players their friends don't like, delete accounts, give away unreleased or proprietary information, or even secretly change features of the game based solely on the wishes of their friends. Quite a few developers have been fired for favors they've done in the name of friendship.

Graeme Bayless & Bryan Walker on Player Communities :::::

Graeme Bayless
(President, Kush
Games—a division of
2K Sports)

Graeme has been directing computer game development for 18 years, and has been in game development for over 25 years. He has shipped over 60 games in his extensive career and has worked on nearly every type of game, ranging from military simulations to action games, from RPGs to sports, and from interactive films to strategy games. Graeme has been a programmer, producer, director, lead designer, and even a quality assurance manager. Prior to Kush/2K, Graeme worked for Crystal Dynamics, Eidos, Sierra, Sega, and Electronic Arts. Graeme is a self-admitted gamer geek, and when he's not at work poring over management documents, he can be found playing nearly every type of game on the market. Beyond computer games, Graeme is a board-miniatures gamer, movie nut, avid reader, and astronomy enthusiast.

There are two key rules for dealing with MMOG communities (and, frankly, they are similar to other communities—just different in scope)…

1. Do NOT lie to your customers. This includes being intentionally misleading, or concealing obvious truths. If you break the bond of trust, you may well find yourself without a community.

2. Be highly communicative. A high degree of interaction shows the public you DO care and ARE listening. If you choose to go down a path that you know will be unpopular with a vocal group…face it head on, be honest and proactive in communication, and then do what you need to do.

By the by . . . community management is a *very* full-time, and very difficult, job. Don't skimp and just assume "your producers can do it." They can . . . but not without sacrificing somewhere else. Give community management the time and support it needs. Enlist your community itself to help.

A veteran developer with over 15 years of experience in the game industry, Bryan is currently serving as Senior Producer at Retro Studios (a Nintendo company). Over the years, he's worked on a wide variety of games and platforms in numerous management, production, and design roles. Some of the more notable titles he's been involved with include *Ultima Online*, the *Metroid Prime* series, and *Sid Meier's Alpha Centauri*. Bryan currently lives in Austin, Texas.

Don't let the inmates run the asylum. While the feedback from vociferous members of your user base can serve as a data point, rise above the ubiquitous ranting by employing as many methods of gathering empirical data as possible. What players say is often quite different from what they really do. Additionally, don't be afraid to surprise the players by giving them something they didn't know they wanted!

Bryan Walker
(Senior Producer,
Retro Studios)

Interaction between your development team and the player community is a sharp, double-edged sword. Such interaction can lead to significant problems—but it can also have a strong, positive effect if handled properly. The members of the development team have the ability to act as powerful and influential ambassadors for the game.

The evolution of MMOGs has caused this effect. Early on, when MMOGs were relatively small projects, the player communities were very tight-knit groups. Developers interacted freely with players, and many of the earliest MMOGS took significant advantage of player suggestions for game features. Over the years, players have come to expect a kind of "right of participation." In a way, they view themselves as honorary members of the development team.

This isn't exactly an unrealistic expectation. Developers still try to leverage the hardcore community. Consider the previous chapter, which discussed hardcore players' involvement and value as marketing evangelists, testers, and a source of ideas. A part of the strategy to create a grassroots, Internet-based, marketing campaign specifically promotes this view.

The trick is to try to extract the good parts out of player-to-developer interaction, while avoiding the pitfalls. This is the primary reason virtually all MMOGs employ a person known as a community manager. In many cases, a small team of 3–5 individuals, led by one specially trained individual, handles community management.

The job of the community manager is to act as a buffer between the public and the development team. They answer questions, relay suggestions, respond on the message boards, and look for trends in the mood of the player base. They are often the first people to learn about negative reactions to new features, as well as to sleuth out bugs and exploits from some of the cheat sites.

Community management is a difficult job. Imagine having to read thousands of messages every day on the boards, organize events and groups, respond to players who are often angry about recent changes or perceived game imbalances, and moderate arguments between players, yet constantly have to remain objective and diplomatic. The worst thing a community manager can do is to enter into a flame war with the players.

Most community managers don't depend on pure intuition to do their jobs. They have a comprehensive set of guidelines and processes for dealing with the public. They are trained to identify important message threads and respond in a timely, diplomatic, decisive manner. They strive to provide a calm and friendly atmosphere for the players to exchange opinions and ideas. They also serve as information gatherers, monitoring the mood of the player base, conducting surveys, and assembling data for both the marketers and the developers to use in their decision-making processes. In fact, the subject has been well researched in a broader sense by Amy Jo Kim in *Community Building on the Web: Secret Strategies for Successful Online Communities.*

When it is time for developers to communicate directly to the public, the community manager is always present, and usually approves all communication. For example, when community chats took place in *Ultima Online*, they were done through a bot program in Internet Relay Chat (IRC).

MMOG players, especially those who are prolific posters on the message boards, are extremely energetic individuals. When they're happy, they're deliriously so. When they're angry, they can become downright ornery. I can clearly recall a situation where a player became so irate over a recent change to the game mechanics, that he hand delivered a death threat to the home mailbox of the game's producer. Yes, players can become that angry.

—*Rick Hall*

Players would ask questions in a public channel, and then the developers would enter their response in a private channel. This response would then be quickly reviewed by the community manager and then sent to the bot to display in the public channel. It was a streamlined process, but it ensured that no developer could make any public comment without approval of the community manager.

Before concluding this section on communities, there is one important topic left to discuss. Who should operate the message boards? Early in the evolution of MMOGs, the developer always created and managed the boards. It was viewed as a standard task. The boards were necessary as one of the more powerful ways to promote a healthy community, so developers ensured their existence.

More and more, the responsibility for these boards has shifted to outside groups. There are quite a number of gateway sites that cater to multiple MMOG communities. Such sites not only accommodate message boards, but they also provide database functions, game wikis containing all known information about the game mechanics and missions, maps, contests, and forums for fan art. They have established their own ways of funding their sites, and, frankly, they are so good at what they do that it would require a tremendous effort by developers to equal them. This effort is just too expensive to duplicate, so many MMOG developers only maintain a small web site with nothing more then news announcements and server status.

For the most part, developers have passed the community torch to these independent sites. Community managers still exist, but instead of haunting only the web sites of their own company, they reach out to the operators of these gateway sites and represent their MMOG in the most popular ones.

As this chapter has shown, the responsibilities of a live team are broad in scope. Live team members are part game designer, part software troubleshooter, part ambassador, part security, part network administrator, and part customer support. Their jobs are challenging and nearly impossible to schedule. They are often a small team that serves as the first and last line of defense for a service that generates many millions of dollars in annual revenues. To meet the variety of multi-faceted challenges they face, the live team must have a substantial amount of carefully documented processes and procedures. They must have robust and rapid communication with customer support and network administration. They must be mentally tough, objective, intelligent, and diplomatic. It is recommended that members of the team who originally constructed the game should be required to serve on the live team for at least 6–12 months after the game launches. In many cases, these creative people don't really want to do this. They see themselves as builders, not maintainers. They want to move on to the next creative endeavor. It would be a mistake to allow this to happen. Good MMOG developers must understand the live environment if they are to build a good game. They must understand the critical necessity for sound documentation of the code base, robust customer-support tools, and the dynamic nature of how the game itself will evolve over time. They must learn to anticipate the need for change in this living environment, so that their future projects will accommodate evolution more easily.

1. Why is customer support essential to a successful launch? What types of difficult situations (and near disasters) can a strong CS team prevent?

2. How does the bug-fixing process differ after launch (in comparison to before launch)? How are exploits addressed?

3. What are 4 types of security attacks, and how can they be prevented? How can a security breach be particularly problematic for an MMOG?

CHAPTER

8

The Business

understanding the bottom line

Key Chapter Questions

- What are the major *costs* associated with running an MMOG service once the game is launched?

- What sorts of game *design* and *technical* decisions can be directly affected by financial considerations?

- What are some of the *legal issues* that must be considered when building an MMOG?

- What are some ways to *monetize* an MMOG besides the traditional subscription model?

- How does the *business model* change when an MMOG is launched in a foreign country?

In this chapter, we will take a look at how the MMOG business model works. We will explore how the legal and financial considerations can impact the way the game is designed and built—and we will also determine how to estimate potential revenues based on both technical performance and sales forecasts.

It's Not a Product, But a Service

Back in the late 1990s, game development was more of an exercise in constructing a discrete product. We designed games, constructed them, put them in a box, sold them to the public, and moved on. There were times when we'd immediately begin work on the sequel, but those efforts typically amounted to either a bunch of new puzzles, weapons, and maps, or a complete rewrite of the old game. There was no middle ground, and little sense of continuity from one project to another.

Working on MMOGs was an incredibly eye-opening experience. The first seven chapters of this book have discussed the substantial differences in project organization, game design, development, and customer support. Alone, this is a vastly different world from single-player games, but it turns out the differences are even deeper. The real key to an MMOG is to look at it as a "service," not a product.

That might sound like a subtle difference, but it profoundly affects the way you think about the game. For example, take a look at some of the latest entries into the MMOG development race. A trend is starting where companies are actually considering giving away the game. These companies aren't worried about revenues from box sales. Instead, they're viewing the game itself as a form of advertisement for the service. The idea is that if it's free, a lot more people will try it. By getting the game into the hands of as many players as possible, it is hoped that more of them will eventually become paying subscribers, where the real money can be made. It's hard to imagine that developers of single-player games would ever consider giving away the game!

The Cost of Doing Business

As noted in previous chapters, a lot of choices must be made that will simultaneously impact the profitability of your company and the public acceptance of your MMOG. To make intelligent choices, it will help to have a general understanding of how much each element of the service will cost. We start with a brief description of the more common costs. Note that for all examples in this section, we will assume approximate costs as of the year 2007.

It's helpful to know that Internet service providers (ISPs) don't usually charge based on the total amount of data that is pushed through over the course of a billing cycle. Rather, they look at the highest data rate that was achieved during the period, and charge based on that. Usually, ISPs base the monthly fee on around 95% of peak bandwidth usage. Thus, for instance, if your game normally wouldn't exceed 100Mbs during prime time, but there was a special in-game event that caused every player to log in all at once, you might experience a spike where the bandwidth usage reached, say, 500Mbs. Your bandwidth costs would therefore be based on 475Mbs, rather than the 100Mbs you might have expected, even if the spike only lasted for a couple of hours. This is often useful to know.

Bandwidth

This cost will be easier to understand if we begin with a simplified example. Assume for a moment that in order to operate, your MMOG must transmit data back and forth to the server at a rate of 1Kbs. Now assume that you have 100 players logged in at once. It is simple to see that to support all 100 players simultaneously, your server must have a network pipe that can handle 100Kbs. Extending the example a little further, a server that could handle 3000 simultaneous players would require a network pipe that could handle 3Mbs. Multiply this by a few dozen or perhaps scores of servers, and the network pipe has to be pretty big.

Don't break out the calculator just yet. There's more. Understand that it's nearly inconceivable that 100% of your players will ever all be online at the same time. It's far more reasonable to assume that at any given time (other than the first month after launch, of course), you're unlikely to see more than 40–50% of your total subscribers logged in at once. That will happen at prime time.

The real measure of your bandwidth costs will come from the combination of your peak simultaneous users and the bandwidth required per character. Some games, like *Fantasy Westward Journey* in China, have extremely low bandwidth requirements. Others, like *Planetside*, require far greater amounts. For the sake of making things easy, it's probably safe to assume that if your MMOG is typical, you can expect to pay somewhere between $0.40 and $0.75 per month per player for bandwidth. Taking a concrete example, we might estimate that an MMOG with 200,000 players will cost $800,000–$1,000,000 a year for bandwidth.

Shot Online has low bandwidth requirements.

PlanetSide has high bandwidth requirements.

Every game will be different, but this is a serviceable rough estimate for now. To get a more accurate estimate, find out the average bandwidth needed to support a given player and multiply this times the expected number of peak simultaneous users. This will give you a peak bandwidth number that you can take to an ISP for an accurate cost.

There are ways to keep this cost under control. Aside from optimizing the bandwidth used per player, there are many creative options. Idling players (it's fairly common for players to step away from their keyboard for periods of time) can have their bandwidth limited until they return, and should probably be disconnected after absences of more than 15–20 minutes.

Another alternative is to try to give players an incentive to play for shorter periods of time. This sounds counterintuitive, but it actually makes sense. In *Ultima Online*, the system of advancement was usage based. The more a player used a given skill, the better that skill got. There were no limits. To get better at anything, players had to use their skills continuously. The result was that they would routinely remain logged in for sessions of 8–10 hours at a stretch. No matter when they logged in, they were likely to overlap their playing time with most other players, causing the number of peak simultaneous users to be high, thus bandwidth usage was high.

:::::*Ultima Online*'s Power Hour

The power hour in *Ultima Online* is a particularly instructive example of how the business model can, and should, influence the game design. In this instance, the feature was implemented into the game for purely financial reasons. The sole driving force behind it was to improve bandwidth costs. Of course, the feature had to be acceptable to the players, and it was. However, without the financial motivator it would never have been considered at all.

Electronic Arts, Inc.

By about the third year of operation, it was decided to find a way to reduce the total amount of time players spent in the game. To accommodate this, a system was introduced that became known as power hour. For the first hour a player was logged in every day, their character's skills advanced at an accelerated rate. But after the power hour was over, the rate of skill increase dropped off dramatically. Thus, although there was nothing preventing them from playing, it became less productive for players to be logged in for more than an hour a day. The result was that players dropped to an average of around 12 hours per week. While they logged in just as often, they played for shorter periods of time, spreading the usage out more evenly. This caused the peak simultaneous user spike to get smaller, and bandwidth costs went down proportionately. The only caveat is that your solution should be designed to limit play hours without causing players to stop playing entirely.

We should also briefly mention bug fixing and continuous content patches in this section. As mentioned in Chapter 2, there are several reasons the size and frequency of client patches should be minimized. You should now add bandwidth costs to those reasons. Clearly, if you implement a very large patch, it will take longer to download. The longer the download takes, the more likely it will be that numerous players will all be drawing large amounts of data simultaneously. Consider the bandwidth spike this can make on patch day, and remember it when you're thinking about some huge client patch that seems incredibly cool.

This section should also give you more to think about when you initially design your MMOG. Keep in mind that MMOGs are distinct from single-player games; you must consider each feature in terms of cost. Some features will increase bandwidth costs. Others will require more customer support costs. Still others will put greater stress on your database. As you work your way through the preproduction process, it's a worthwhile exercise to step back and make a ballpark estimate regarding how much the service is going to cost to operate. You may just change your mind about a few things.

Personnel

Most people are surprised when they find out for the first time just how many people it takes to staff a typical MMOG. Let's take a moment and make a quick count. We'll continue with our theoretical MMOG that supports 200,000 players, and we'll use the following conservative estimates on staff:

- **Expansion team**—12 persons
- **Network operations**—3 persons (requires round-the-clock attention)
- **In-game customer support**—15 persons
- **Phone support**—4 persons
- **Live Team**—8 persons
- **Community management**—2 persons
- **Marketing**—1 person
- **Management**—4 persons (2 producers, 1 studio manager, 1 customer support manager)

Thus, just a quick count gives us 55 people on the support staff. Different companies will emphasize different aspects of the business and have different totals, but the preceding figures are, if anything, conservative. Depending on the location of your company (clearly the region in which you are located will affect salaries), whether you pay benefits for everyone, and taxes, this will probably put your personnel costs at somewhere between $2.5 million and $4.7 million a year. This is a fixed cost that won't change much.

Even a conservative support staff for a typical MMOG will be similar in size to the original team that developed the game, and will be only marginally cheaper. When you think about it in these terms, operating an MMOG is basically like funding development forever. Be prepared for this.

Also note that unlike bandwidth, the support staff won't increase proportionately with the number of subscribers. If the number of subscribers were to suddenly double, you might need a few more in-game support employees and maybe another couple of phone support people, but the other teams would remain largely the same. Thus, the personnel costs would increase only slightly, even if the number of subscribers increased dramatically.

Unfortunately, the reverse is also true. Cut the number of subscribers in half, and although that means you can reduce the in-game support and phone support, virtually everything else must still remain the same. The personnel cost per player will rise.

To put it succinctly, this means that smaller subscriber numbers will create an inefficient business. The profit per customer gets worse and worse as the subscribers decrease. If the subscriber numbers increase, so too will the profit per customer. The relatively fixed nature of the personnel costs makes an MMOG a somewhat nonlinear business model.

Hardware Costs

Somehow, this part of the MMOG business inevitably seems to be radically misunderstood. Developers seem to gravitate to extreme ends of the spectrum, with some failing to consider hardware costs at all, and others envisioning servers that cost millions of dollars each. Naturally, reality lies somewhere in between.

Hardware will consist almost exclusively of servers. With just some basic information, you should be able to adequately predict how much this will cost. Again, for the sake of consistency, we'll work with our theoretical 200,000-subscriber model.

The first thing we need to know is how many players a given server can accommodate simultaneously. This will vary considerably based on the type of MMOG you're building and the resources consumed by each player. We'll use a rough approximation here, since an average MMOG server can accommodate somewhere between 2,000 and 5,000 simultaneous players. Let's say our theoretical MMOG server can handle 3,000 players.

The next thing we need to know is how powerful each server must be. Again, this varies greatly from game to game, but a typical machine might consist of perhaps 60–70 processors costing something like $75,000.

Next, we have to have some information about our login servers and database boxes. Continuing to choose fairly standard numbers, it's typical for a single MMOG database box, perhaps costing $20,000 to be able to meet the needs of several game servers simultaneously. For our example, let's just assume that we need one database box for every four servers. Likewise, we'll assume that one similarly priced login server can meet the needs of 10 game servers.

If we work with the assumption that our peak simultaneous users will be somewhere in the neighborhood of 40%, then that means we can expect, on average, to have to deal with 80,000 players at once. Pull out your abacus, and that means you'll need approximately 27 game servers, 7 database boxes, and 3 login servers. At the costs listed earlier, that comes to roughly $2.23 million.

Understand that this is a very rough estimate, based on a lot of assumptions. More than anything else, the point is to show a simple way to get a ballpark idea of how much things are going to cost. This number is subject to change based on current hardware costs, peak simultaneous users, and the performance of the game, but at least it gives us an idea.

You should also consider the timing of when you will have to purchase your servers. Early in the development process, you'll probably only need one for your developers. It's important for them to construct the game on the hardware that it will be on once it launches. Don't get cheap here and force them to develop the game on an underpowered little box in the corner. The more differences there are between the development environment and the final live environment, the more critical mistakes will be made.

When you get into beta, you'll need another server so that your beta community can have something to play on while the development team continues to work on theirs. You might even want a third server if you want to let QA test in a separate environment. That's a choice you'll have to make at some point. You'll also need your login server and database box at this stage.

As you approach launch, you'll have to start purchasing the bulk of your servers. It typically takes some lead time to order, ship, and configure each server, so it's not uncommon to start acquiring the bulk of them a couple of months before the game launches.

It's also important to remember our graphs from the previous chapter. Usage will be much higher in that first week than later on. If you don't acquire enough hardware to properly handle that usage spike, then you'll either need to live with the consequences, or figure out a plan to keep the spike from being too high.

Once your MMOG launches, your continuing hardware costs won't disappear completely even if the subscriber level becomes static. Computers are fussy creatures, and with so many of them humming away, day in and day out, things are bound to wear out. Expect the occasional RAID drive to fail, system RAM to break, or CPU to fry. It's not usually a gigantic expense, but if you're trying to be accurate, discuss this with your network administrator to get an estimate of maintenance costs.

Colocation Facilities

While we're on the subject of servers, have you ever wondered where they are physically located? A fairly common assumption is that they are somewhere in the same building as the developer. After all, wouldn't we want them nearby so we could maintain them and deal with problems quickly?

Certainly, it would be convenient if the servers were nearby. Unfortunately, the question isn't about the server hardware; it's about the network. The previous section alluded to the huge network connection that MMOG servers require. Most buildings simply aren't wired to handle this amount of data traffic. It's possible to improve the office facilities to be able to handle it, but that's not the only problem. It turns out that most service providers charge significantly more money to run that amount of bandwidth to your location. Often, very high bandwidth can cost 50% more when delivered to your site.

ISPs often provide *colocation* services, allowing you to put your MMOG servers at their location. Colocating your servers is inconvenient, and you have to rent out physical space at the ISP for your server racks, but in the end it's quite a bit cheaper than locating them at your office. This means your network administrators will need ready physical access to the ISP, and can expect to travel back and forth a good bit. It also means that in the event that your ISP goes out of business (a disconcertingly common occurrence these days) or you find a better deal on bandwidth somewhere else, you may find yourself scrambling to pull off the very tricky maneuver of moving. Shutting down servers, taking them apart, moving them across town, putting them back together, and booting them back up can cause outages to the game service that will anger your players.

Development Costs

This is the granddaddy of costs for MMOGs. Currently, a typical MMOG costs $15–20 million or more to build, takes 36–42 months of time, and requires a development team of perhaps 50–70 persons, not including vendors.

If you've been paying attention while you've been reading this book, you should have a pretty good idea why development costs are so high. By definition, MMOGs are very large in scope. With a goal of hundreds or thousands of hours of game play, an MMOG requires a huge space for players to explore, and a tremendous amount of content.

But as large an undertaking as the content is, the server and support infrastructure effectively double this effort. It's not enough to just make a huge game. MMOGs require highly efficient network programming, databases, login servers, patch servers, account management, server side programming, God clients, server monitoring tools, carefully documented procedures and processes, and a fully staffed customer support team in order to launch.

It never fails the first time a company attempts to build an MMOG for the executive team to go the extra mile in trying to figure out ways to cut costs and schedule. There are plenty of examples where an executive team ordered developers to build an MMOG in 12–18 months, and do it for half the cost. Like good little soldiers, the developers wander back to their cubicles to make the attempt. Overwhelmed by the impossibility of the task, they either fail outright or the project winds up massively over budget and behind schedule. More often than not, it costs more and takes longer than if they'd started with the proper resources in the first place.

It's therefore appropriate to give some two-way advice. Executives and developers should both spend some time at the start of the preproduction process laying out a high-level plan. It's imperative for both parties to have precise expectations. Before committing definitely to undertake an MMOG project, you should each agree on some realistic goals for budget, schedule, and project scope. Avoid the temptation of cutting corners simply for the sake of cutting corners.

If done properly, MMOGs are capable of generating enormous revenues. Some analysts have projected that *World of Warcraft* may perhaps generate as much as a billion dollars a year! Of course you shouldn't count on numbers like that, but even a modest MMOG of 110,000 subscribers, each paying a $15 monthly subscription fee, can net $20 million in annual revenues. If the MMOG lasts for five years, not at all uncommon for an MMOG, that's $100 million in total revenues, not counting earnings from retail sales. In the face of numbers like this, quibbling over a few dollars or a couple of months in the schedule is just plain silly.

Courtesy of Blizzard Entertainment, Inc.

World of Warcraft

The moral here is that it's okay to watch the budget and schedule like a hawk, but this is not the time to be cheap. MMOGs are not an investment for the faint of heart. While it's foolish to spend $30 million on development, it's equally foolish to spend $3 million. Go ahead and try to save a couple of million in development costs. You might just turn a $300 million money-printing machine into a set of very expensive coasters for your coffee table. It's happened before.

Middleware

While true that it's inherent to a successful executive's personality to display hyper-sensitivity to issues of efficiency, developers must also accept their share of stereo-typical blame. At Origin, when developers displayed this annoying idiosyncrasy we referred to it as the Not-Invented-Here Syndrome.

Any reasonably skilled programmer might have a problem looking at another programmer's work and somehow not mutter the comment, "I could do that better." In other words, if they didn't invent it, they don't like it. It's instinctive. It's built into their DNA. This attitude is partly what makes them good at what they do. Unfortunately, this attitude is also financially unreasonable. Let's take a quick look at the simple example of 3D renderers, a subject that's near and dear to most graphics programmers' hearts.

This kind of comment is so incredibly dumb on so many levels it's almost hard to know how to begin a response. It's best to just start with some totally ridiculous assumptions. Let's just assume that your programmer is somehow smarter than John Carmack or Tim Sweeney (co-founder of id Software and founder of Epic Games, respectively). Try not to laugh. We're not at the really ridiculous part yet.

> There are a plethora of existing 3D game engines that are available on the commercial market, covering a wide array of functionality and levels of quality. Companies such as id Software, Epic, Crytek, and many others have some of the best-performing, most technically sophisticated 3D game engines available on the planet. Yet despite this, programmers tell me with a totally straight face that they could "make something better if given half a chance." I haven't just heard this once, by the way. I've heard it dozens of times, in dozens of different forms, from dozens of different programmers.
>
> —*Rick Hall*

Let's further assume that despite the fact that engines such as Quake, Unreal, or the CryENGINE have been effectively under development for many years, with huge engineering teams, your programmer and his five teammates can crank out something a little better. Along with this, they'll produce all of the accompanying content-generation tools, scripting languages, shaders, and support for a reasonable variety of PC hardware. Let's say they can do it in 18 months. Heck, let's say 12 months. Seriously, stop laughing.

To start with, six programmers for a year will already cost you twice as much as you'd pay for the latest version of the Unreal Engine. This alone is enough to make any responsible executive want to kill the idea of building your own engine. Why pay twice as much for the same result?

Unreal Editor

Added to this is the concept of opportunity cost. Basically, what this means is, even if you could build an equivalent to CryENGINE more cheaply than buying it, you still lose time. Even if you could do it in a year, that's a year of lost development time, since virtually nothing else in the game can be started without the engine.

Programmers have heard these arguments before, and some have adopted an arsenal of reasons they should still build their own engine. They might tell you that the source code isn't documented well enough, the engine has too much legacy game code in it, or the network code isn't powerful enough. They might tell you that it's too difficult to modify, or there's too much work involved in making it run on a server. They might even call it spaghetti code.

Feel free to accept all of their reasons if you like. It makes no difference. Sure, there will be work involved in removing legacy code. Yes, you may have to document some of the engine yourself. Yep, the network code isn't powerful enough. Great, it's tough to adapt to your purposes, and wasn't written for UNIX or Linux. Awesome.

But you know what? Almost no challenge is unsolvable. While your team of programmers spends the next year working out all of those issues, the rest of the development team can be building the game. That's the beauty of having the engine from day one. Everyone can be productive from the start.

There are plenty of other useful middleware products available. With a little digging, you can find billing software, patch tools, animation engines, content-generation tools, video and audio streaming software, networking software, and a whole range of other handy libraries. If you're working with a publisher that has built an MMOG before, you can probably take code from them as well.

Take anything you can buy or import from a publisher. This isn't the time for egos to get in the way. If you put your mind to it, you can take a great quantity of discrete, modular components and cobble them together Lego-style to assemble a basic MMOG engine pretty quickly.

Naturally, many of these components won't be perfectly suited to your application right out of the box. No one said it would be easy. However, spending time adapting existing software to a specific need is always more efficient than building custom applications from scratch.

Licenses

One potentially major cost when developing an MMOG is the choice of whether or not to utilize an existing intellectual property (IP). (Since this section is about costs, we will only consider IPs that are owned by some external party, and must be purchased or licensed from that party.) This strategy has paid off well on single-player games, but before reflexively mimicking that strategy for an MMOG project, let's analyze it first.

There are quite a few IP-based MMOGs already on the market or currently under development. Properties such as *Dungeons & Dragons*, *The Matrix*, *Star Trek*, *Star Wars*, *The Lord of the Rings*, and *Lineage* are the most obvious that come to mind. The first question we should ask ourselves is: "What can we expect the value of this IP to add to our MMOG?"

Funcom

Age of Conan

The subjective component of the answer might well be the topic of an entire book. Rather than tackle that here, let's just consider things on a more abstract level. As we stated earlier, the key benefit an IP should bring to any game is a ready-made, enthusiastic audience. It should guarantee us a certain minimum number of potential customers, and those customers should be counted on to help create a buzz about the game as development nears its completion. Thus, an IP contributes both customers and advertisement.

These customers will be anxious to get their hands on the game. The more attached they are to the IP, the more likely they will be to purchase the game in that first month when it launches. As we've already shown in the first graph in Chapter 7, most MMOGs jump out of the gates quickly, but after a couple of months, growth will begin to level out. If the game was well done, subscriptions will increase slowly but steadily. If not, it will stagnate or begin to decline.

Some MMOGs that have utilized IPs have already demonstrated that a popular property alone cannot sustain subscriber levels. After the initial burst of enthusiasm, subscriptions in the MMOG will inevitably fall if the game is poorly done or doesn't capture the essence of the property—no matter how popular the IP may be.

Thus, it appears that the major contribution value of an IP to an MMOG is composed primarily of some significant percentage of the subscribers generated in the first month or two. After that, the success or failure of the product in the long term is almost entirely determined by the quality of the game, not the IP.

So far, this sounds pretty similar to what we should expect in a single-player game. The difference between MMOGs and single-player games is the nature of the licensing agreement. Owners of IPs will traditionally sell the rights to their property either based on a percentage of box sales, or an agreed-upon flat fee. When dealing with MMOGs, however, they invariably want a percentage of the subscription revenues.

If viewed carefully, this represents a very bad deal for the MMOG developer. The IP only substantively contributes to the box sales in the first couple of months. After that, its value quickly dwindles in comparison to the relative quality of the game. If the license agreement requires the developer to continue paying a royalty on subscriptions, this means the owner of the IP is effectively leeching revenues to which their property made no contribution. In other words, you'd be letting them profit from your labor as well as from the value of their property.

In some extreme cases, the owner of the IP may receive far more than anyone would ever agree to pay as a flat fee. Consider once again the case of our theoretical 200,000-subscriber MMOG. Let's say the owner of the IP demands 5% of box sales and 5% of subscription revenues. Assuming the MMOG sustained an average of 200,000 subscribers over five years, and three expansions were released in addition to the original game, this would result in royalty payments totaling more than $10 million. Most developers would find $10 million to be a very excessive licensing fee for a property that only drove a few hundred thousand customers to the shelves.

In the case of more popular properties, where several million customers might be expected, the numbers get even crazier. If we assume that the IP was popular enough to drive 3 million players to the stores, and we further assume that 2 million of them liked the game enough to want to subscribe to it, this would net the owner of the IP more than $100 million over the course of five years. So far, even the most expensive IP hasn't approached that staggering level!

So why do some MMOG developers pay royalties to obtain IPs anyway? If a developer is risk averse or doesn't have a lot of cash floating around, they may use the long-term royalty lure as a means of mitigating their risks. Rather than pay a large flat fee up front, they pay a greatly reduced fee, and then offer a royalty. The idea is that if the product fails, at least a lot of unrecoverable money wasn't spent on the IP. If it succeeds, they'll end up paying more in the long run, but they'll also be making more themselves.

The best way to look at an IP is to simply assume that it drives box sales in the first couple of months, and perhaps helps maintain player interest for a few months afterward. To be generous, call it a year. Thus, either the royalty shouldn't extend beyond the first year, or it should have a cap. If the owner of the IP won't agree to either of those or to a reasonable flat fee, you should seriously reconsider whether it's worth it in the long run.

Facing Financial Reality

The biggest challenge I feel MMOG developers now face is financial reality—in short, the barriers that cost of entry and subscriber acquisition/retention represent. Post-development expenses such as server hardware and rack space, bandwidth, 24/7 customer service, billing systems, and "live" team support are considerable. Developing a game that is financially feasible in those regimes *and* contains a feature set that can compete with the market leaders is a very daunting task. The dominant games are already funding large teams and future expansions with substantial revenue streams, so a new project will have to be truly exceptional to differentiate itself to players *and* be profitable enough to attract publisher/investor interest.

—*Bryan Walker (Senior Producer, Retro Studios)*

Legal Issues

It's the nature of the world in which we live that as any business grows, the number of predatory lawyers who attempt to profit from it grows as well. MMOGs are certainly no exception, and there are quite a few legal issues with which you should acquaint yourself before entering this industry. Knowledge of them may affect your customer support policies, community management, game design, programming methodology, or even marketing.

Volunteers

In September of 2000, a now-famous class-action lawsuit (Reab v. Electronic Arts) was filed. Similar to the class action lawsuit filed against AOL in May of 1999 (Hallisey and William v. America Online Communities, Inc.), the lawsuit against EA alleged that volunteers were de facto employees, entitled to compensation under the Fair Labor Standards Act.

The case was eventually settled, but without debating its merits, we can still consider its impact. Allowing players to perform certain volunteer functions has the potential to be attacked in court. It is acceptable for players to provide these services completely on their own, but it's legally safest if you ignore it and do not assist in any way. Providing players with special tools that are unavailable to others, helping to organize them in any way, compensating them with free accounts, or any other assistance or acknowledgement of their efforts simply opens the door to litigation.

Considering this lawsuit, developers must take care when designing features such as player justice systems, guide programs, and player-generated quest systems. A developer cannot selectively allocate to specific players any tool that implies authority of one player over another. Anything available to one player must be available to all.

Digital Asset Ownership

Since the late 1990s, players have had an increasing tendency to sell their virtual, in-game possessions for real-world money on eBay. Even then, certain rare items, gold, houses, and even powerful characters—collectively digital assets—could sell for literally thousands of dollars. There are documented cases of individuals (usually outside the United States) forming small companies staffed with dozens of game players who are paid to play MMOGs all day and acquire assets for resale on eBay.

Although this practice would not bother most MMOG developers in principle, it must be carefully considered. If digital assets have an acknowledged intrinsic value in the real world, what happens if your database crashes and players lose those assets? What happens when the number of subscribers finally dips low enough that you decide to shut the service down? Clearly, if you shut the service down, all digital assets disappear. Is your company liable for their implied value in such cases?

To see how MMOG developers address this question, try reading the Terms of Service agreement. You may have noticed that upon installing an MMOG for the first time, or after any patch, an annoying, long legal screen appears. Almost no one ever reads this. It's called the Terms of Service, or TOS.

The TOS usually covers a variety of topics. In particular, the TOS often explicitly states that the player does not own his or her character or anything that character possesses or achieves. In a sense, it's more like you are renting the character from the developer, rather than owning it personally. The TOS also usually has language addressing the right to terminate the account of any player for any reason, thus allowing CS representatives to ban unruly players without legal repercussions.

In practice, the developer usually takes no official stance against players selling items on eBay. They make a point of legally stating their ownership of any digital asset, but then turn a blind eye as players sell them back and forth anyway. It's a way for everyone to have their cake and eat it too. The players can get maximum enjoyment out of their game, and the company is legally protected.

> Ebay transactions had an unintended side effect at Origin. Players would routinely sell *Ultima Online* gold on eBay for cash. Depending on how much gold was currently available in the game world, it affected the asking price on eBay. For a while, it was actually theoretically possible to track virtual inflation in-game, based on the price of gold on Ebay. It was like some sort of surreal, third-world, virtual commodities exchange.
>
> —*Rick Hall*

User-Generated Content

The thought of providing a set of tools that allows players to extend the game by generating their own content seems like a perfectly natural idea in an MMOG. What better way is there for the game to grow and expand over time than to allow the players to be the builders of their own world? It's perfect.

Well, not really. Even this idea has certain legal ramifications. Imagine if you designed a tool that allowed players to create their own 3D models and bring them into the game. Wouldn't it be fun to see the wide variety of amazing things that the more talented players could dream up? Wouldn't it make the world a more diverse and interesting place if players could build their own houses and vehicles too?

It would be fun until the first time some player plagiarized copyrighted material. It's inevitable that players would build models that were exact copies of existing characters, places, or other objects from movies, comics, or books. Sooner or later, the real owners of those properties would want to slap a lawsuit on someone, and guess who would find themselves in court?

The same principle applies if you allow players to create music, custom sound clips, video, or even large amounts of text. Most of them will probably just have fun being creative, but it's inevitable that some won't be able to resist the temptation of sharing their favorite songs, movies, fictional characters, or even books. This is where you can get into trouble.

The difficulty lies in the fact that it's efficient to distribute such assets through the server. The server has the bandwidth to ensure that if crowds of people are all viewing a user-generated asset, it can be quickly distributed to anyone who comes close enough. Thus, the process would probably be for the player to create the content offline, upload it, and then allow the server to distribute it efficiently. Naturally, if your server is found to be illegally distributing copyrighted materials, you will probably be found legally liable.

Some developers have proposed the solution of all user-generated content requiring approval. It would be uploaded someplace where a representative of the company could review it to make sure it wasn't profane or plagiarized, before being accepted by the game.

This solution has two obvious flaws. First of all, depending on the amount of content the players generate, it might prove impossible to review it all without hiring an army of censors. Second, it might still be possible for obscure properties that the censors don't recognize to sneak through the system. Inevitably, this solution probably can't work.

The second solution is to simply avoid routing user-generated content through the server. With peer-to-peer connections, it might be inefficient, but it would still be possible to get content from one user to another. Then again, this creates the added problem of a potential security hole that might allow players to hack each other's computers, so it's not a perfect solution either.

Piracy

Earlier, we mentioned the problem of so-called gray servers. This is when a player duplicates the functionality of your server, and then attracts several other people to play on his or her server instead. Often, they don't bother to re-create the client side at all. The client usually consists of a staggering amount of assets, and besides, yours will serve the purpose quite nicely.

The operators of these gray servers can and should be pursued in the United States. Once located, they aren't difficult to remove, and it's even possible to sue for compensation. Unfortunately, copyright laws aren't enforced as rigorously in other countries, so the problem persists overseas.

The best way to combat piracy is to protect your data stream. The only way a server can be reproduced is if the data traffic coming across the network can be deciphered. The better your encryption, the less likely it will be that anyone can duplicate your server.

Ironically, if the encryption fails, the next best tactic is to make frequent client-side patches. Every time the client is patched, corresponding changes can be made to the server code to make the previous client incompatible with the new server. This isn't a problem for your players, since they are automatically patched to the new version the next time they log in. This presents a problem for the operator of the gray server. The players on this server will want the latest patches, fixes, and content. They'll want to patch to the latest version every time it comes out. However, to support the latest version, the gray server operator must hack into it again, figure out the new changes, and change the server accordingly. This can take time, during which any of the players who have patched to the newest version won't be able to play on the gray server. The more often you patch, the more difficult you make it for the gray server operator to keep up.

Most often, they'll simply settle for keeping an old, out-of-date version of the game, and not support new versions. That's too much work. Alas, eventually for the players on the gray server, the game will quickly become static and out of date. It will become progressively more unattractive to them and many of them will eventually leave.

Payday

There are a couple of different models for generating revenues from an MMOG. Each model shares one thing in common: the goal of repeatedly extracting relatively small amounts of money from every subscriber over a long period of time. The resultant stable and predictable revenue stream makes MMOGs unusual in the gaming industry. Rather than producing the typical roller coaster of revenue that comes from 18 months of expenditures followed by 3 months of income, the MMOG produces a stable, predictable income, month after month.

The most common model contains two sources of income: the box revenues and the subscription revenues. The box revenues are identical to single-player games. Depending on the cost of manufacturing and the retail price, each box that is sold will generate somewhere around $20–$30 for the developer.

Once the boxes reach the consumer, it is customary to provide the player with the first month's subscription for free, so they can try the game and see if they like it. Beginning in the second month, a subscription fee is charged. This fee varies from MMOG to MMOG, but $15 a month is fairly typical.

It is important to recognize that although you can count on nearly everyone who purchases the box to try the game during the free trial month, not everyone will ultimately opt to pay for the monthly subscription. Inevitably some buyers won't care for the game, and will quit playing after a few days or weeks. We'll refer to the percentage of players who buy the box and then pay at least one month of subscription fees as the conversion rate. Thus, if 100 people buy the game, and 30 days later we find 72 of them have started paying for the monthly subscription, this would infer a conversion rate of 72%. In the real world, we never see a 100% conversion rate. Each game will demonstrate a long-term conversion rate trend that usually falls somewhere between 50% and 80%.

Now let's follow the timeline of our trusty theoretical 200,000-subscriber MMOG, beginning with launch day. We'll try to understand how players are acquired. In the following table, we'll see cumulative totals for the number of boxes sold, the total number of players playing the game, and the total number of subscribers (meaning those who have begun paying the monthly subscription fee).

Diagram by Per Olin

Day	Total Boxes Sold	Total Players	Subscribers
1	65,000	65,000	0
5	178,150	147,679	0
10	203,302	158,835	0
15	213,022	158,084	0
20	221,902	161,878	0
25	230,462	168,792	0
30	239,342	175,955	57,200
45	261,982	193,074	139,201
60	274,822	200,000	155,868

Notice that by Day 5, the total players entry is more than 30,000 lower than the number of boxes sold. This represents those players who have bought the game and decided that they don't care for it. Thus, by this point, 18% of the purchasers of the game are already gone. Others will last a week or two longer, but by the time things stabilize at Day 60, this theoretical model shows roughly a 65% conversion rate. Our model in this case assumes an 18% churn. Since the number of boxes sold between Day 10 and Day 15 is only about 4.9% of the total, it can't keep up with the churn. This explains why the total number of players actually decreases between Day 10 and Day 15.

We also don't start receiving subscription revenues until after the first free month. At that point, they'll start showing up 30 days after they first purchased and installed the game. The effect is that subscribers typically lag behind total players. Often, when an MMOG claims to have 200,000 subscribers, it means 200,000 people are playing, but probably only somewhere between 170,000 and 180,000 are actually paying. At any given point in time, no matter how long the MMOG has been running, some percentage of the total players will be in their trial month, thus not yet paying. Every month some players leave and new players join. This means that the total subscribers are always lower than the total players.

Once your subscriber level stabilizes, you'll see a fairly predictable churn each month. As you will recall, churn is different from conversion rate. Churn refers to those who were formerly paying subscribers, and have decided to terminate their subscription. Thus, conversion rate and churn will both affect the subscriber numbers. If you can accurately forecast total box sales, conversion rate, and churn, the revenue calculation is easily deduced.

As a final note, it is important to make the distinction between total players and subscribers. The subscriber number determines your revenues, while the total player number will impact your bandwidth costs. Be sure to perform each calculation properly if you want more accurate revenue forecasts.

Free Box

Experience has shown that the average subscriber eventually winds up paying three or four times as much money in subscription fees as they did to purchase the box at retail. This means that approximately 75% of the total revenues come from subscription fees.

An interesting experimental model might follow from this realization. If developers began distributing the game for free, instead of charging for it at retail, it would wind up reaching a potentially much larger audience. Assuming the conversion rate and churn remain as before, it is conceivable that more income will be generated this way purely from subscription fees.

Micropayments

As the industry continues to evolve, some developers have arrived at the conclusion that many players exhibit a certain reluctance to commit themselves to the idea of a subscription. To them, a subscription represents a monthly bill much like a credit card payment or electric bill. Viewed in this light, they consider the entire idea with a negative predisposition, and they shy away from subscription-based games entirely.

Ironically, the resistance probably doesn't stem from an inability to afford $15 a month. More likely, it is simply the commitment that players don't like. In response to this possibility, pioneering companies like NCsoft and Sony Online Entertainment have begun experimenting with a new way to monetize MMOGs with what is known as *micropayments*.

The concept is simple. The player purchases the game at retail and may then play as long as possible without paying a subscription fee; instead, the MMOG will offer a wide variety of features, weapons, maps, and assets for a small charge—such as $0.50–$1.00 each. The player is under no obligation to buy anything more, but the assumption is that if they enjoy playing, they will most likely purchase some items over time.

The model is reminiscent of the card game *Magic: The Gathering*. Those who have played this game will understand. When you first buy the game, you are supplied with a starter deck that contains a small number of random cards. This starter deck is adequate to play the game without purchasing more cards, but it only contains a tiny fraction of the thousands that are available.

©Wizards of the Coast. Used with Permission.

Magic: The Gathering Online

In practice, everyone who decides they enjoy the game will purchase many, many extra packs of cards. Your authors can readily admit to personally spending hundreds of dollars over the course of a year on *Magic* cards when the game was in its heyday. Ironically, had the publishers of this card game attempted to sell every card available in one, giant box, we would have thought that price was insane. In the end, they got it out of us anyway.

This is the attitude targeted for exploitation in a micropayment model. The developer hopes that if players get hooked on their "free" game, they will wind up spending far more money on extras than they would have on subscription fees. If the *Magic: The Gathering* game is any indicator, they may be on to something.

Alternative Billing Methods

In Chapter 6, we discussed demographics at length. One of the things you may have noticed is that MMOG audiences include at least some percentage of players who are under the age of 18. A potential problem arises for these players, especially if they don't have their own credit card. Monthly billing is most easily accomplished simply by supplying credit card information. In addition to younger players, it has been observed that people in some foreign countries exhibit a cultural aversion to credit cards. Japan, for instance, has a noticeably lower instance of credit card owners than the United States.

For those players who don't have a credit card, paying a monthly subscription fee can be problematic. Sending a check to the game service every month is certainly possible, but not everyone cares to undertake that inconvenience. For this reason, MMOG developers have some alternative methods of paying for subscriptions. The three most common methods are the following:

- **Paypal**—Since Paypal accounts can withdraw money directly from a bank account, some players prefer this form of payment.
- **Cell phones**—Some overseas MMOG developers have begun experimenting with cell phone billing. To accomplish this, players simply call a number each month, punch some buttons to identify themselves, and receive a subscription fee in their monthly cell phone bills.
- **Game time cards**—A game time card is sold at the same retailer where the game can be purchased. Much like a prepaid phone card, it contains a code number that can be entered into the player's game account. Game time cards usually come in 30-day, 90-day, or even 180-day varieties. Typically, cards that cover a subscription longer than 30 days offer a progressive discount. If you include this form of billing, be sure to compensate for it in your revenue calculations, because this discount means that 90-day or 180-day game time card purchasers will actually be paying less than the usual subscription fee.

PTER REVIEW:::

the fact that MMOGs are a service rather than a product affect the associated busi-
in terms of technology, cost, personnel, and other resources?

me legal issues associated with user-generated content and digital asset ownership?
done to prevent these issues from occurring?

e payment methods associated with MMOGs? Discuss the benefits and disadvan-
method.

Foreign Markets

We have noted in previous chapters how the possibility of launching an MMOG in
foreign markets can affect design decisions. In addition to this, some foreign markets
will also affect cost and revenue calculations. Understanding how the business works
in different countries is important if you plan to release your MMOG in other countries besides the United States. The three regions that present the most significant
differences are Japan, South Korea, and China.

Japan

Aside from stylistic preferences and the lower percentage of credit cards, the other
significant difference between Japan and the U.S. market has to do with their hardware. In Japan, there are far more game players who play on laptops than in the
United States. There is a tendency in U.S. markets to favor more powerful desktop
systems, thus many developers focus their technical efforts on ensuring compatibility with them, often to the exclusion of less powerful laptops. To maximize
subscriber numbers in Japan, it is strongly recommended that laptops be explicitly
included in the compatibility testing phase.

South Korea

In South Korea, few online gamers play their games from home. Overwhelmingly,
the custom is to turn online game playing into a social event by gathering at Internet
game rooms. An Internet game room is a large, open area that is filled with PCs.
Players are charged about a dollar an hour, and for this fee they are free to wander
the room and play any game they like at no further charge. This difference affects
both the revenue model and the account management features substantially.

To illustrate how MMOGs work in an Internet game room, let's consider an example. Let's call your MMOG *Game X*. If someone wants to play *Game X*, they must
find a computer in the game room that has it installed. Not every computer in the
room will have every game on it.

Upon finding a computer with *Game X* on it, the player sits down to play. Let's
assume they have never played *Game X* before. Since they are already paying the
owner of the game room a dollar an hour, they certainly won't want to pay you
as well. Thus, the process of opening an account in an MMOG must be free in a
game room.

The person plays *Game X* for a couple of hours a day for a week or two, but then some obligation prevents them from returning to the game room for a month. When they finally do return, let's say they want to pick up where they left off. They expect to be able to just log back in and continue playing.

Nexon/KRU

Shattered Galaxy

This is very different from the way things would work in the United States. In the United States, the player must have paid for the subscription to log back in a month later and continue playing. If the fee had not been paid, the account would have been automatically suspended. However, as we've just learned, the player in a game room is already paying an hourly fee and expects the subscription itself to be free.

So how does the MMOG developer get money out of this? What they do is provide a number of seats to the Internet game room. The number of seats is the maximum number of simultaneous players allowed to play *Game X* in that Internet game room at any given time.

Let's assume the game room in question has purchased five seats for *Game X*. Each seat will cost the game room, say, $60 a month. Thus, the game room is paying a total of $300 a month to the MMOG developer for the five seats. For this fee, any number of players can play *Game X*, but no more than five simultaneously.

Clearly, the more popular the game, the more seats the game room owner will need to purchase. If the five seats combined see more than 300 total hours of use in a given month, the owner of the game room will make a profit. If not, the owner is likely to reduce the number of paid seats for next month.

This model is quite different from a standard subscription model, and it requires special versions of the account management so that accounts won't be closed. It also makes the total subscriber numbers far less clear. If you think about it, since

Courtesy of NCsoft

Lineage: The Blood Pledge

an MMOG account in an Internet game room never actually closes, how can we truly know how many players are still playing? Over the years, the number of accounts can only go up.

This is why we see numbers showing millions of subscribers for games like *Lineage* in South Korea. It's extremely unlikely that everyone who ever opened an account in *Lineage* is still actively playing, but there's no way to tell for sure.

Value Added Tax

For those MMOG developers considering releasing in the European Union, you might also want to in VAT. The nature of this tax will have an impact been known to surprise smaller MMOG deve ence with international business.

China

China, too, centers on an Internet gar identical to the South Korean mode' potential market size in China is e doing business are much smaller about a dollar an hour, but Chi

This may sound like it can't width and customer suppor a healthy profit. Anyone you that a small profit fr profit from a small nur

The business overv most of the larger that the service- complex and p sible to effect interrelatior of depend

CHAPTER

Endgame

bringing everything together

Key Chapter Questions

- What are some essential *design* issues associated with developing an MMOG?

- What are some essential *technical* issues associated with developing an MMOG?

- What are some essential *business* issues associated with developing an MMOG?

- What are some thoughts on the *future* of MMOG development?

- How can you prepare for a *career* in MMOG development?

In this final chapter, we recap many of the key concepts that must be kept in mind when building an MMOG. This list is not necessarily all-encompassing—but it should be consulted from time to time during the entire development process.

In addition to a reference, this chapter serves as a glimpse into the future of MMOG development. It also provides some guidelines for entering a career as an MMOG developer.

Design Issues

All massively multiplayer online games (MMOGs) have unique gameplay structures, markets, and social features that distinguish themselves from games that are played "offline" with a limited number of players. Here are just a few *design* issues associated with creating an MMOG:

- **Lifestyle Thinking**—Remember that an MMOG is more of a lifestyle than a game. This world will be the player's home for a year or two. Make it feel that way.
- **Latency**—Compensate for latency in your design, or live with the fact that players with better connections will have an advantage.
- **Community**—Communities cannot form easily without lots of tools for communication and organization. The more you provide, the stronger the community can be.
- **Sacred Cows**—Don't discard ideas simply because you've always been told "that isn't done in MMOGs." MMOGs are such a new genre of games that conventional wisdom doesn't always apply. This holds true for design, programming, art, marketing, and business models. Don't blindly accept a sacred cow, or you may just create an unintentional copy of an existing game.
- **Virtual Economy**—If you're not aware of how money enters and leaves the game world, you'll probably wind up with inflation problems.
- **Cultural Considerations**—Don't think purely from an American point of view. If there's a chance your game will launch in other countries, find out how each culture will react to your MMOG's play style, art, and music.
- **Quantification**—Always remember that players need lots of ways to quantify themselves, show off what they've accomplished, and feel unique.
- **Monetization Model**—Know how your game will be monetized. A subscription-based model will require different designs from a micropayment model.

After two years of teaching game design classes at the university, the most common request students have made of me is to provide checklists. They want a step-by-step procedure for everything. They don't usually like it the first time I tell them that every project is different, and I'd prefer they learn how to arrive at their own conclusions rather than working from a list that can't possibly cover every scenario. There are times when checklists are appropriate, but I think that they should act as a review of what we have already learned, rather than substituting for comprehension.

—*Rick Hall*

- **Razor Statement**—This is a one-line description of the essence of your game. Use it as a razor, especially when designing your core mechanic.

- **Core Mechanic**—Be sure that whatever activity the players will spend the majority of their time doing is fun. Don't let all the other features distract you from this.

- **Mind Mapping**—Mind maps are useful brainstorming tools. Remember to try to explore second-order ideas.

- **Tone Words**—There's a vast difference between a predatory dragon and a bumbling dragon. Use tone words to clarify your version of the flavor of the world.

- **Production Value**—Remember that it's the details that bring a world to life. You can't possibly include too much detail in your world.

- **The Uncanny Valley**—Take care that your aesthetic doesn't fall into the uncanny valley.

- **Audience Types**—Remember Bartle's four: achievers, explorers, socializers, and killers.

- **Mechanical Themes**—Settle on a fundamental mechanical theme when designing the core mechanic.

- **Customization**—Remember that an MMOG represents one big crowd. Players need as many tools as possible to enable them to stand out and be unique.

- **Traffic Control**—Find ways in the game design to keep players naturally spread out across the world, rather than clustered together in crowds.

- **Demographics**—Understand your audience and what entertains them before trying to build a game for them.

- **Think Like a Marketer**—If you can't explain what makes your game unique, a marketer won't be able to either.

- **The Audience Dynamic**—Remember to build mechanisms into the design that allow hardcore players to interact with casual players and vice versa. Don't allow them to become separate camps.

- **Multiplayer Balance**—Take care in balancing the game. Remember that players will tend to gang up on each other or look for underpowered players to use as victims.

- **Elder Game**—Once players achieve the highest level or powers in the game, you must have things for them to do going forward or they will become bored and quit the game.

An example of in-game housing: an empty house in *EverQuest II* that is ready to be decorated and equipped.

Technology Issues

MMOG development involves many unique *technology* issues that exist before, during, and after launch. Here are just a few technology issues that every aspiring MMOG developer should anticipate:

Illustration by Ben Bourbon

- ■ **Load Balancing**—Remember that no matter how good the design is at traffic control, players will sometimes all congregate in close proximity to each other. How will your engine deal with this?

- ■ **Tools Are the Key to Everything**— Providing tools for things such as content creation, testing, bug reporting, server monitoring, and AI will allow your team to create a much larger, more densely populated, bug-free, high-performing world.

- ■ **Bandwidth**—Be as efficient as possible with how much bandwidth each player uses. Remember that bandwidth usage directly affects profitability.

- ■ **Database**—Get a database administrator (DBA) to build your database if at all possible. If done incorrectly, this can be the cause of enormous problems.

- ■ **"Not Invented Here" (NIH) Syndrome**—Don't scoff at off-the-shelf technology. Anything that can be adapted for your use is more efficient than coding it yourself. Remember opportunity costs.

- ■ **Infrastructural Needs**—Remember that in addition to the game, you're going to have to build login servers, databases, patch servers, pipelines, account management, billing systems, God clients, server-monitoring tools, content-generation tools, and process documentation for the live team. Remember to include things like this in your schedules.

- ■ **Security**—Never trust the client. Validate everything on the server side. Protect your data stream as if your life depends on it. Remember, it's your small team against potentially hundreds of hackers who will be entertained if they can crash your server.

- ■ **Server Side Performance**—This is another issue that affects the bottom line financially. The more players that each server can manage simultaneously, the lower your hardware costs will be. AI must be given particular attention.

- ■ **Development Server**—Don't work on a cheap imitation of a server during development. As early as possible, settle on your final server architecture and develop the game on that exact hardware.

- *Rapid Progress*—As early as possible, get a complete architecture running. This includes not only the development server mentioned earlier, but a login server, patcher, and account database. Don't wait until halfway through production to put this together for the first time. Do it in pre-production.

- *Document Everything*—Remember that this game will probably be running for long after you've moved on to other projects. It's imperative that every technical aspect be well documented, and the documentation must be easily accessible.

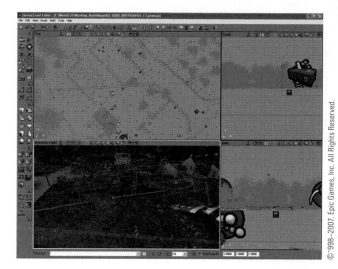

Unreal Editor

- *D-Day*—Launch week is going to be traumatic. Don't plan on vacations this month just because the game has launched. Brace for impact!

- *Compatibility Testing*—Remember to test your code on hardware and operating system configurations that reflect any region in which the game may be launched.

Business Issues

Many developers do not consider the significance of *business* issues that are specific to MMOG development. However, elements such as customer support and live teams provide the life blood of most MMOGs. Here are a few business issues that we've discussed in previous chapters:

- *Set Your Expectations*—If you assume an MMOG is some kind of get-rich-quick scheme, you probably shouldn't attempt the project. It's a huge, lengthy, risky undertaking. If done properly, it can be extremely profitable, but cutting corners during development is dangerous in the extreme.

- *Begin Marketing Early*—Building a grass roots community is necessary well before the game launches. Work with the development team all through the process, not just as production approaches completion. Make a marketing schedule during the pre-production phase. Marketing can be particularly useful early in demographic research.

- *Customer Support*—Remember that customer support representatives must come on board many months before the game launches. Budget and schedule accordingly.

Illustration by Ben Bourbon

- **Business Model**—Since the monetization scheme can dramatically affect the design and technology, settle on this right from the start.
- **Live Team**—Begin work on the first expansion immediately after the game launches. Remember to staff the expansion team separately from the live team. Trying to get double duty out of the live team or splitting their time will probably result in completely unpredictable schedules.
- **Server Hardware Plan**—Remember the timing of when you should buy server hardware. The development team needs a server at the start. Later you'll need servers for QA and beta testing, and then the public servers must be in place before launch.
- **Foreign Markets**—Different regions will have distinct impacts on your business. Make sure the development team is aware of any constraints your decisions impose. Assume that for major territories outside of the country, you'll need small foreign offices.
- **Churn and Conversion Rate**—These variables are important factors when calculating revenues. Plan not only to estimate them for your financial plan, but to track them for the entire lifetime of the project. They will change as the game gets older.
- **Community Management**—Make sure you remember to staff a person or two to manage the community. They will be your voice to the players. Development team members probably shouldn't be allowed to directly communicate to the public without supervision by the community manager.
- **Legal Issues**—Acquaint yourself with legal issues specific to MMOGs. They are natural targets for lawsuits.
- **Community VIPs**—Identify as many hardcore community leaders personally as you can. Target them as VIPs, and get them involved. They can be very useful as evangelists, especially if they are armed with insider information, tools for creating their own web sites, and early beta versions of the game.

Courtesy of Maggie the Jackcat

Maggie the Jackcat (*Asheron's Call*) is the epitome of the community VIP.

Back To the Future

From everything you've read so far, you've probably realized a valuable skill to possess in the development of computer games is an ability to predict the future. From the day your project first gets underway, you have to guess what will be popular, successful, and competitive two to three years later when the game finally ships. A lot can change in those intervening years. New technology might make your game obsolete before it even ships. A competitor may do the same thing you're doing, only ship it earlier, making you look like a bandwagon jumper. Popular culture and tastes may change to the point that your subject matter is no longer trendy.

All of this is no different from most games of any genre. The thing that magnifies the problem for MMOGs is that they're intended to last many years after they ship. That means that while typical game makers must predict the industry advances 2–3 years in the future, developers of MMOGs would ideally like to look forward 7–10 years.

As it happens, perhaps the most common question asked of game developers follows exactly that thinking. Everyone always wants to know: "So, what do you think will be the next great innovations in MMOGs?" If you ever have to answer this kind of question, keep in mind that your answer will be recorded and seemingly forgotten, only to be pulled from a dusty file drawer 10 years down the road. No one ever forgets.

Given that caveat, it's at least safe to assume that in the near future, we're going to see MMOGs expand to a number of new and interesting genres besides just RPGs. Military simulations of all kinds are already in the works as well as a couple of different RTS games, FPS titles, and even a racing game has been done. It's not hard to believe that every conceivable genre of game will make its way to an MMOG world fairly quickly.

What's Next?

Eventually, everyone will be able to create their own virtual worlds if they like, in the same way that they can create their own Web pages or Web 2.0 pages today. Yes, that does mean they'll mainly be dreadful—but some will be absolutely wonderful.

—Richard Alan Bartle
(Professor, Essex University)

The future of online game development can be summed up with one term: cooperative gameplay. MMOGs for years have embraced cooperative play as a cornerstone to the business; you gather with friends, go online, club monsters, and take their treasure. What we have not seen, until relatively recently, is an explosion in coop gameplay for non-MMOGs. I believe this is changing, and it will need to change more. Being able to play games primarily as a cooperative online experience will change the face of non-MMOGs, and it will definitely help expand the game market to more and more "non-gamers."

—Graeme Bayless
(President, Kush Games—a division of 2K Sports)

The online game industry will grow, but linearly with the rest of the player market. MMOGs are different, not better. Many people will still prefer the more personal and less time-consuming single-player experiences.

—Denis Papp
(Chief Technology Officer, TimeGate Studios)

I feel that a significant degree of gamer drift is quite likely as the paradigms currently employed by the market leaders run their course and become passé. Trying to get another medieval "Men In Tights" or "VR Life" MMOG project off the ground would likely be a non-starter. Developers should think about how they can capitalize on a market that would probably be more fragmented and savvy in its expectations after they migrate out of what are today's "Big Things."

—Bryan Walker
(Senior Producer, Retro Games)

The online gaming market will grow at a minimum of 9% annually. A decade or so from now, theaters will no longer exist in the classic sense—and the vast majority of our population will prefer its entertainment to be interactive.

—Mario "Thunderbear" Orsini
(Executive Producer, Team Orbit/Academy of Game Entertainment Technology [AGET])

The online environment will become more and more like *Second Life*, but with deeper involvement and seamless integration into real life. Also, there will be a larger variety of flavors—different worlds for different tastes. . . Online also needs more gesture-based interfaces. How about an MMORPG for the Wii?

—David Javelosa
(Professor, Santa Monica College)

It's also safe to assume that further exploration of the business model will take place. *Second Life* has already shown a creative approach that allows players to make money by generating their own content. Other games are also experimenting with what you might call quasi-real economies (in which real-world money is spent for virtual assets). Expect more of that, to be sure.

None of this is particularly innovative, of course. Incorporating new genres and expanding on business models is very iterative. It's completely in keeping with the kind of slow evolution that we've seen take place in MMOGs since the mid-1990s. Truly revolutionary ideas are few and far between. It's reasonable to expect that the standard iterative improvements and incremental changes will comprise the majority of the near-term future for MMOGS. As always, most developers will choose to refine and improve in small bits from product to product, rather than go out on a limb to try something experimental. Experimental ideas represent an unknown risk. No one knows if they'll work or not, and the gaming industry is notoriously risk averse.

For those few adventurous souls who embark on the quest to do something truly unique, however, the MMOG represents a wealth of fascinating, untapped possibilities. Sooner or later a developer will conceive of an entirely new game genre for an MMOG, rather than simply retrofitting an existing game genre into a massively multiplayer environment. Look for that game genre to utilize the human social aspects that are inherent to this environment, rather than fireballs, grenade launchers, and plasma cannons for a core mechanic.

:::::: *Second Life* as an Educational Tool

Author Jeannie Novak is producer and lead designer on a project that utilizes the *Second Life* (*http://www.secondlife.com*) multi-user virtual environment as a learning system. (Although *Second Life* might be described more appropriately as a social network, it has the capacity to exhibit features of an MMOG.) The Business Communications course behaves like a process simulation game with some role-playing, adventure, and strategy elements. During the course, students ("player characters") learn the inner workings of a fictional corporation through real-world scenarios. They will also discover how to communicate with other employees ("non-player characters") within the corporate environment. This is a big step forward in integrating games into education. Eventually, all courses may be taught as games. All games involve "covert learning"—often unintended by the developers. The reverse can also be true: All courses could conceivably involve "covert gaming"! This is just the beginning of an educational revolution. See *http://www.simteach. com* for forums discussing using *Second Life* as an educational environment.

Surveying construction of a Business Communications educational simulation game being built in *Second Life*.

It might be interesting to see an MMOG that is based in popularity and politics, where players can form their own governments, societies, and political parties. Perhaps we'll see games based on an exchange of real information, similar in function to what the Internet already does, but put into game form. Alternative reality games based on conspiracy theories and shadow governments seem like a natural fit too. Everyone loves a good conspiracy.

In the future, MMOGs will also probably place far more emphasis on crossing over into different platforms, which is starting to be called trans-medial access. This is where a game incorporates cell phones, instant messaging, email, iPods, or anything else that allows people to communicate. The visionary-but-failed game *Majestic* already used this technique, but look for it to be used far more extensively in the future.

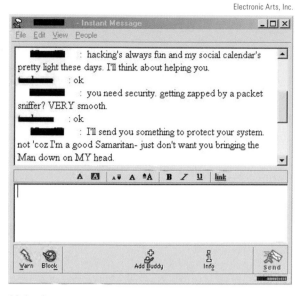

Majestic

The Matrix is only a science fiction movie, but in a way the lines between reality and *virtual reality* are continuing to blur. Massively multiplayer games that are designed around social interactions, incorporate trans-medial access, have quasi-real economies, exchange real information, and allow people to form almost shadow societies aren't far off. When they arrive and players start investing the usual amount of time and money into them, who's to say they won't begin to constitute their own reality?

Ken Finney on the Future of MMOGs:::::

Kenneth Finney was a commercial and industrial software engineer from the 1980s until the mid-1990s. He is an associate developer for GarageGames (Torque Game Engine), and an author of three books on game development (including *3D Game Programming All In One*). Kenneth has also been an instructor in the Game Art & Design program at the Art Institute of Toronto since 2004.

Kenneth C. Finney (Author, Cengage/ Delmar Learning; Instructor, Art Institute of Toronto)

I think the future is in player-directed real-time content creation. This would include story generation, as well as art resources. The companies with the best real-time online content-generation tools will be the market leaders. I think that the player market roughly doubles every five years. It seems like we are currently in a big growth spurt, so it's likely that the player base of 2012 will be double that of today's.

Busting Down the MMOG Developer Door

For those readers who are interested in developing MMOGs, you'll quickly find that it's something of an incestuous culture. Most MMOG developers recognize the enormous complexity of their genre, and are typically hesitant to hire people who don't have several years of experience developing them already. It's the age-old problem of not being able to get a job without experience, but not being able to get experience without a job.

At some level, MMOG developers understand this. In a perfect world they'd only hire MMOG veterans, but there aren't enough to go around. The more MMOGs that begin development, the bigger the problem becomes. Developers have no choice but to hire outside of the family, like it or not.

As an outsider, then, your best bet is to become totally immersed in existing MMOGs as a player. Play a variety of MMOGs long before you apply for a job. If you don't have a couple of level 70 *WoW* characters, a castle in *UO*, an all-powerful villain or two in *City of Villains*, or haven't made a ton of real money in *Second Life*, they'll probably think you're simply not knowledgeable enough or dedicated enough to make MMOGs. What they want are fanatics, like themselves. Nothing less will do.

> Depending on what kind of job you want, other skills are valuable. As a programmer, you can stand out from the crowd if you're a network expert or a gifted database programmer. A good friend of mine got his first job in MMOGs partly because he was a network programming Linux-head, and partly because he had the most "Realm Points" on his server in *Dark Age of Camelot*.
>
> —Rick Hall

Courtesy of NCsoft

City of Villains

As an artist or designer, you really want to be an expert with level-building tools. If you can put together great-looking environments in *Unreal*, *Torque*, *Neverwinter Nights*, etc., especially if you are good at scripting, you also have an advantage. They'll want to know that you understand things such as traffic control, optimization, and vertical space. The less they have to teach you, the more attractive you are to them.

> **D**o as much on your own as you can until you absolutely have to work with somebody else. Keep your vision pure! Remember you are there for the end user; that is your only gauge for success.
>
> —David Javelosa
> (Professor, Santa
> Monica College)

Deborah Baxtrom on Becoming an Online Game Developer:::::

Deborah has an MFA in screenwriting/directing from Columbia University in NYC. She has written and/or directed two award-winning short films and has optioned several feature length screenplays. She also developed a game story and characters for a course taught at the Art Institute of Pittsburgh—Online Division. She teaches for AiP-OD and has also worked as a story analyst, entertainment journalist, and script doctor.

Make sure you develop interesting characters first. My students sometimes prefer to emphasize gameplay and epic storylines rather than taking the time to develop interesting characters. As a result, the entire project generally falls flat.

Deborah Baxtrom
(Writer & Filmmaker;
Instructor, Art Institute
of Pittsburgh—Online
Division)

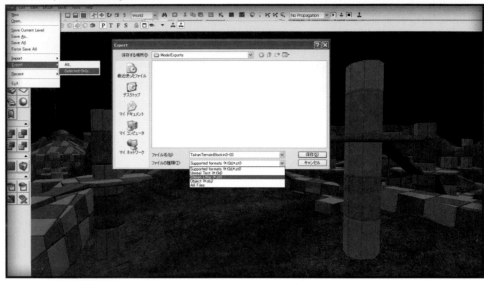

Unreal Editor

It also helps if you're an active blogger, have your own web page, post on MMOG chat boards religiously, and are generally well known in an MMOG community or two. Quite a few MMOG developers have gotten into the industry primarily because they were well known as players. Like anything else in life, knowing the right people, even if only online, can open doors for you.

And there you have it. MMOGs represent a huge, complex, confusing, fascinating new universe. Luckily, numerous pioneering companies have emerged since the mid-1990s that were willing to stumble their way through the fog of the unknown and provide the rest of us with a clearer vision of what MMOGs can be. As the industry has grown, so too has our understanding of how it works. Now that the fog has begun to lift and we are able to see MMOGs in their entirety, it appears that they have evolved into a totally different species of game. They are not merely larger versions of single-player games. They are living, breathing, and evolving entities. It might be more appropriate to say that they have been born instead of launched.

> To invent, you need a good imagination and a pile of junk.
>
> —*Thomas Edison*

By the way, for those readers who looked askance at the above quote by Edison, look a little deeper. What Edison was trying to say in his own humorous way was that ordinary things can become amazing new inventions if only you view them from a different perspective. Rather than focus on worn-out, formulaic processes, we've attempted to provide high-level, conceptual constraints—showing not only individual considerations, but also the ways they interact with each other and with the MMOG as a whole. Only by understanding the nature of the challenges is it possible to conceive of revolutionary solutions.

::: CHAPTER REVIEW :::

1. Moving beyond the mindmapping phase you went through earlier, how will you use what you've learned in this book to create a prototype of your own MMOG idea?

2. Create a hypothetical career plan for yourself with regard to online game development. Will you start a company of your own, join an existing independent project, or approach one of the top online game developers or publishers?

3. What are your thoughts on the future of online game development? Do you agree or disagree with some of the predictions in this chapter?

Resources

There's a wealth of information on game development and related topics discussed in this book. Here is just a sample list of books, news sites, organizations, and events you should definitely explore!

News

Blues News—www.bluesnews.com

Computer Games Magazine—www.cgonline.com

Game Daily Newsletter—www.gamedaily.com

Game Developer Magazine—www.gdmag.com

Gamers Hell—www.gamershell.com

Game Music Revolution (GMR)—www.gmronline.com

Game Rankings—www.gamerankings.com

GamesIndustry.biz—www.gamesindustry.biz

GameSlice Weekly—www.gameslice.com

GameSpot—www.gamespot.com

GameSpy—www.gamespy.com

Game Industry News—www.gameindustry.com

GIGnews.com—www.gignews.com

Internet Gaming Network (IGN)—www.ign.com

Metacritic—www.metacritic.com

MMOGChart.com—www.mmogchart.com

Music4Games.net—www.music4games.net

Next Generation—www.next-gen.biz

1UP—www.1up.com

PC Gamer—www.pcgamer.com

Star Tech Journal [technical side of the coin-op industry]—www.startechjournal.com

UGO Networks (Underground Online)—www.ugo.com

Video Game Music Archive—www.vgmusic.com

Wired Magazine—www.wired.com

Directories & Communities

Apple Developer Connection—developer.apple.com

Betawatcher.com—www.betawatcher.com

Fat Babies.com [game industry gossip]—www.fatbabies.com

Gamasutra—www.gamasutra.com

GameDev.net—www.gamedev.net

Game Development Search Engine—www.gdse.com

GameFAQs—www.gamefaqs.com

Game Music.com—www.gamemusic.com

Games Tester—www.gamestester.com

GarageGames—www.garagegames.com

Machinima.com—www.machinima.com

Moby Games—www.mobygames.com

Overclocked Remix—www.overclocked.org

PS3—www.ps3.net

Wii-Play—www.wii-play.com

Xbox.com—www.xbox.com

XBOX 360 Homebrew—www.xbox360homebrew.com
    [includes XNA developer community]

Organizations

Academy of Interactive Arts & Sciences (AIAS)—www.interactive.org

Academy of Machinima Arts & Sciences—www.machinima.org

Association of Computing Machinery (ACM)—www.acm.org

Business Software Alliance (BSA)—www.bsa.org

Digital Games Research Association (DiGRA)—www.digra.org

Entertainment Software Association (ESA)—www.theesa.com

Entertainment Software Ratings Board (ESRB)—www.esrb.org

Game Audio Network Guild (GANG)—www.audiogang.org

International Computer Games Association (ICGA)—www.cs.unimaas.nl/icga

International Game Developers Association (IGDA)—www.igda.org

SIGGRAPH—www.siggraph.org

Events

Consumer Electronics Show (CES)
January—Las Vegas, NV
www.cesweb.org

Game Developers Conference (GDC)
February—San Francisco, CA
www.gdconf.com

D.I.C.E. Summit (AIAS)
March—Las Vegas, NV
www.dicesummit.org

SIGGRAPH (ACM)
Summer—Los Angeles, CA; San Diego, CA; Boston, MA (location varies)
www.siggraph.org

E3 Business & Media Summit
July—Santa Monica, CA
www.e3expo.com

Tokyo Game Show (TGS)
Fall—Japan
tgs.cesa.or.jp/english/

Austin Game Developers Conference
September—Austin, TX
www.gameconference.com

IndieGamesCon (IGC)
October—Eugene, OR
www.indiegamescon.com

E for All Expo
October—Los Angeles, CA
www.eforallexpo.com

Colleges & Universities

Here is a list of schools that have strong game degree or certificate programs:

Academy of Art University—www.academyart.edu

Arizona State University—www.asu.edu

Art Center College of Design—www.artcenter.edu

Art Institute of Pittsburgh - Online Division—www.aionline.edu

The Art Institutes—www.artinstitutes.edu

Carnegie Mellon University/Entertainment Technology Center—www.cmu.edu

DeVry University—www.devry.edu

DigiPen Institute of Technology—www.digipen.edu

Expression College for Digital Arts—www.expression.edu

Full Sail Real World Education—www.fullsail.edu

Guildhall at SMU—guildhall.smu.edu

Indiana University MIME Program—www.mime.indiana.edu

Iowa State University—www.iastate.edu

ITT Technical Institute—www.itt-tech.edu

Massachusetts Institute of Technology (MIT)—media.mit.edu

Rensselaer Polytechnic Institute—www.rpi.edu

Ringling College of Art & Design—www.ringling.edu

Santa Monica College Academy of Entertainment & Technology—academy.smc.edu

Savannah College of Art & Design—www.scad.edu

Tomball College—www.tomballcollege.com

University of California, Los Angeles (UCLA) - Extension—www.uclaextension.edu

University of Central Florida - Florida Interactive Entertainment Academy—fiea.ucf.edu

University of Southern California (USC) - Information Technology Program—itp.usc.edu

University of Southern California (USC) School of Cinematic Arts—interactive.usc.edu

Vancouver Film School—www.vfs.com

Westwood College—www.westwood.edu

Books & Articles

Adams, E. (2003). *Break into the game industry.* McGraw-Hill Osborne Media.

Adams, E. & Rollings, A. (2006). *Fundamentals of game design.* Prentice Hall.

Ahearn, L. & Crooks II, C.E. (2002). *Awesome game creation: No programming required. (2ⁿᵈ ed).* Charles River Media.

Ahlquist, J.B., Jr. & Novak, J. (2007). *Game development essentials: Game artificial intelligence.* Cengage Delmar.

Aldrich, C. (2003). *Simulations and the future of learning.* Pfeiffer.

Aldrich, C. (2005). *Learning by doing.* Jossey-Bass.

Allison, S.E. et al. (March 2006). "The development of the self in the era of the Internet & role-playing fantasy games. *The American Journal of Psychiatry.*

Atkin, M. & Abercrombie, J. (2005). "Using a goal/action architecture to integrate modularity and long-term memory into AI behaviors." *Game Developers Conference.*

Axelrod, R. (1985). *The evolution of cooperation.* Basic Books.

Bartle, R.A. (1996). "Hearts, clubs, diamonds, spades: Players who suit MUDs." http://www.mud.co.uk/richard/hcds.htm

Bates, B. (2002). *Game design: The art & business of creating games.* Premier Press.

Beck, J.C. & Wade, M. (2004). *Got game: How the gamer generation is reshaping business forever.* Harvard Business School Press.

Bethke, E. (2003). *Game development and production.* Wordware.

Brandon, A. (2004). *Audio for games: Planning, process, and production.* New Riders.

Brin, D. (1998). *The transparent society.* Addison-Wesley.

Broderick, D. (2001). *The spike: How our lives are being transformed by rapidly advancing technologies.* Forge.

Brooks, D. (2001). *Bobos in paradise: The new upper class and how they got there.* Simon & Schuster.

Business Software Alliance. (May 2005). "Second annual BSA and IDC global software piracy study." http://www.bsa.org/globalstudy

Campbell, J. (1972). *The hero with a thousand faces.* Princeton University Press.

Campbell, J. & Moyers, B. (1991). *The power of myth.* Anchor.

Castells, M. (2001). *The Internet galaxy: Reflections on the Internet, business, and society.* Oxford University Press.

Castronova, E. (2005). *Synthetic worlds: The business and culture of online games.* University of Chicago Press.

Chase, R.B., Aquilano, N.J. & Jacobs, R. (2001). *Operations management for competitive advantage (9ᵗʰ ed).* McGraw-Hill/Irwin

Cheeseman, H.R. (2004). *Business law (5ᵗʰ ed).* Pearson Education, Inc.

Chiarella, T. (1998). *Writing dialogue.* Story Press.

Christen, P. (November 2006). "Serious expectations" *Game Developer Magazine.*

Cooper, A., & Reimann, R. (2003). *About face 2.0: The essentials of interaction design.* Wiley.

Cornman, L.B. et al. (December 1998). A fuzzy logic method for improved moment estimation from Doppler spectra. *Journal of Atmospheric & Oceanic Technology*.

Cox, E. & Goetz, M. (March 1991). Fuzzy logic clarified. *Computerworld*.

Crawford, C. (2003). *Chris Crawford on game design*. New Riders.

Crowley, M. (2004). "'A' is for average." *Reader's Digest*.

Csikszentmihalyi, M. (1991). *Flow: The psychology of optimal experience*. Perennial.

DeMaria, R. & Wilson, J.L. (2003). *High score!: The illustrated history of electronic games*. McGraw-Hill.

Dunniway, T. & Novak, J. (2008). *Game development essentials: Gameplay mechanics*. Cengage Delmar.

Egri, L. (1946). *The art of dramatic writing: Its basis in the creative interpretation of human motives*. Simon and Schuster.

Erikson, E.H. (1994). *Identity and the life cycle*. W.W. Norton & Company.

Erikson, E.H. (1995). *Childhood and society*. Vintage.

Escober, C. & Galindo, J. (2004). Fuzzy control in agriculture: Simulation software. *Industrial Simulation Conference 2004*.

Evans, A. (2001). *This virtual life: Escapism and simulation in our media world*. Fusion Press.

Feare, T. (July 2000). "Simulation: Tactical tool for system builders." *Modern Materials Handling*.

Friedl, M. (2002). *Online game interactivity theory*. Charles River Media.

Fruin, N. & Harringan, P. (Eds.) (2004). *First person: New media as story, performance and game*. MIT Press.

Fullerton, T., Swain, C. & Hoffman, S. (2004). *Game design workshop: Designing, prototyping & playtesting games*. CMP Books.

Galitz, W.O. (2002). *The essential guide to user interface design: An introduction to GUI design principles and techniques*. (2nd ed.). Wiley.

Gamma, E., Helm, R., Johnson, R. & Vlissides, J. (1995). *Design patterns: Elements of reusable object-oriented software*. Addison-Wesley.

Gardner, J. (1991). *The art of fiction: Notes on craft for young writers*. Vintage Books.

Gee, J.P. (2003). *What video games have to teach us about learning and literacy*. Palgrave Macmillan.

Gershenfeld, A., Loparco, M. & Barajas, C. (2003). *Game plan: The insiders guide to breaking in and succeeding in the computer and video game business*. Griffin Trade Paperback.

Giarratano, J.C. & Riley, G.D. (1998). *Expert systems: Principles & programming (4th ed)*. Course Technology.

Gibson, D., Aldrich, C. & Prensky, M. (Eds.) (2006). *Games and simulations in online learning*. IGI Global.

Gladwell, M. (2000). *The tipping point: How little things can make a big difference*. New York, NY: Little Brown & Company.

Gladwell, M. (2007). *Blink: The power of thinking without thinking*. Back Bay Books.

Gleick, J. (1987). *Chaos: Making a new science*. Viking.

Gleick, J. (1999). *Faster: The acceleration of just about everything.* Vintage Books.

Gleick, J. (2003). *What just happened: A chronicle from the information frontier.* Vintage.

Godin, S. (2003). *Purple cow: Transform your business by being remarkable.* Portfolio.

Godin, S. (2005). *The big moo: Stop trying to be perfect and start being remarkable.* Portfolio.

Goldratt, E.M. & Cox, J. (2004). *The goal: A process of ongoing improvement (3rd ed).* North River Press.

Gordon, T. (2000). *P.E.T.: Parent effectiveness training.* Three Rivers Press.

Hamilton, E. (1940). *Mythology: Timeless tales of gods and heroes.* Mentor.

Heim, M. (1993). *The metaphysics of virtual reality.* Oxford University Press.

Hight, J. & Novak, J. (2007). *Game development essentials: Game project management.* Cengage Delmar.

Hornyak, T.N. (2006). *Loving the machine: The art and science of Japanese robots.* Kodansha International.

Hsu, F. (2004). *Behind Deep Blue: Building the computer that defeated the world chess champion.* Princeton University Press.

Hunt, C.W. (October 1998). "Uncertainty factor drives new approach to building simulations." *Signal.*

Jensen, E. (2006). *Enriching the brain: How to maximize every learner's potential.* John Wiley & Sons.

Isla, D. (2005). "Handling complexity in the *Halo 2* AI." Game Developers Conference.

Johnson, S. (1997). *Interface culture: How new technology transforms the way we create & communicate.* Basic Books.

Johnson, S. (2006). *Everything bad is good for you.* Riverhead.

Jung, C.G. (1969). *Man and his symbols.* Dell Publishing.

Kent, S.L. (2001). *The ultimate history of video games.* Prima.

King, S. (2000). *On writing.* Scribner.

Knoke, W. (1997). *Bold new world: The essential road map to the twenty-first century.* Kodansha International.

Koster, R. (2005). *Theory of fun for game design.* Paraglyph Press.

Krawczyk, M. & Novak, J. (2006). *Game development essentials: Game story & character development.* Cengage Delmar.

Kurzweil, R. (2000). *The age of spiritual machines: When computers exceed human intelligence.* Penguin.

Laramee, F.D. (Ed.) (2002). *Game design perspectives.* Charles River Media.

Laramee, F.D. (Ed.) (2005). *Secrets of the game business. (3rd ed).* Charles River Media.

Levy, P. (2001). *Cyberculture.* University of Minnesota Press.

Lewis, M. (2001). *Next: The future just happened.* W.W.Norton & Company.

Mackay, C. (1841). *Extraordinary popular delusions & the madness of crowds.* Three Rivers Press.

McConnell, S. (1996). *Rapid development.* Microsoft Press.

McCorduck, P. (2004). *Machines who think: A personal inquiry into the history and prospects of artificial intelligence (2nd ed)*. AK Peters.

McKenna, T. (December 2003). "This means war." *Journal of Electronic Defense.*

Mencher, M. (2002). *Get in the game: Careers in the game industry.* New Riders.

Meyers, S. (2005). *Effective C++: 55 specific ways to improve your programs and designs (3rd ed)*. Addison-Wesley.

Michael, D. (2003). *The indie game development survival guide.* Charles River Media.

Montfort, N. (2003). *Twisty little passages: An approach to interactive fiction.* MIT Press.

Moravec, H. (2000). *Robot.* Oxford University Press.

Morris, D. (September/October 2004). Virtual weather. *Weatherwise.*

Morris, D. & Hartas, L. (2003). *Game art: The graphic art of computer games.* Watson-Guptill Publications.

Muehl, W. & Novak, J. (2007). *Game development essentials: Game simulation development.* Cengage Delmar.

Mulligan, J. & Patrovsky, B. (2003). *Developing online games: An insider's guide.* New Riders.

Mummolo, J. (July 2006). "Helping children play." *Newsweek.*

Murray, J. (2001). *Hamlet on the holodeck: The future of narrative in cyberspace.* MIT Press.

Negroponte, N. (1996). *Being digital.* Vintage Books.

Nielsen, J. (1999). *Designing web usability: The practice of simplicity.* New Riders.

Novak. J. (2007). *Game development essentials: An introduction. (2nd ed.)*. Cengage Delmar.

Novak, J. & Levy, L. (2007). *Play the game: The parents guide to video games.* Cengage Course Technology PTR.

Novak, J. (2003). "MMOGs as online distance learning applications." University of Southern California.

Oram, A. (Ed.) (2001). *Peer-to-peer.* O'Reilly & Associates.

Patow, C.A. (December 2005). "Medical simulation makes medical education better & safer." *Health Management Technology.*

Peck, M. (January 2005). "Air Force's latest video game targets potential recruits." *National Defense.*

Piaget, J. (2000). *The psychology of the child.* Basic Books.

Piaget, J. (2007). *The child's conception of the world.* Jason Aronson.

Pohflepp, S. (January 2007). "Before and after Darwin." *We Make Money Not Art.* (http://www.we-make-money-not -art.com/archives/009261.php)

Prensky, M. (2006). *Don't bother me, Mom: I'm learning!* Paragon House.

Ramirez, J. (July 2006). "The new ad game." *Newsweek.*

Rheingold, H. (1991). *Virtual reality.* Touchstone.

Rheingold, H. (2000). *Tools for thought: The history and future of mind-expanding technology.* MIT Press.

Robbins, S.P. (2001). *Organizational behavior (9th ed)*. Prentice-Hall, Inc.

Rogers, E.M. (1995). *Diffusion of innovations.* Free Press.

Rollings, A. & Morris, D. (2003). *Game architecture & design: A new edition.* New Riders.

Rollings, A. & Adams, E. (2003). *Andrew Rollings & Ernest Adams on game design.* New Riders.

Rouse, R. (2001) *Game design: Theory & practice (2ⁿᵈ ed).* Wordware Publishing.

Salen, K. & Zimmerman, E. (2003). *Rules of play.* MIT Press.

Sanchanta, M. (2006 January). "Japanese game aids U.S. war on obesity: Gym class in West Virginia to use an interactive dance console." *Financial Times.*

Sanger, G.A. [a.k.a. "The Fat Man"]. (2003). *The Fat Man on game audio.* New Riders.

Saunders, K. & Novak, J. (2007). *Game development essentials: Game interface design.* Cengage Delmar.

Schildt, H. (2006). *Java: A beginner's guide (4ᵗʰ ed).* McGraw-Hill Osborne Media.

Schomaker, W. (September 2001). "Cosmic models match reality." *Astronomy.*

Sellers, J. (2001). *Arcade fever.* Running Press.

Shaffer, D.W. (2006). *How computer games help children learn.* Palgrave Macmillan.

Standage, T. (1999). *The Victorian Internet.* New York: Berkley Publishing Group.

Strauss, W. & Howe, N. (1992). *Generations.* Perennial.

Strauss, W. & Howe, N. (1993). *13th gen: Abort, retry, ignore, fail?* Vintage Books.

Strauss, W. & Howe, N. (1998). *The fourth turning.* Broadway Books.

Strauss, W. & Howe, N. (2000). *Millennials rising: The next great generation.* Vintage Books.

Strauss, W., Howe, N. & Markiewicz, P. (2006). *Millennials & the pop culture.* LifeCourse Associates.

Stroustrup, B. (2000). *The C++ programming language (3ʳᵈ ed).* Addison-Wesley.

Trotter, A. (November 2005). "Despite allure, using digital games for learning seen as no easy task." *Education Week.*

Tufte, E.R. (1983). *The visual display of quantitative information.* Graphics Press.

Tufte, E.R. (1990). *Envisioning information.* Graphics Press.

Tufte, E.R. (1997). *Visual explanations.* Graphics Press.

Tufte, E.R. (2006). *Beautiful evidence.* Graphics Press.

Turkle, S. (1997). *Life on the screen: Identity in the age of the Internet.* Touchstone.

Van Duyne, D.K. et al. (2003). *The design of sites.* Addison-Wesley.

Vogler, C. (1998). *The writer's journey: Mythic structure for writers. (2ⁿᵈ ed).* Michael Wiese Productions.

Welch, J. & Welch, S. (2005). *Winning.* HarperCollins Publishers.

Weizenbaum, J. (1984). *Computer power and human reason.* Penguin Books.

Williams, J.D. (1954). *The compleat strategyst: Being a primer on the theory of the games of strategy.* McGraw-Hill.

Wolf, J.P. & Perron, B. (Eds.). (2003). *Video game theory reader.* Routledge.

Wong, G. (November 2006). "Educators explore 'Second Life' online." *CNN.com* (http://www.cnn.com/2006/TECH/11/13/second.life.university/index.html)

Wysocki, R.K. (2006). *Effective project management (4ᵗʰ ed).* John Wiley & Sons.

Index

Foreign Markets

We have noted in previous chapters how the possibility of launching an MMOG in foreign markets can affect design decisions. In addition to this, some foreign markets will also affect cost and revenue calculations. Understanding how the business works in different countries is important if you plan to release your MMOG in other countries besides the United States. The three regions that present the most significant differences are Japan, South Korea, and China.

Japan

Aside from stylistic preferences and the lower percentage of credit cards, the other significant difference between Japan and the U.S. market has to do with their hardware. In Japan, there are far more game players who play on laptops than in the United States. There is a tendency in U.S. markets to favor more powerful desktop systems, thus many developers focus their technical efforts on ensuring compatibility with them, often to the exclusion of less powerful laptops. To maximize subscriber numbers in Japan, it is strongly recommended that laptops be explicitly included in the compatibility testing phase.

South Korea

In South Korea, few online gamers play their games from home. Overwhelmingly, the custom is to turn online game playing into a social event by gathering at Internet game rooms. An Internet game room is a large, open area that is filled with PCs. Players are charged about a dollar an hour, and for this fee they are free to wander the room and play any game they like at no further charge. This difference affects both the revenue model and the account management features substantially.

To illustrate how MMOGs work in an Internet game room, let's consider an example. Let's call your MMOG *Game X*. If someone wants to play *Game X*, they must find a computer in the game room that has it installed. Not every computer in the room will have every game on it.

Upon finding a computer with *Game X* on it, the player sits down to play. Let's assume they have never played *Game X* before. Since they are already paying the owner of the game room a dollar an hour, they certainly won't want to pay you as well. Thus, the process of opening an account in an MMOG must be free in a game room.

The person plays *Game X* for a couple of hours a day for a week or two, but then some obligation prevents them from returning to the game room for a month. When they finally do return, let's say they want to pick up where they left off. They expect to be able to just log back in and continue playing.

This is very different from the way things would work in the United States. In the United States, the player must

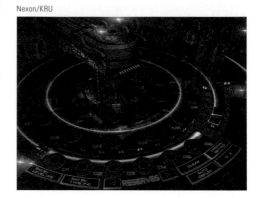

Nexon/KRU

Shattered Galaxy

have paid for the subscription to log back in a month later and continue playing. If the fee had not been paid, the account would have been automatically suspended. However, as we've just learned, the player in a game room is already paying an hourly fee and expects the subscription itself to be free.

So how does the MMOG developer get money out of this? What they do is provide a number of seats to the Internet game room. The number of seats is the maximum number of simultaneous players allowed to play *Game X* in that Internet game room at any given time.

Let's assume the game room in question has purchased five seats for *Game X*. Each seat will cost the game room, say, $60 a month. Thus, the game room is paying a total of $300 a month to the MMOG developer for the five seats. For this fee, any number of players can play *Game X*, but no more than five simultaneously.

Clearly, the more popular the game, the more seats the game room owner will need to purchase. If the five seats combined see more than 300 total hours of use in a given month, the owner of the game room will make a profit. If not, the owner is likely to reduce the number of paid seats for next month.

This model is quite different from a standard subscription model, and it requires special versions of the account management so that accounts won't be closed. It also makes the total subscriber numbers far less clear. If you think about it, since

Courtesy of NCsoft

Lineage: The Blood Pledge

an MMOG account in an Internet game room never actually closes, how can we truly know how many players are still playing? Over the years, the number of accounts can only go up.

This is why we see numbers showing millions of subscribers for games like *Lineage* in South Korea. It's extremely unlikely that everyone who ever opened an account in *Lineage* is still actively playing, but there's no way to tell for sure.

1. How does the fact that MMOGs are a service rather than a product affect the associated business model in terms of technology, cost, personnel, and other resources?

2. What are some legal issues associated with user-generated content and digital asset ownership? What can be done to prevent these issues from occurring?

3. What are some payment methods associated with MMOGs? Discuss the benefits and disadvantages of each method.

For those MMOG developers considering releasing a game in any member country in the European Union, you might also want to investigate the Value Added Tax, or VAT. The nature of this tax will have an impact on your revenue models, and it has been known to surprise smaller MMOG developers who don't have much experience with international business.

China

China, too, centers on an Internet game room model. In all respects but two it is identical to the South Korean model. The two pronounced differences are: 1) the potential market size in China is enormous; and 2) both the revenues and cost of doing business are much smaller. South Korean game rooms typically charge players about a dollar an hour, but Chinese game rooms are more like a nickel an hour.

This may sound like it can't possibly be worth doing, but because the costs for bandwidth and customer support are likewise much lower, it's still quite possible to make a healthy profit. Anyone who has ever read a biography about Henry Ford can tell you that a small profit from a large number of people is vastly superior to a large profit from a small number of people.

The business overview presented in this chapter has given a high-level picture of most of the larger considerations of the MMOG industry. There can be no doubt that the service-oriented nature of MMOGs produces implications that are far more complex and pervasive than those experienced by single-player games. It is impossible to effectively design and build an MMOG without fully understanding the interrelations between the game and the service. Together, they form a complex web of dependencies that cannot and should not be separated.